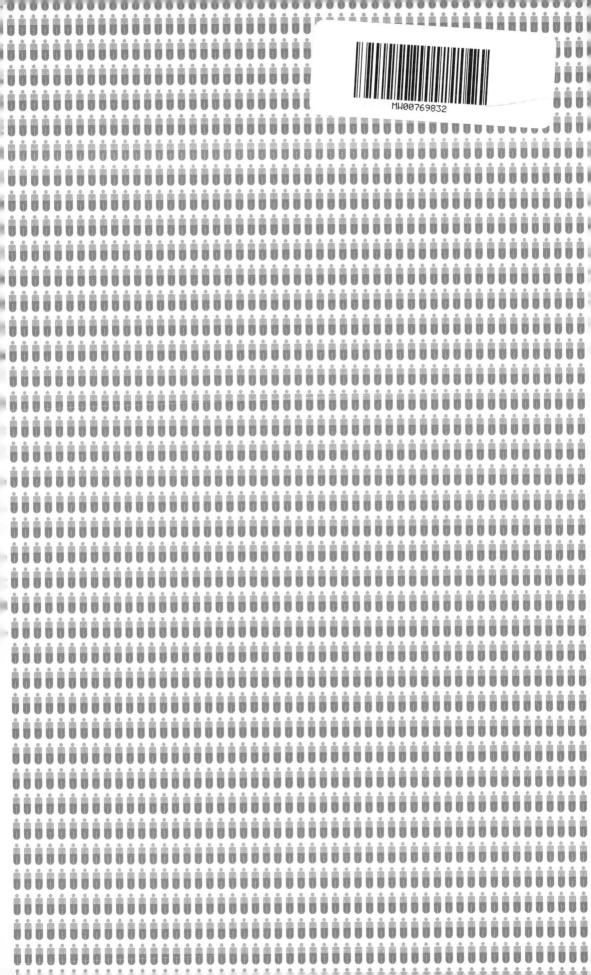

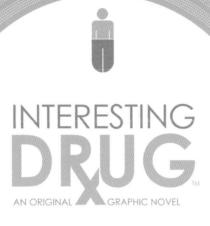

# INTERESTING DRUG

AN ORIGINAL GRAPHIC NOVEL

SHAUN **MANNING**

ANNA **WIESZCZYK**

Published by
ARCHAIA™

ROSS RICHIE CEO & Founder
JACK CUMMINS President • MARK SMYLIE
Founder of Archaia • MATT GAGNON Editor-in-Chief
FILIP SABLIK VP of Publishing & Marketing • STEPHEN CHRISTY
VP of Development • LANCE KREITER VP of Licensing & Merchandising
PHIL BARBARO VP of Finance • BRYCE CARLSON Managing Editor
MEL CAYLO Marketing Manager • SCOTT NEWMAN Production Design Manager
IRENE BRADISH Operations Manager • DAFNA PLEBAN Editor • SHANNON WATTERS
Editor • ERIC HARBURN Editor • REBECCA TAYLOR Editor • IAN BRILL Editor • CHRIS ROSA
Assistant Editor • ALEX GALER Assistant Editor • WHITNEY LEOPARD Assistant Editor • JASMINE
AMIRI Assistant Editor • CAMERON CHITTOCK Assistant Editor • HANNAH NANCE PARTLOW
Production Designer • KELSEY DIETERICH Production Designer • DEVIN FUNCHES E-Commerce &
Inventory Coordinator • ANDY LIEGL Event Coordinator • BRIANNA HART Executive Assistant • AARON
Ferrara Operations Assistant • JOSE MEZA Sales Assistant • ELIZABETH LOUGHRIDGE Accounting Assistant

ARCHAIA™    INTERESTING DRUG, May 2014.
Published by Archaia, a division of Boom Entertainment. Inc.

BOOM! Studios. 5670 Wilshire Boulevard, Suite 450. Los Angeles,
CA 90036-5679. Printed in China. First Printing.
ISBN: 978-1-60886-424-9, eISBN: 978-1-61398-278-5

# INTERESTING
# DRxUG™

WRITTEN AND CREATED BY
**SHAUN MANNING**

ILLUSTRATED BY
**ANNA WIESZCZYK**

LETTERS BY
**ED BRISSON & FRANK J. BARBIERE**

EDITED BY
**REBECCA TAYLOR**

DESIGN AND COVER BY
**SCOTT NEWMAN**

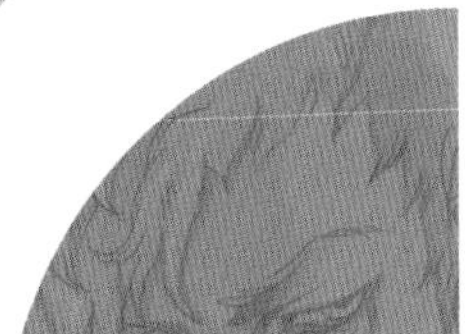

CHAPTER
ONE

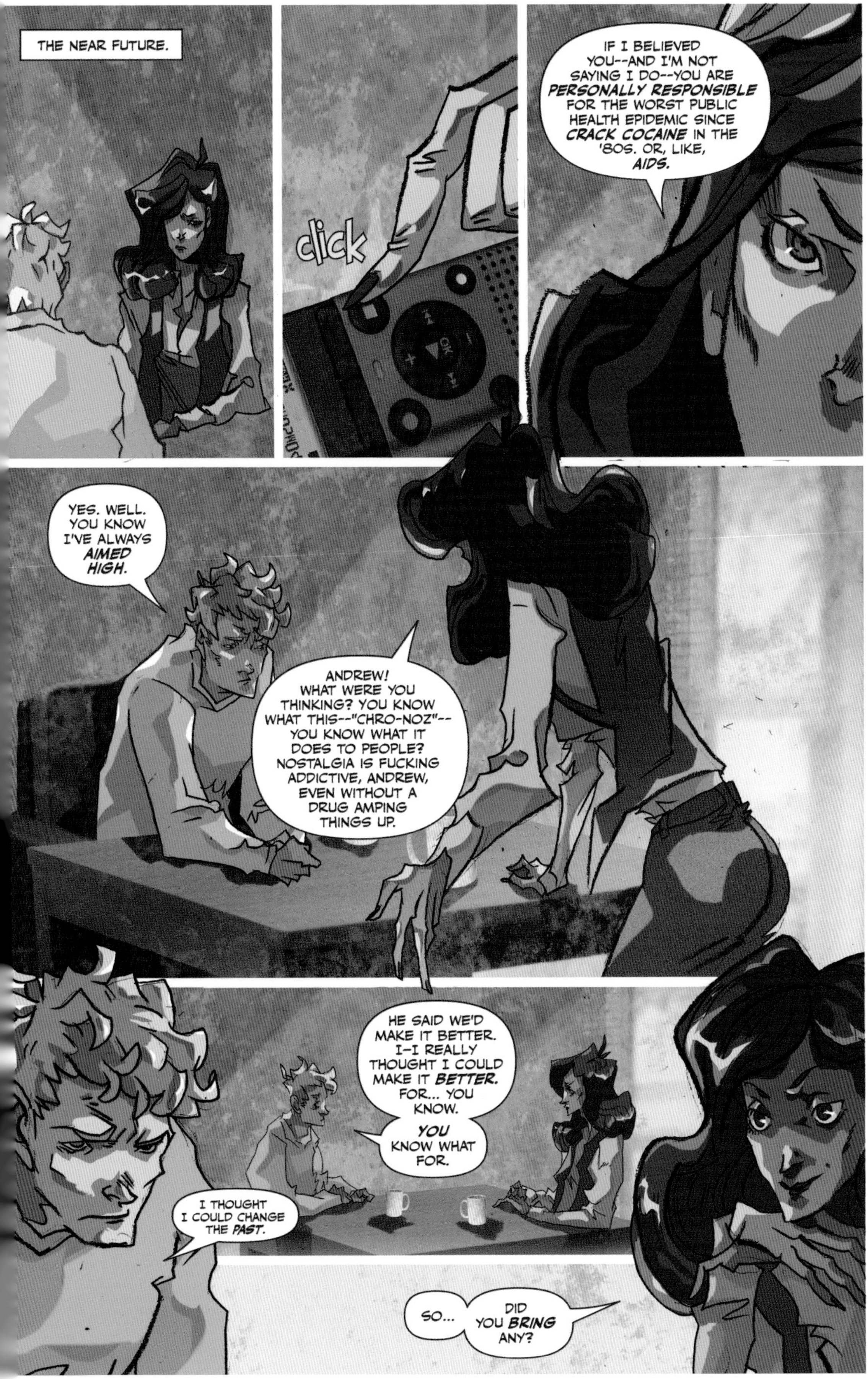
THE NEAR FUTURE.
click
IF I BELIEVED YOU--AND I'M NOT SAYING I DO--YOU ARE PERSONALLY RESPONSIBLE FOR THE WORST PUBLIC HEALTH EPIDEMIC SINCE CRACK COCAINE IN THE '80S. OR, LIKE, AIDS.
YES. WELL. YOU KNOW I'VE ALWAYS AIMED HIGH.
ANDREW! WHAT WERE YOU THINKING? YOU KNOW WHAT THIS--"CHRO-NOZ"--YOU KNOW WHAT IT DOES TO PEOPLE? NOSTALGIA IS FUCKING ADDICTIVE, ANDREW, EVEN WITHOUT A DRUG AMPING THINGS UP.
HE SAID WE'D MAKE IT BETTER. I--I REALLY THOUGHT I COULD MAKE IT BETTER. FOR... YOU KNOW.
YOU KNOW WHAT FOR.
I THOUGHT I COULD CHANGE THE PAST.
SO...
DID YOU BRING ANY?

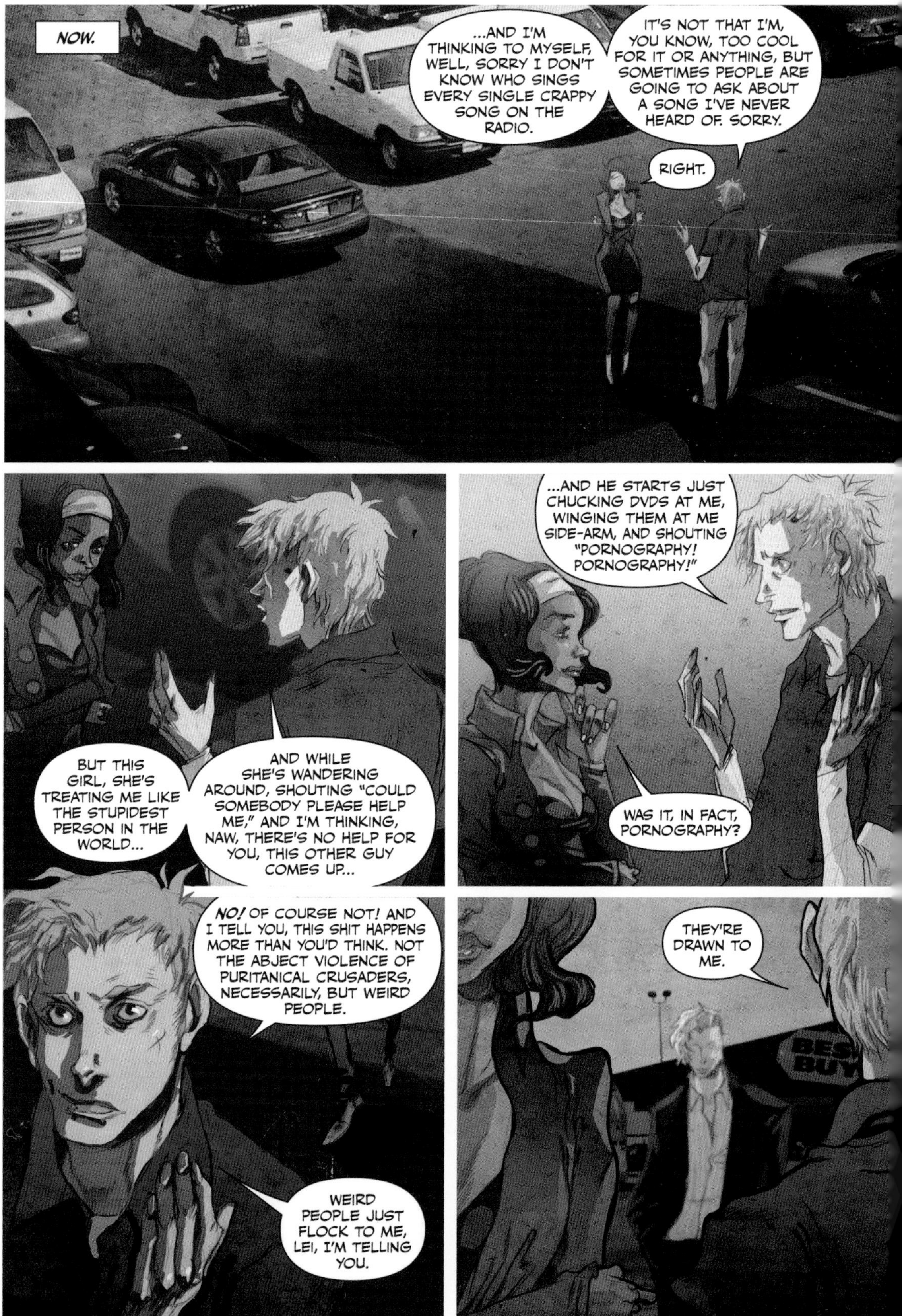
NOW.
...AND I'M THINKING TO MYSELF, WELL, SORRY I DON'T KNOW WHO SINGS EVERY SINGLE CRAPPY SONG ON THE RADIO.
IT'S NOT THAT I'M, YOU KNOW, TOO COOL FOR IT OR ANYTHING, BUT SOMETIMES PEOPLE ARE GOING TO ASK ABOUT A SONG I'VE NEVER HEARD OF. SORRY.
RIGHT.
BUT THIS GIRL, SHE'S TREATING ME LIKE THE STUPIDEST PERSON IN THE WORLD...
AND WHILE SHE'S WANDERING AROUND, SHOUTING "COULD SOMEBODY PLEASE HELP ME," AND I'M THINKING, NAW, THERE'S NO HELP FOR YOU, THIS OTHER GUY COMES UP...
...AND HE STARTS JUST CHUCKING DVDS AT ME, WINGING THEM AT ME SIDE-ARM, AND SHOUTING "PORNOGRAPHY! PORNOGRAPHY!"
WAS IT, IN FACT, PORNOGRAPHY?
NO! OF COURSE NOT! AND I TELL YOU, THIS SHIT HAPPENS MORE THAN YOU'D THINK. NOT THE ABJECT VIOLENCE OF PURITANICAL CRUSADERS, NECESSARILY, BUT WEIRD PEOPLE.
WEIRD PEOPLE JUST FLOCK TO ME, LEI, I'M TELLING YOU.
THEY'RE DRAWN TO ME.
BEST BUY

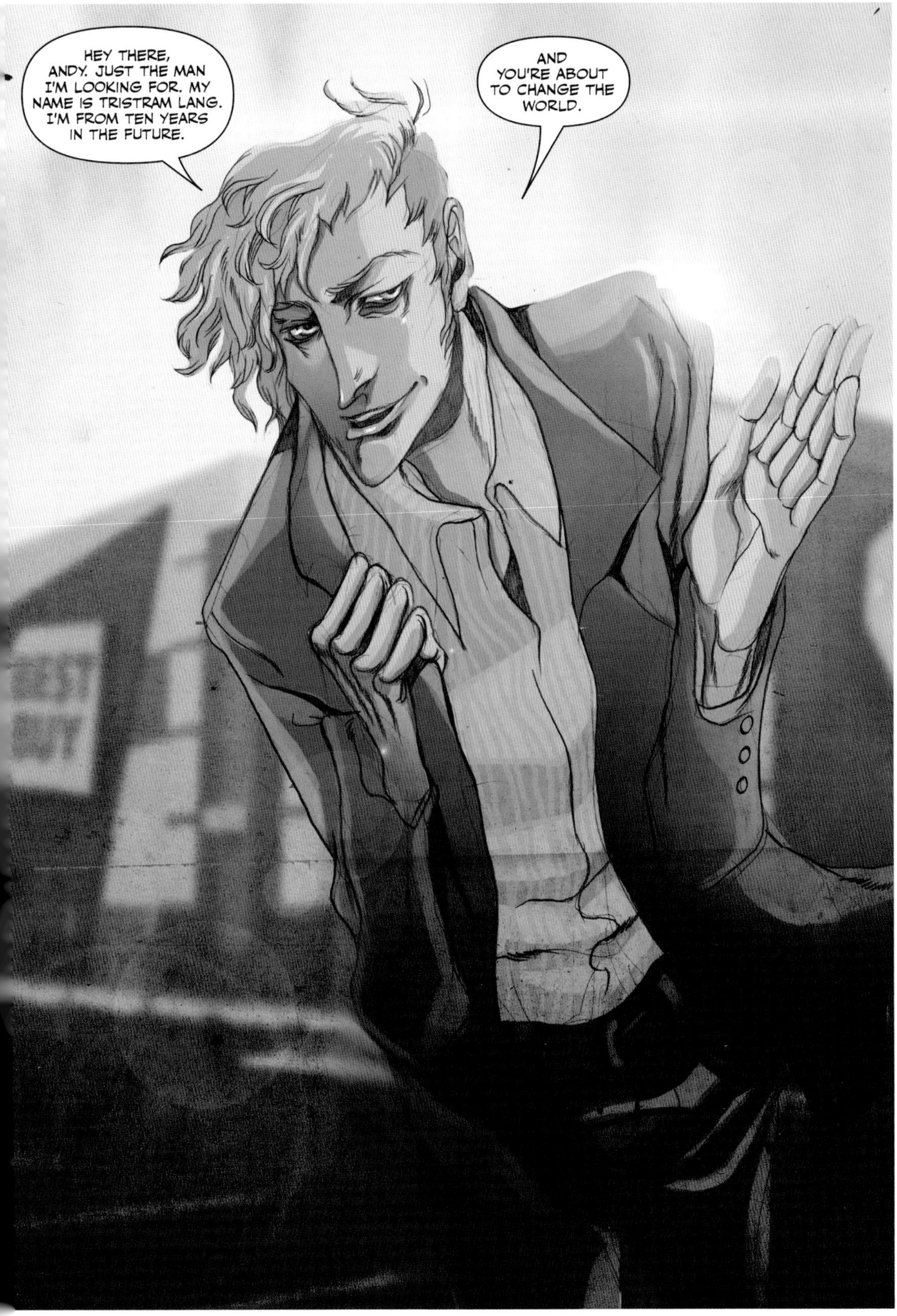
HEY THERE, ANDY. JUST THE MAN I'M LOOKING FOR. MY NAME IS TRISTRAM LANG. I'M FROM TEN YEARS IN THE FUTURE.
AND YOU'RE ABOUT TO CHANGE THE WORLD.

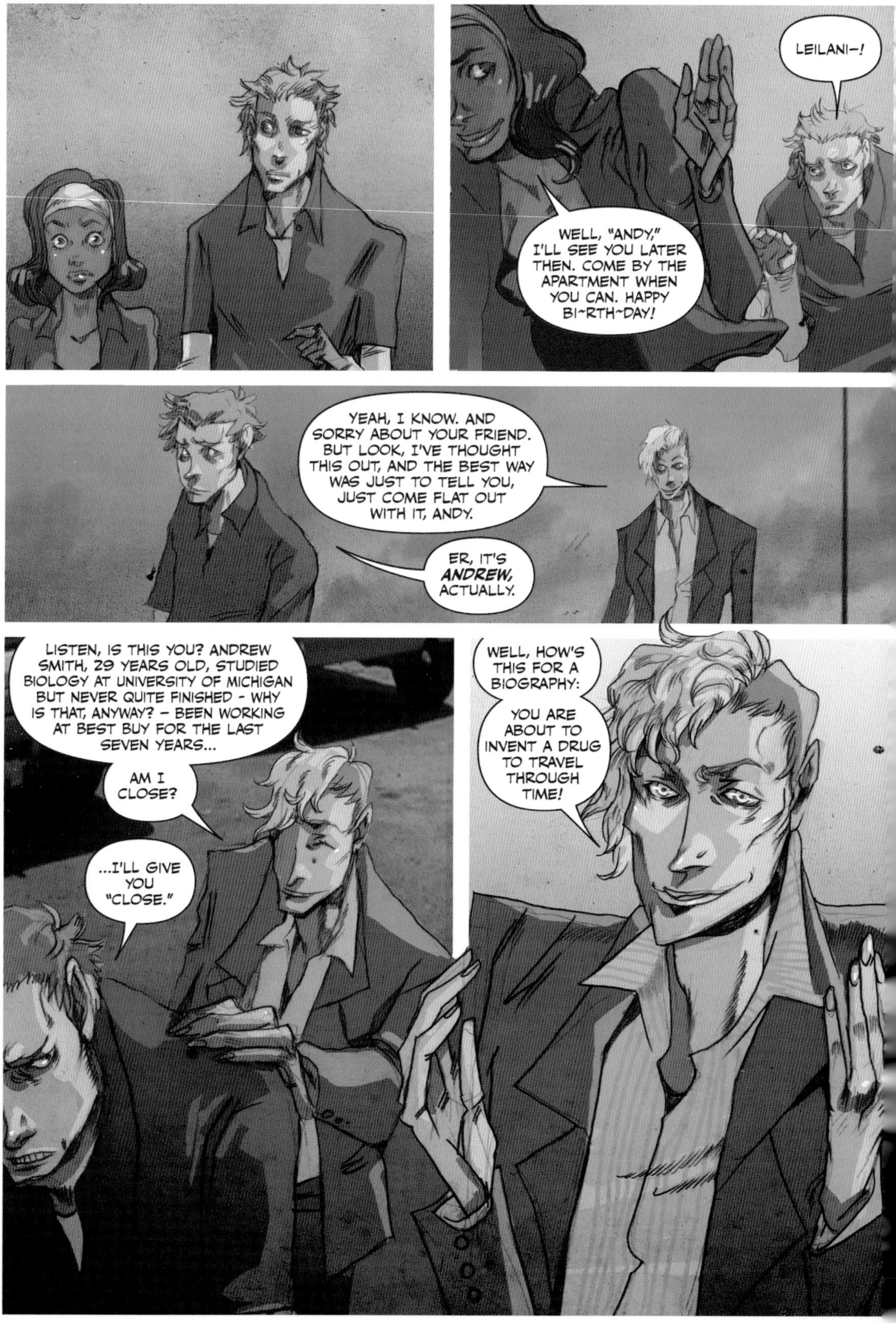
LEILANI—!
WELL, "ANDY," I'LL SEE YOU LATER THEN. COME BY THE APARTMENT WHEN YOU CAN. HAPPY BI~RTH~DAY!
YEAH, I KNOW. AND SORRY ABOUT YOUR FRIEND. BUT LOOK, I'VE THOUGHT THIS OUT, AND THE BEST WAY WAS JUST TO TELL YOU, JUST COME FLAT OUT WITH IT, ANDY.
ER, IT'S ***ANDREW,*** ACTUALLY.
LISTEN, IS THIS YOU? ANDREW SMITH, 29 YEARS OLD, STUDIED BIOLOGY AT UNIVERSITY OF MICHIGAN BUT NEVER QUITE FINISHED - WHY IS THAT, ANYWAY? — BEEN WORKING AT BEST BUY FOR THE LAST SEVEN YEARS...
AM I CLOSE?
...I'LL GIVE YOU "CLOSE."
WELL, HOW'S THIS FOR A BIOGRAPHY:
YOU ARE ABOUT TO INVENT A DRUG TO TRAVEL THROUGH TIME!

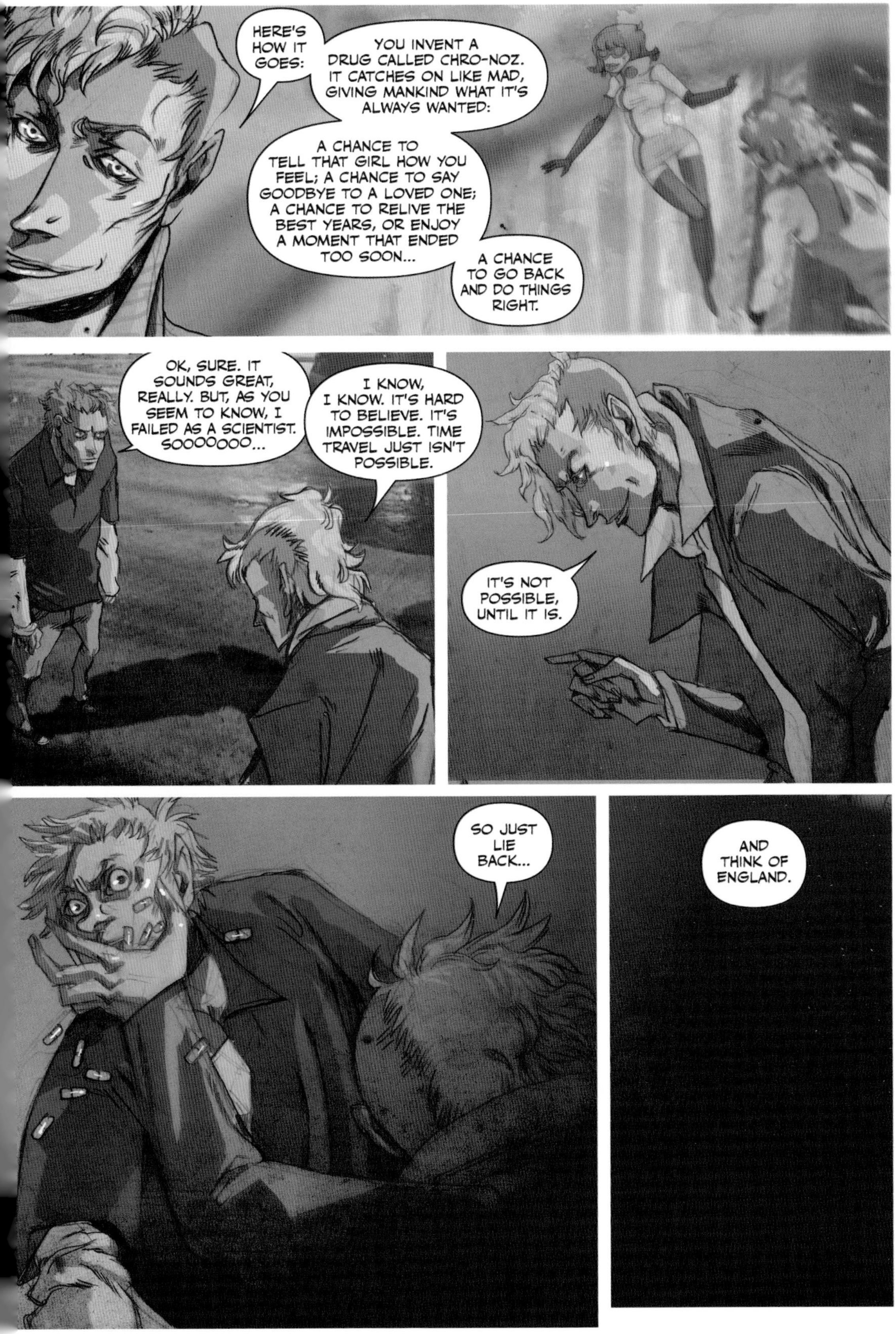
HERE'S HOW IT GOES:
YOU INVENT A DRUG CALLED CHRO-NOZ. IT CATCHES ON LIKE MAD, GIVING MANKIND WHAT IT'S ALWAYS WANTED:
A CHANCE TO TELL THAT GIRL HOW YOU FEEL; A CHANCE TO SAY GOODBYE TO A LOVED ONE; A CHANCE TO RELIVE THE BEST YEARS, OR ENJOY A MOMENT THAT ENDED TOO SOON...
A CHANCE TO GO BACK AND DO THINGS RIGHT.
OK, SURE. IT SOUNDS GREAT, REALLY. BUT, AS YOU SEEM TO KNOW, I FAILED AS A SCIENTIST. SOOOOOOO...
I KNOW, I KNOW. IT'S HARD TO BELIEVE. IT'S IMPOSSIBLE. TIME TRAVEL JUST ISN'T POSSIBLE.
IT'S NOT POSSIBLE, UNTIL IT IS.
SO JUST LIE BACK...
AND THINK OF ENGLAND.

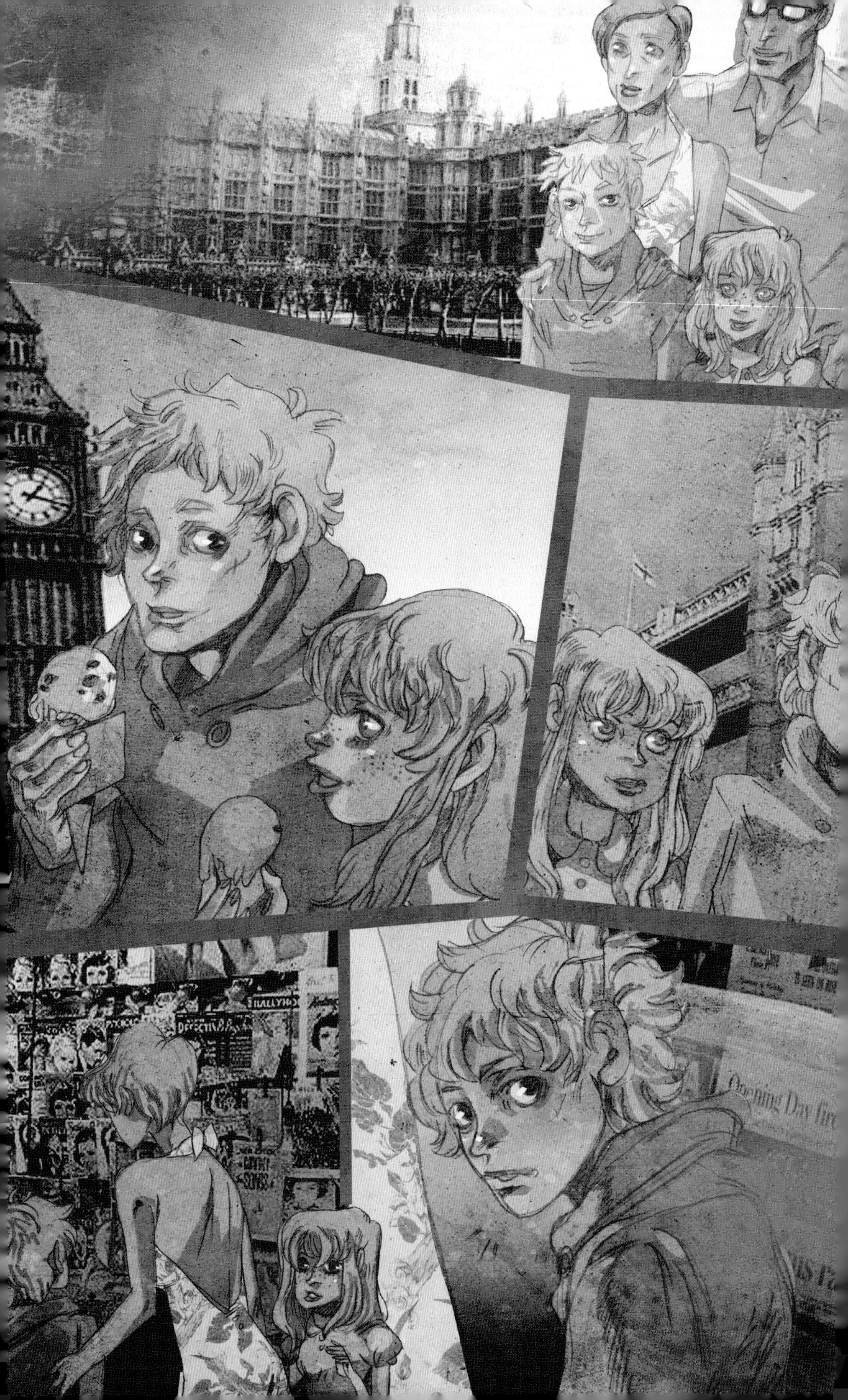

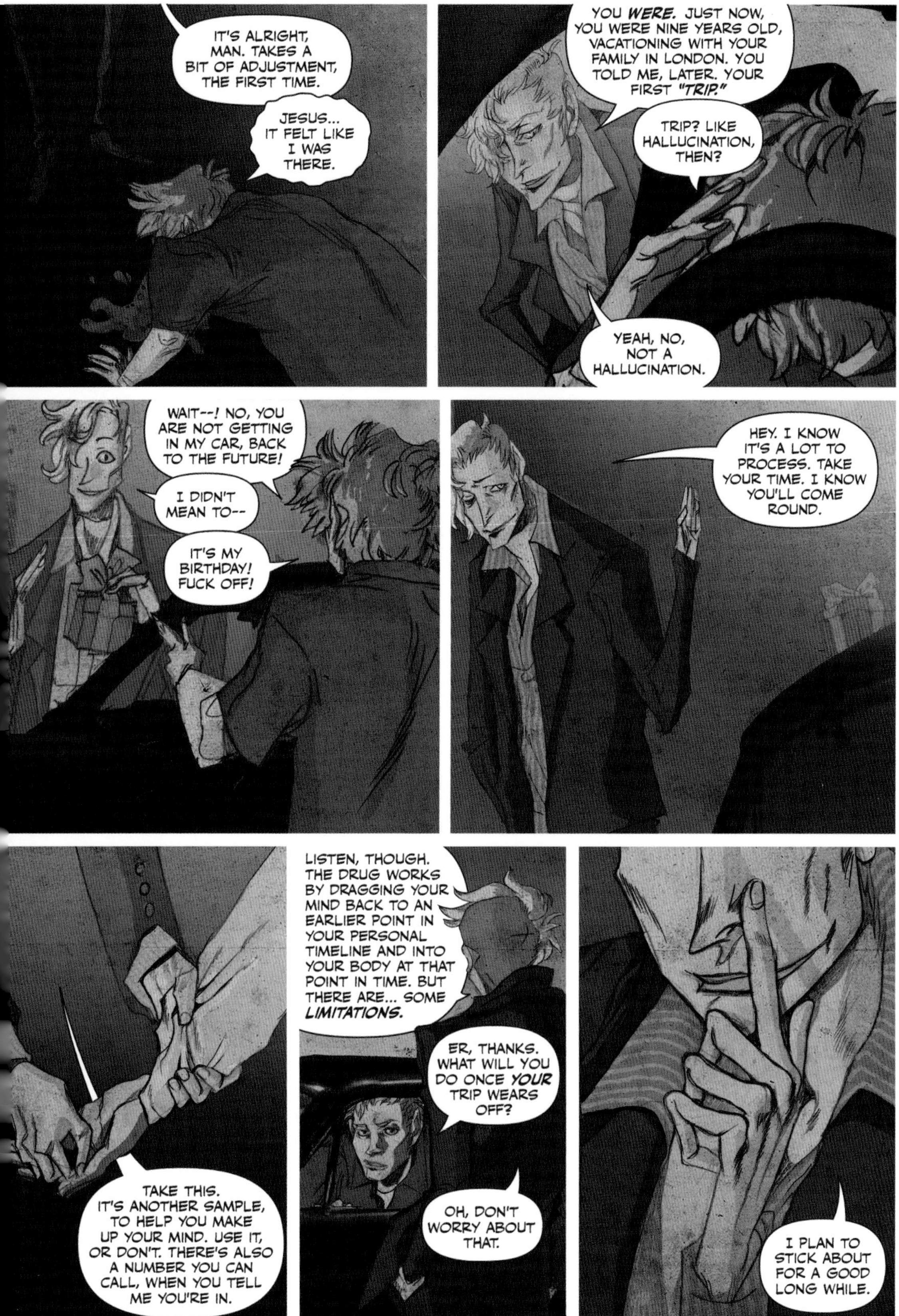
IT'S ALRIGHT, MAN. TAKES A BIT OF ADJUSTMENT, THE FIRST TIME.
JESUS... IT FELT LIKE I WAS THERE.
YOU *WERE.* JUST NOW, YOU WERE NINE YEARS OLD, VACATIONING WITH YOUR FAMILY IN LONDON. YOU TOLD ME, LATER. YOUR FIRST *"TRIP."*
TRIP? LIKE HALLUCINATION, THEN?
YEAH, NO, NOT A HALLUCINATION.
WAIT--*!* NO, YOU ARE NOT GETTING IN MY CAR, BACK TO THE FUTURE!
I DIDN'T MEAN TO--
IT'S MY BIRTHDAY*!* FUCK OFF*!*
HEY. I KNOW IT'S A LOT TO PROCESS. TAKE YOUR TIME. I KNOW YOU'LL COME ROUND.
TAKE THIS. IT'S ANOTHER SAMPLE, TO HELP YOU MAKE UP YOUR MIND. USE IT, OR DON'T. THERE'S ALSO A NUMBER YOU CAN CALL, WHEN YOU TELL ME YOU'RE IN.
LISTEN, THOUGH. THE DRUG WORKS BY DRAGGING YOUR MIND BACK TO AN EARLIER POINT IN YOUR PERSONAL TIMELINE AND INTO YOUR BODY AT THAT POINT IN TIME. BUT THERE ARE... SOME ***LIMITATIONS.***
ER, THANKS. WHAT WILL YOU DO ONCE *YOUR* TRIP WEARS OFF?
OH, DON'T WORRY ABOUT THAT.
I PLAN TO STICK ABOUT FOR A GOOD LONG WHILE.

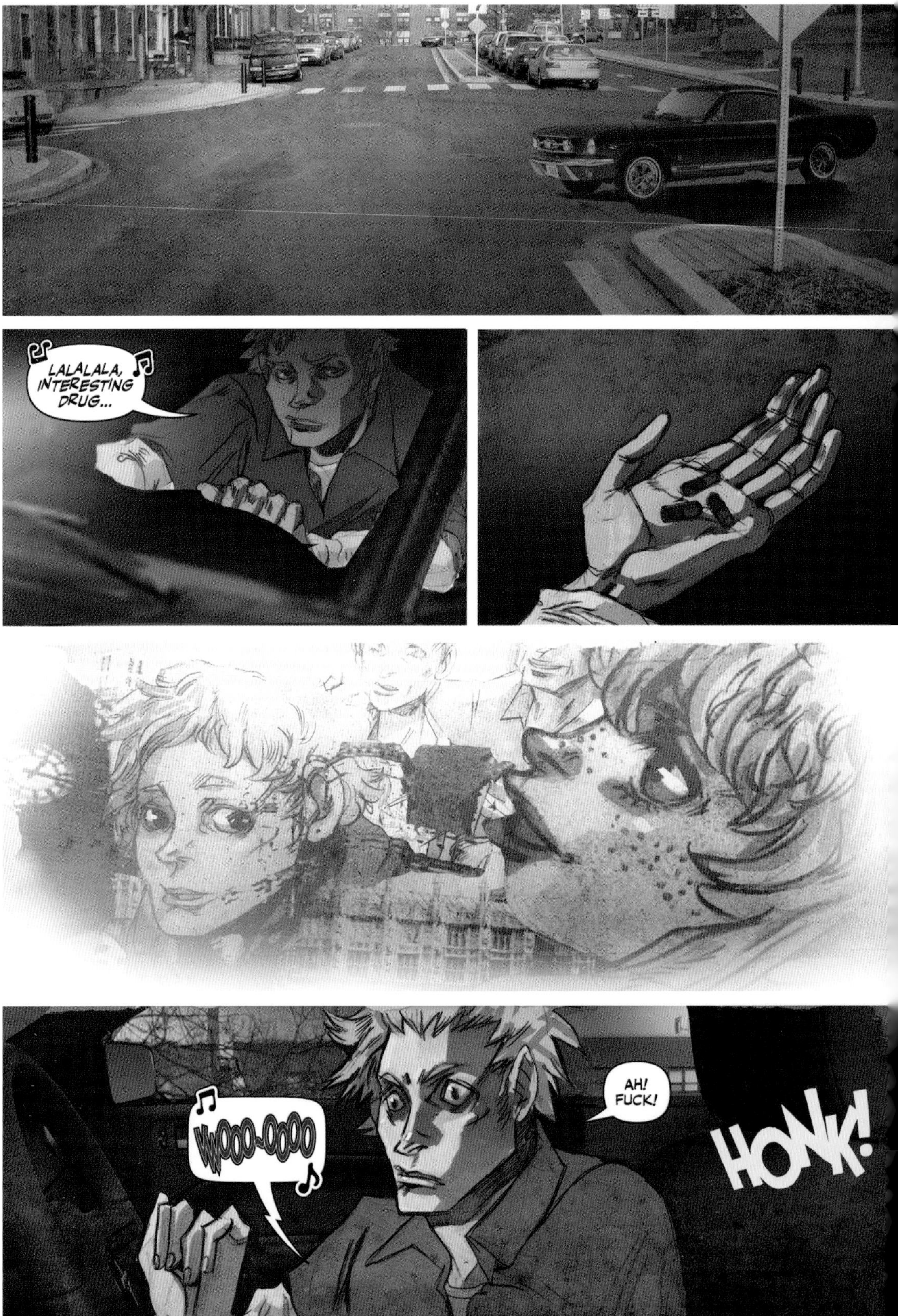
LALALALA, INTERESTING DRUG...
WOOO-OOOO
AH! FUCK!
HONK!

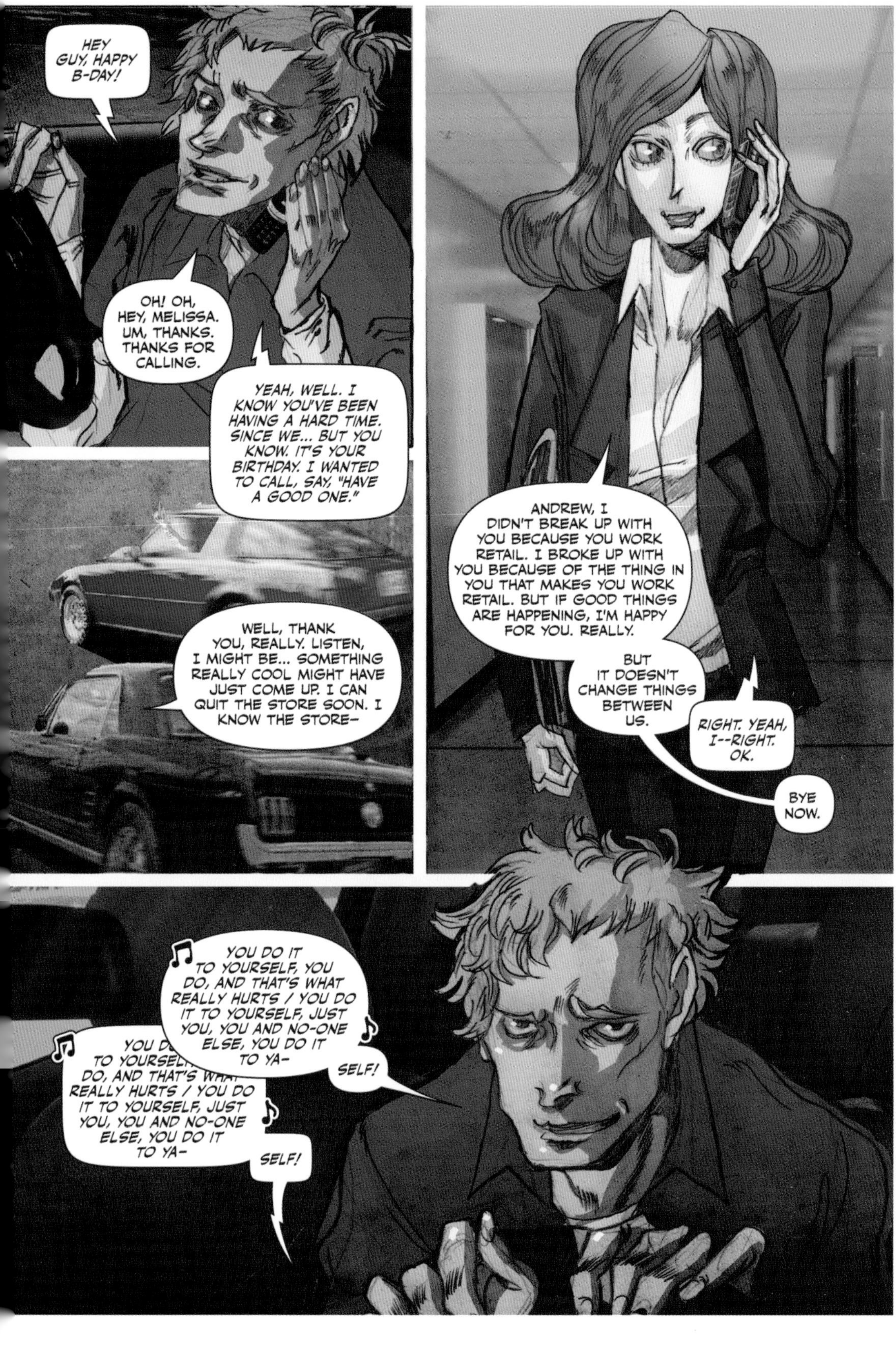
HEY GUY, HAPPY B-DAY!
OH! OH, HEY, MELISSA. UM, THANKS. THANKS FOR CALLING.
YEAH, WELL. I KNOW YOU'VE BEEN HAVING A HARD TIME. SINCE WE... BUT YOU KNOW. IT'S YOUR BIRTHDAY. I WANTED TO CALL, SAY, "HAVE A GOOD ONE."
WELL, THANK YOU, REALLY. LISTEN, I MIGHT BE... SOMETHING REALLY COOL MIGHT HAVE JUST COME UP. I CAN QUIT THE STORE SOON. I KNOW THE STORE–
ANDREW, I DIDN'T BREAK UP WITH YOU BECAUSE YOU WORK RETAIL. I BROKE UP WITH YOU BECAUSE OF THE THING IN YOU THAT MAKES YOU WORK RETAIL. BUT IF GOOD THINGS ARE HAPPENING, I'M HAPPY FOR YOU. REALLY.
BUT IT DOESN'T CHANGE THINGS BETWEEN US.
RIGHT. YEAH, I--RIGHT. OK.
BYE NOW.
YOU DO IT TO YOURSELF, YOU DO, AND THAT'S WHAT REALLY HURTS / YOU DO IT TO YOURSELF, JUST YOU, YOU AND NO-ONE ELSE, YOU DO IT TO YA–
SELF!
REALLY HURTS / YOU DO IT TO YOURSELF, JUST YOU, YOU AND NO-ONE ELSE, YOU DO IT TO YA–
SELF!

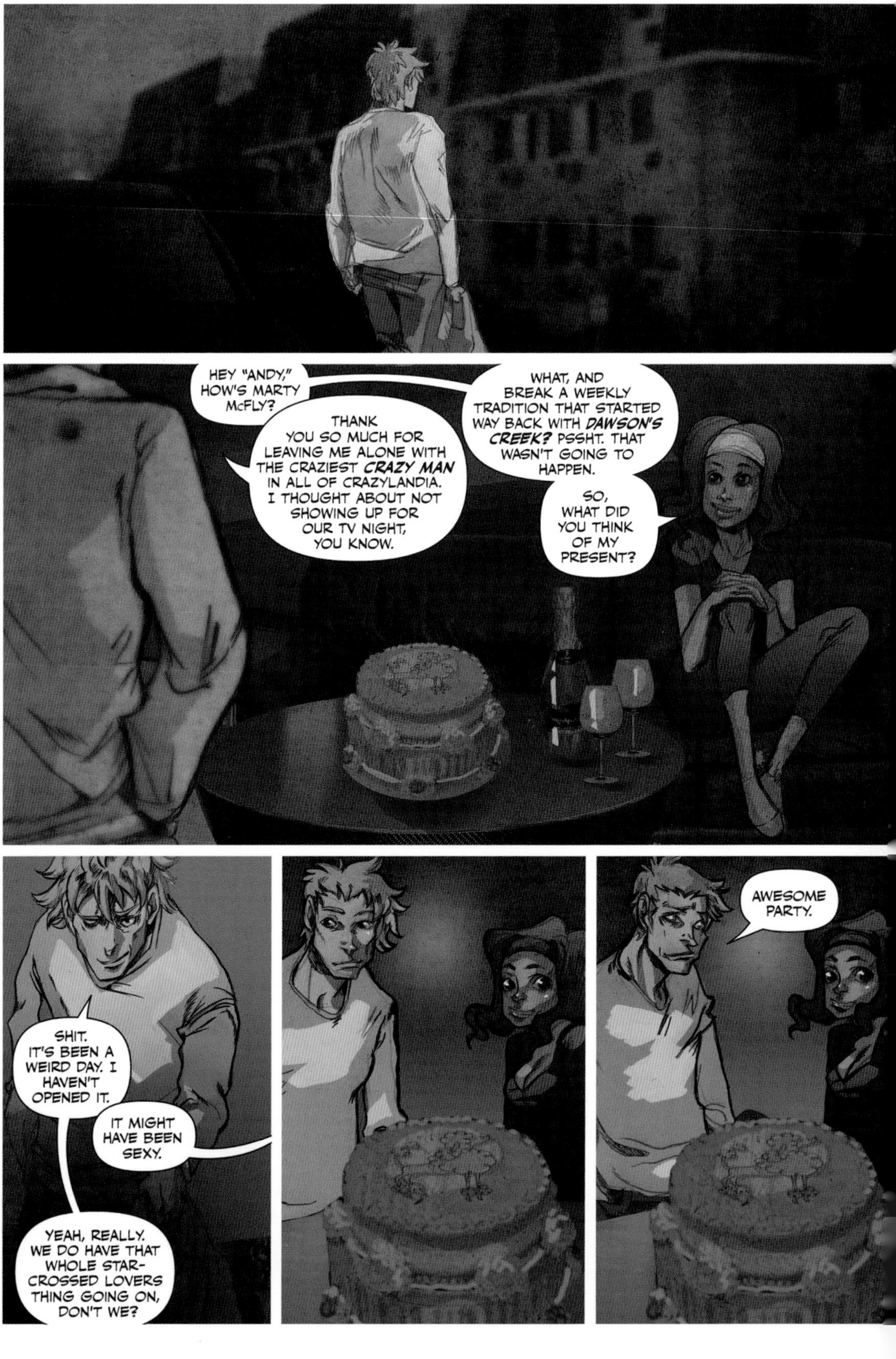
HEY "ANDY," HOW'S MARTY McFLY?
THANK YOU SO MUCH FOR LEAVING ME ALONE WITH THE CRAZIEST CRAZY MAN IN ALL OF CRAZYLANDIA. I THOUGHT ABOUT NOT SHOWING UP FOR OUR TV NIGHT, YOU KNOW.
WHAT, AND BREAK A WEEKLY TRADITION THAT STARTED WAY BACK WITH DAWSON'S CREEK? PSSHT. THAT WASN'T GOING TO HAPPEN.
SO, WHAT DID YOU THINK OF MY PRESENT?
SHIT. IT'S BEEN A WEIRD DAY. I HAVEN'T OPENED IT.
IT MIGHT HAVE BEEN SEXY.
YEAH, REALLY. WE DO HAVE THAT WHOLE STAR-CROSSED LOVERS THING GOING ON, DON'T WE?
AWESOME PARTY.

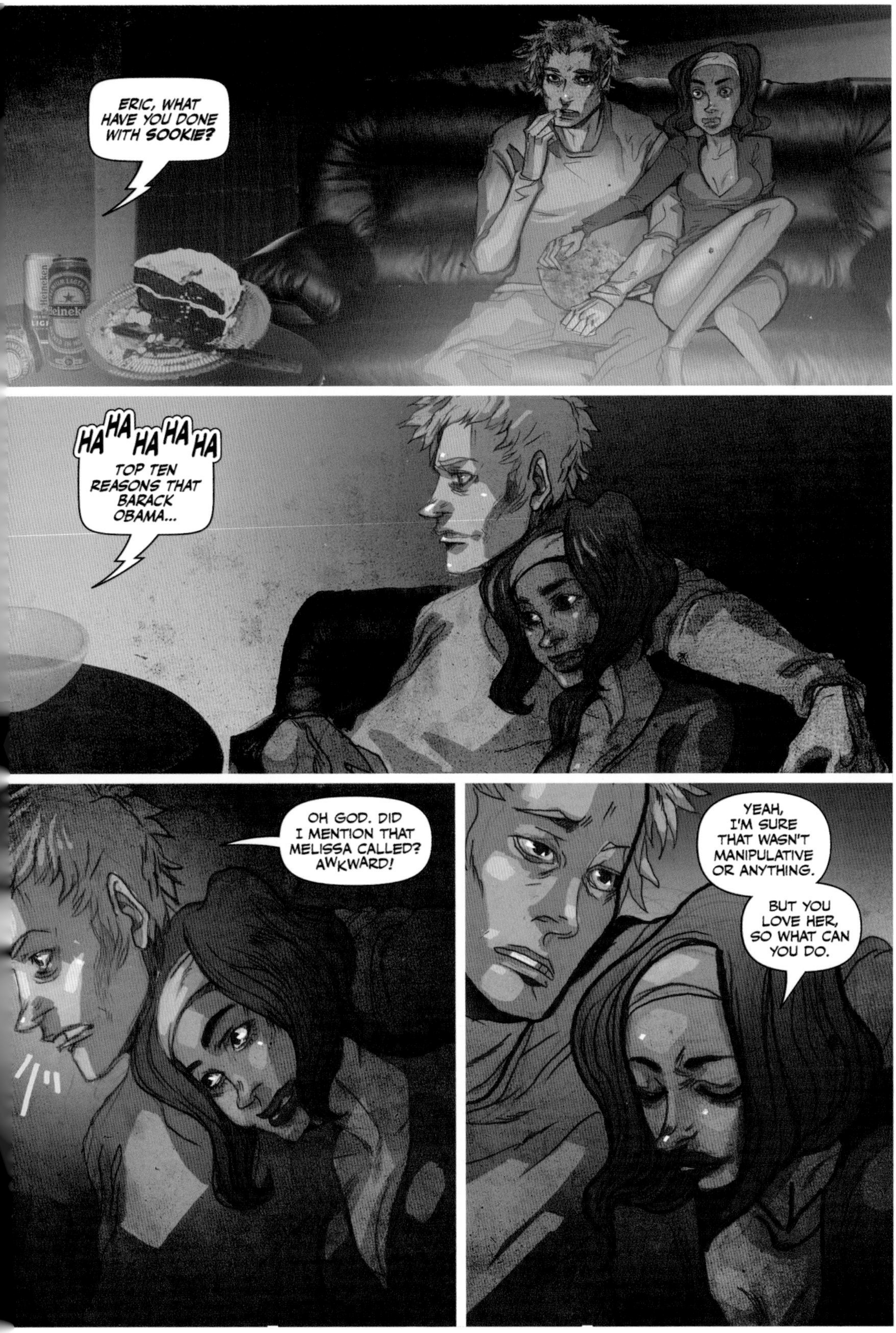
ERIC, WHAT HAVE YOU DONE WITH SOOKIE?
Heineken
HAHAHAHAHAHA
TOP TEN REASONS THAT BARACK OBAMA...
OH GOD. DID I MENTION THAT MELISSA CALLED? AWKWARD!
YEAH, I'M SURE THAT WASN'T MANIPULATIVE OR ANYTHING.
BUT YOU LOVE HER, SO WHAT CAN YOU DO.

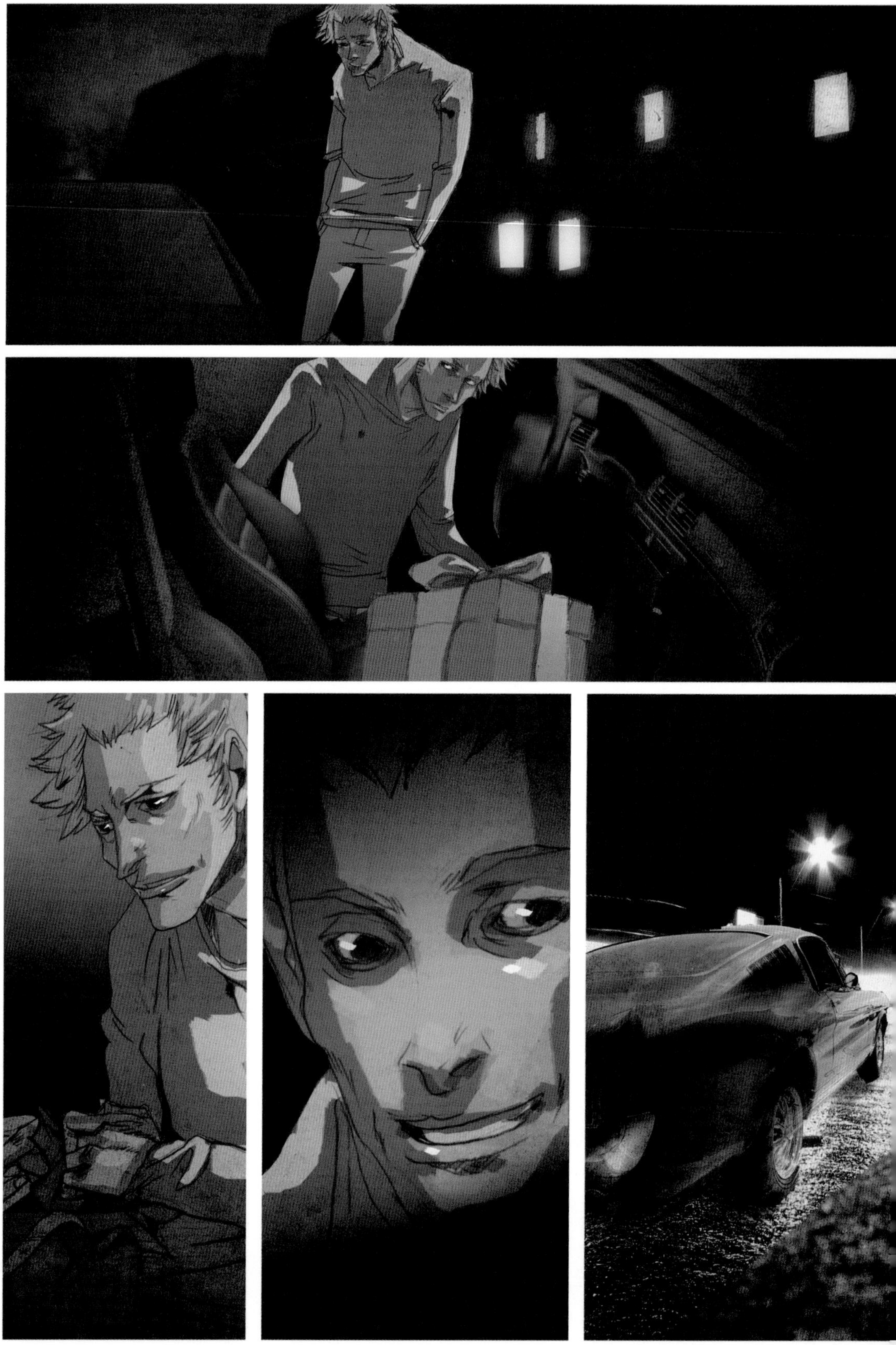

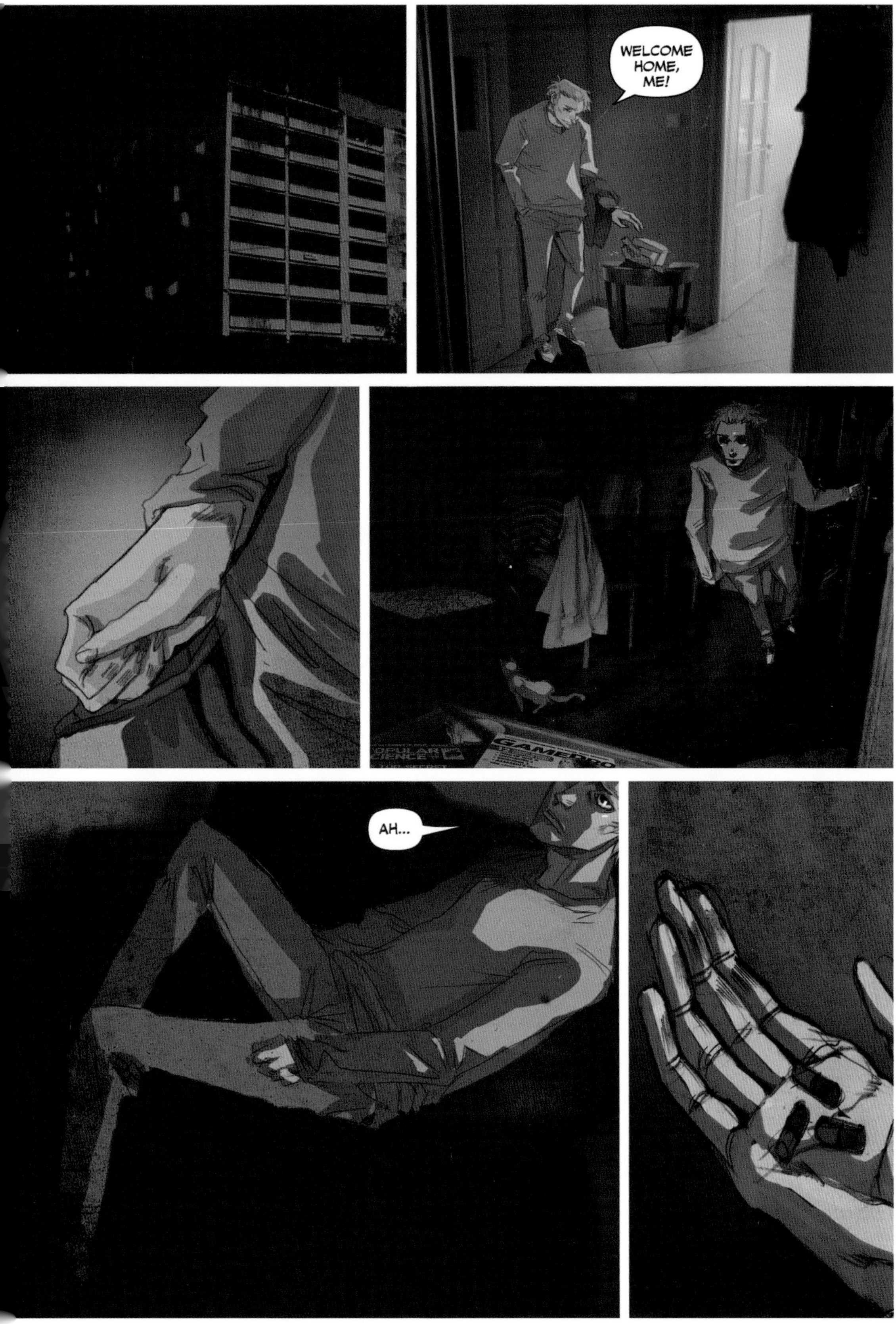
WELCOME HOME, ME!
AH...

SO, DRUGS, IT'S JUST YOU AND ME. SHOULD I RELIVE MY GLORY DAYS-- HA!--OR CHANGE THE WORLD?

RIGHT. DON'T BE A DICK, ANDREW.

MM. A BIT CREEPY. AGAIN: DON'T BE A DICK.

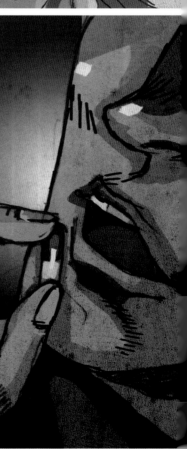

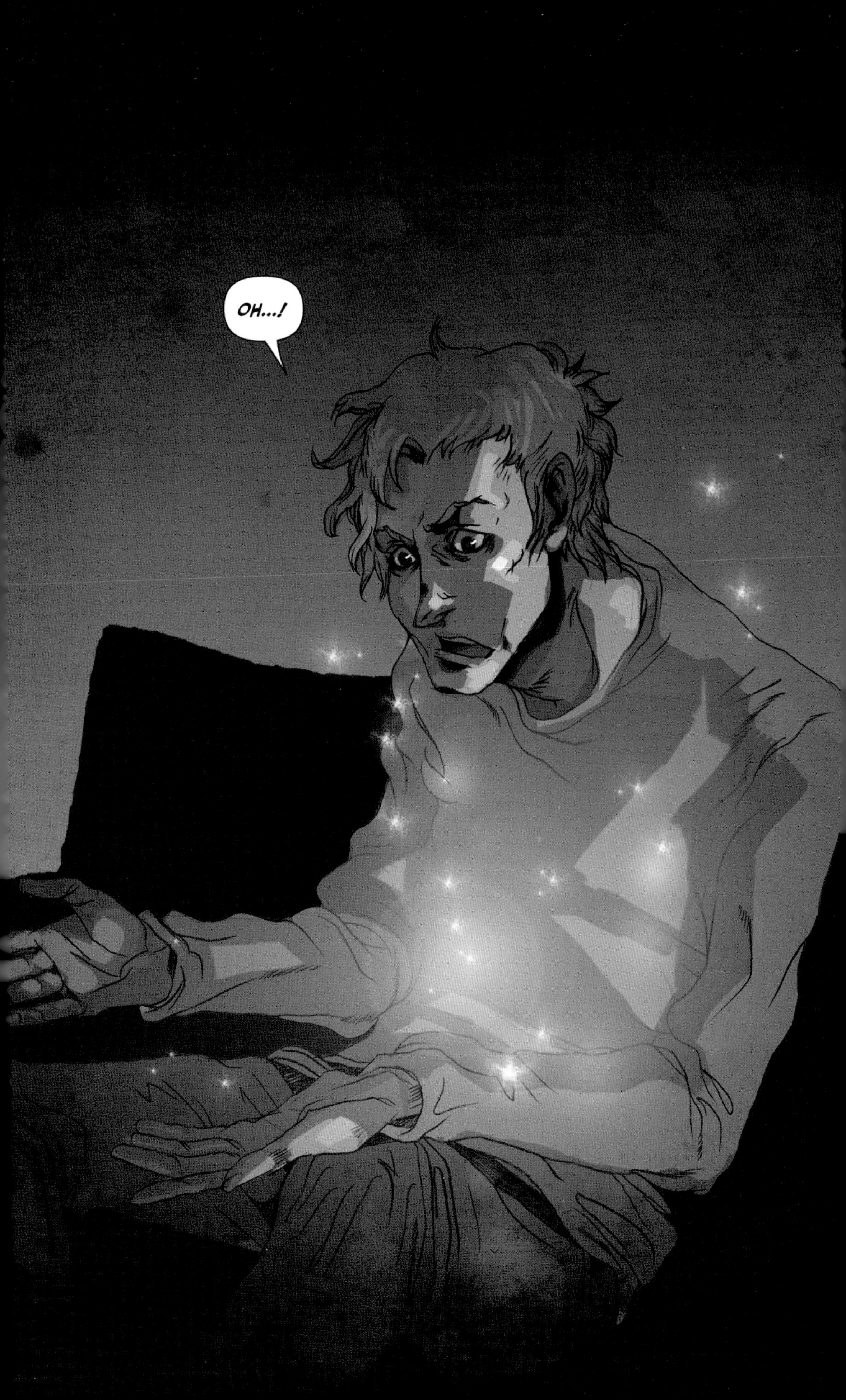
OH...!

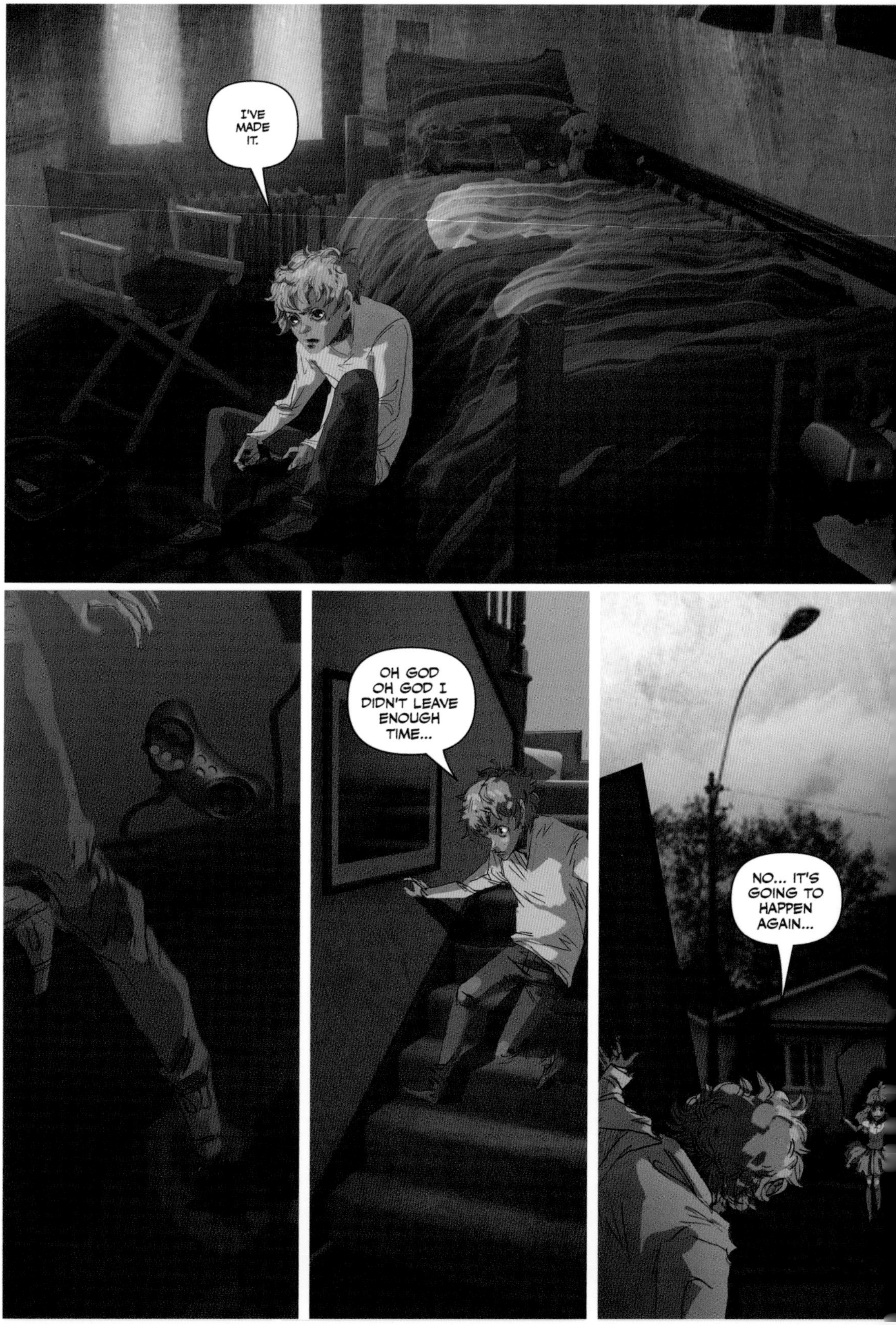
I'VE MADE IT.
OH GOD OH GOD I DIDN'T LEAVE ENOUGH TIME...
NO... IT'S GOING TO HAPPEN AGAIN...

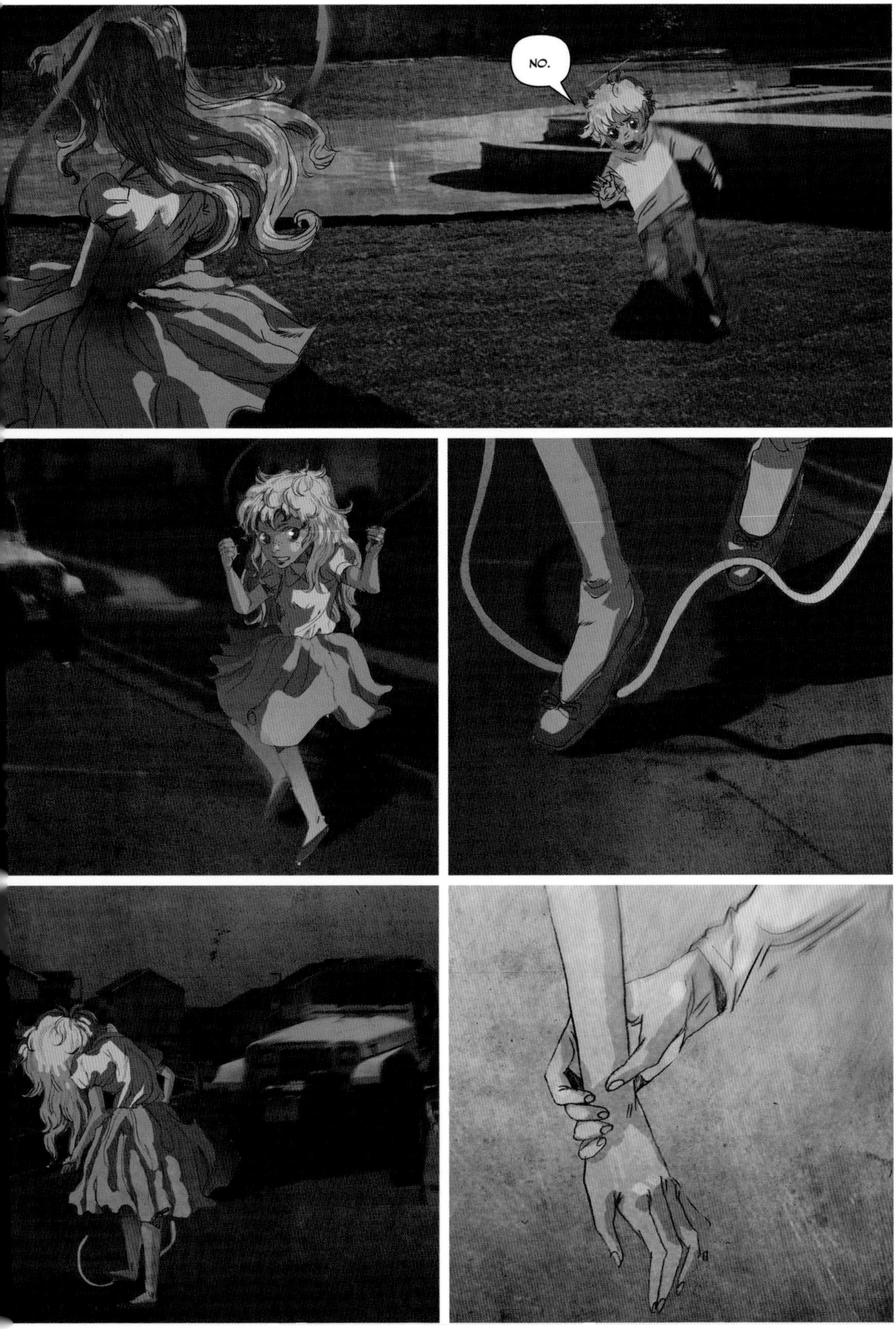
NO.

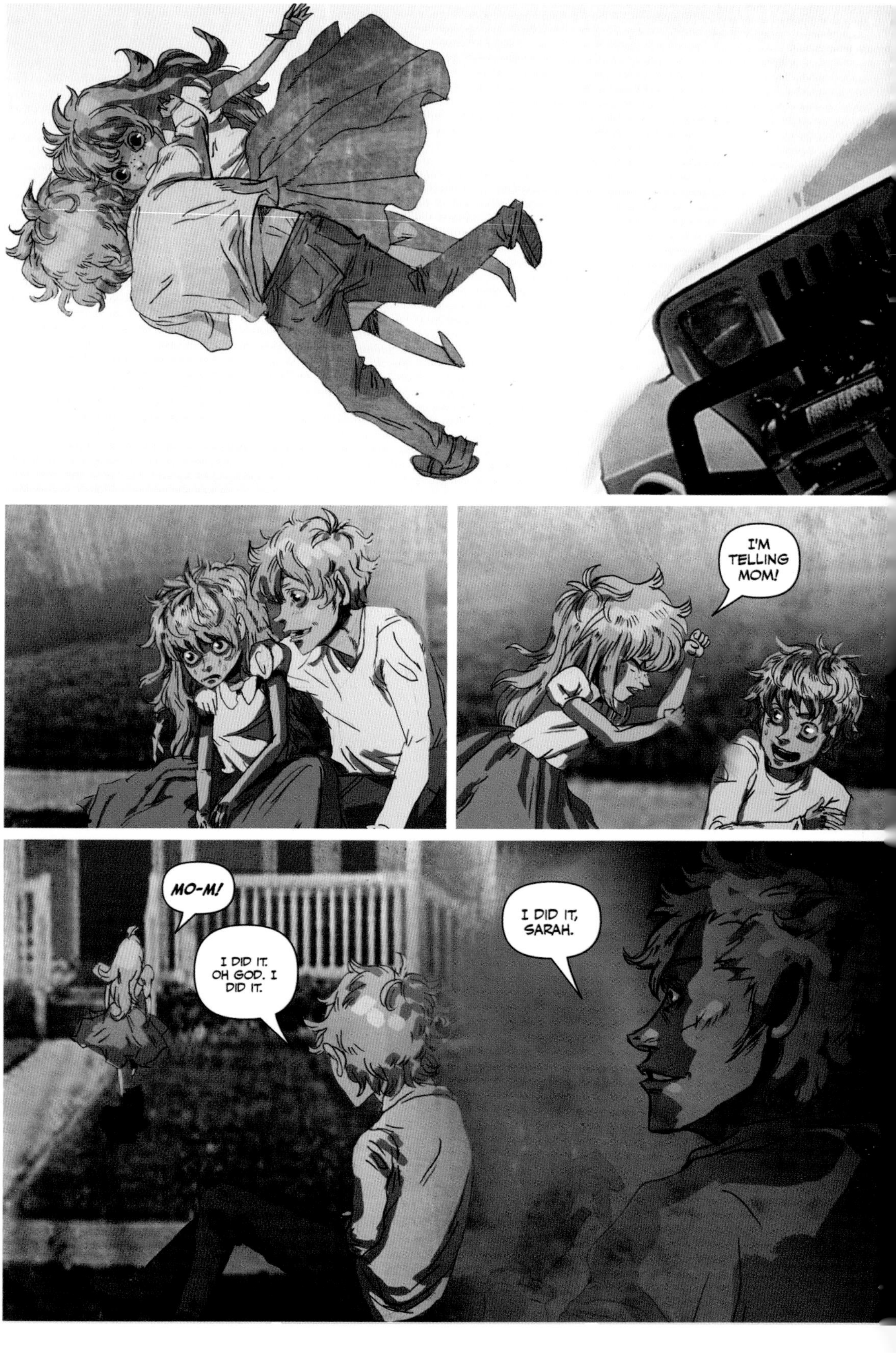
I'M TELLING MOM!
MO-M!
I DID IT. OH GOD. I DID IT.
I DID IT, SARAH.

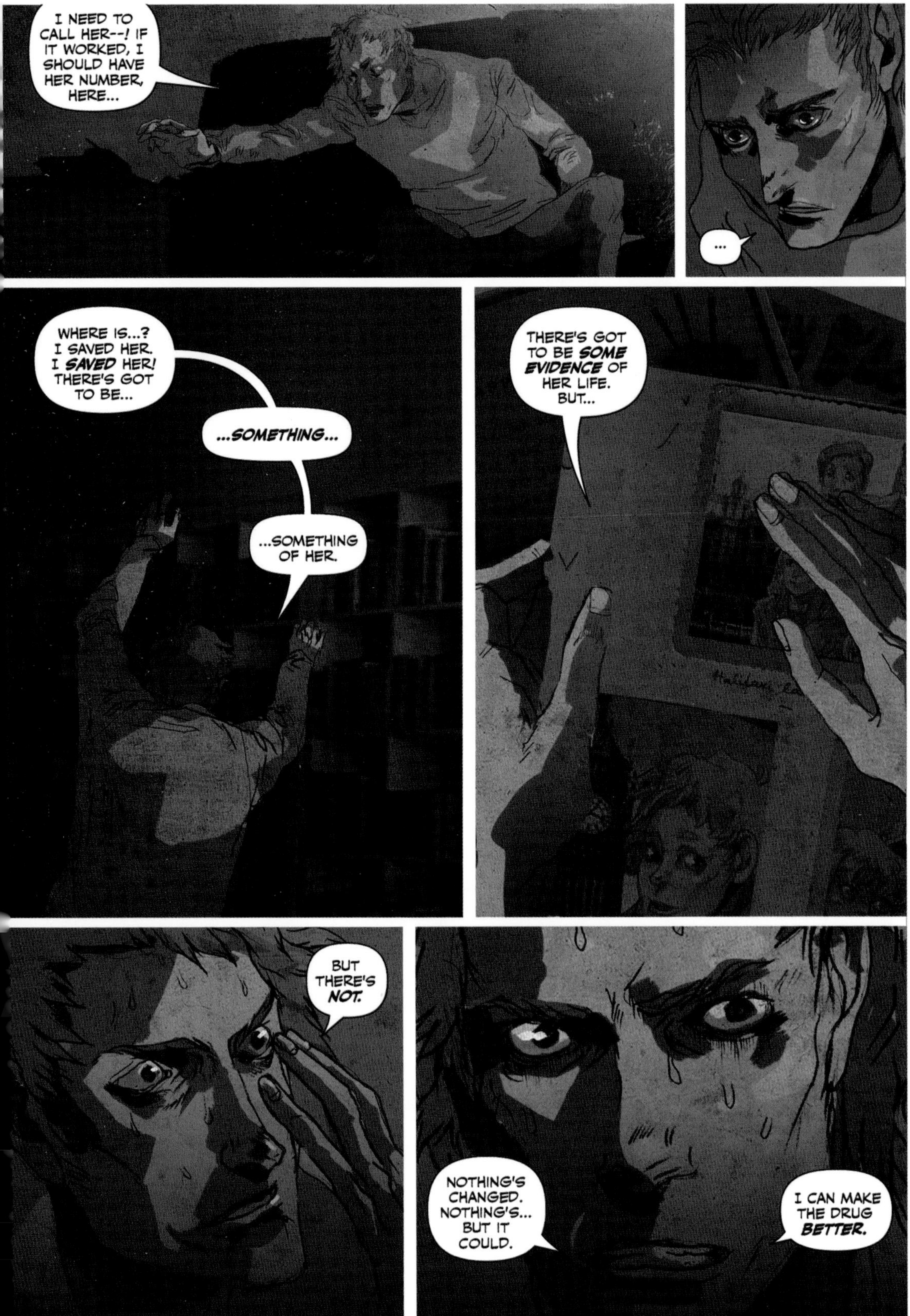
I NEED TO CALL HER--! IF IT WORKED, I SHOULD HAVE HER NUMBER, HERE...
...
WHERE IS...? I SAVED HER. I *SAVED* HER! THERE'S GOT TO BE...
*...SOMETHING...*
...SOMETHING OF HER.
THERE'S GOT TO BE *SOME EVIDENCE* OF HER LIFE. BUT...
BUT THERE'S *NOT.*
NOTHING'S CHANGED. NOTHING'S... BUT IT COULD.
I CAN MAKE THE DRUG *BETTER.*

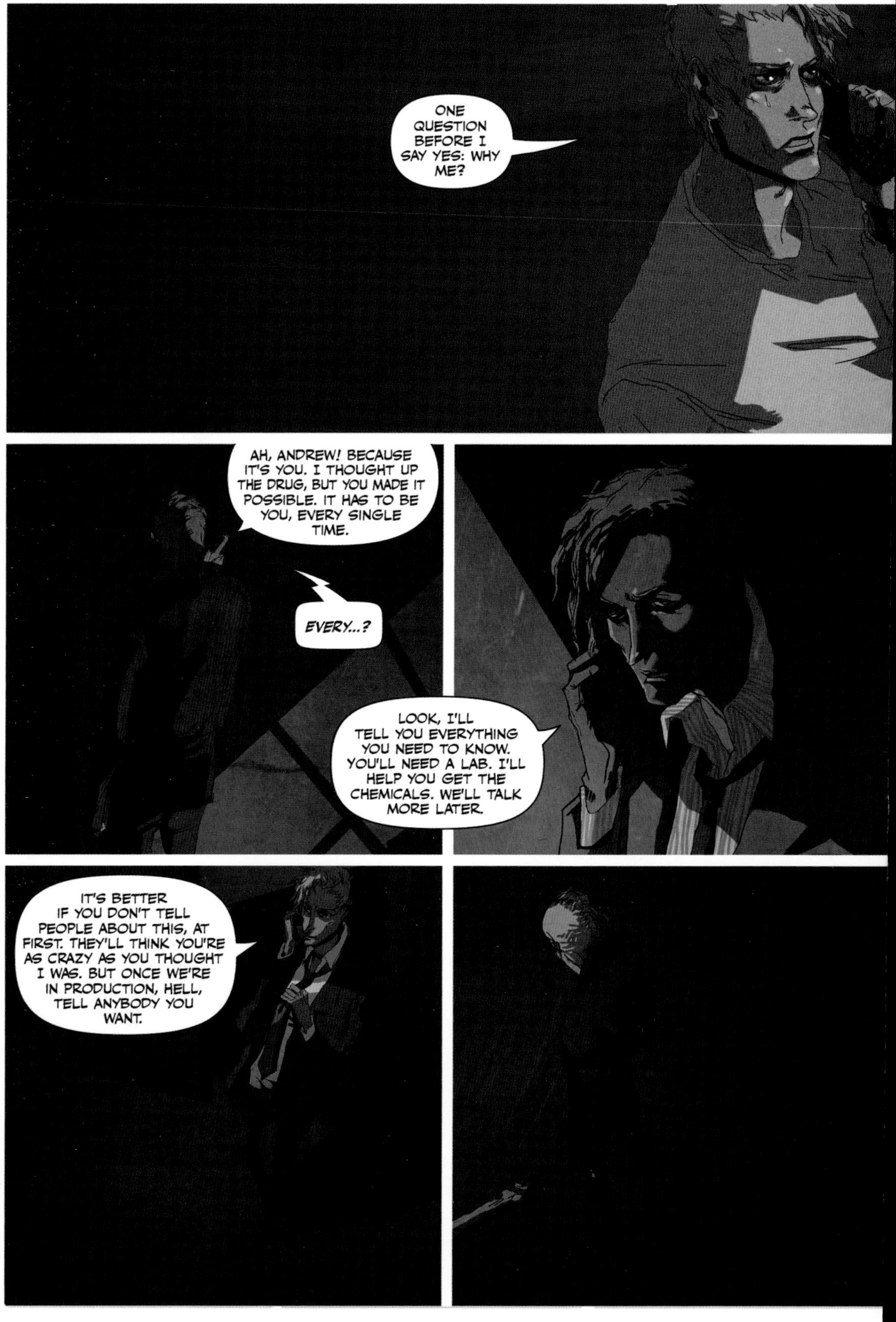
ONE QUESTION BEFORE I SAY YES: WHY ME?
AH, ANDREW! BECAUSE IT'S YOU. I THOUGHT UP THE DRUG, BUT YOU MADE IT POSSIBLE. IT HAS TO BE YOU, EVERY SINGLE TIME.
EVERY...?
LOOK, I'LL TELL YOU EVERYTHING YOU NEED TO KNOW. YOU'LL NEED A LAB. I'LL HELP YOU GET THE CHEMICALS. WE'LL TALK MORE LATER.
IT'S BETTER IF YOU DON'T TELL PEOPLE ABOUT THIS, AT FIRST. THEY'LL THINK YOU'RE AS CRAZY AS YOU THOUGHT I WAS. BUT ONCE WE'RE IN PRODUCTION, HELL, TELL ANYBODY YOU WANT.

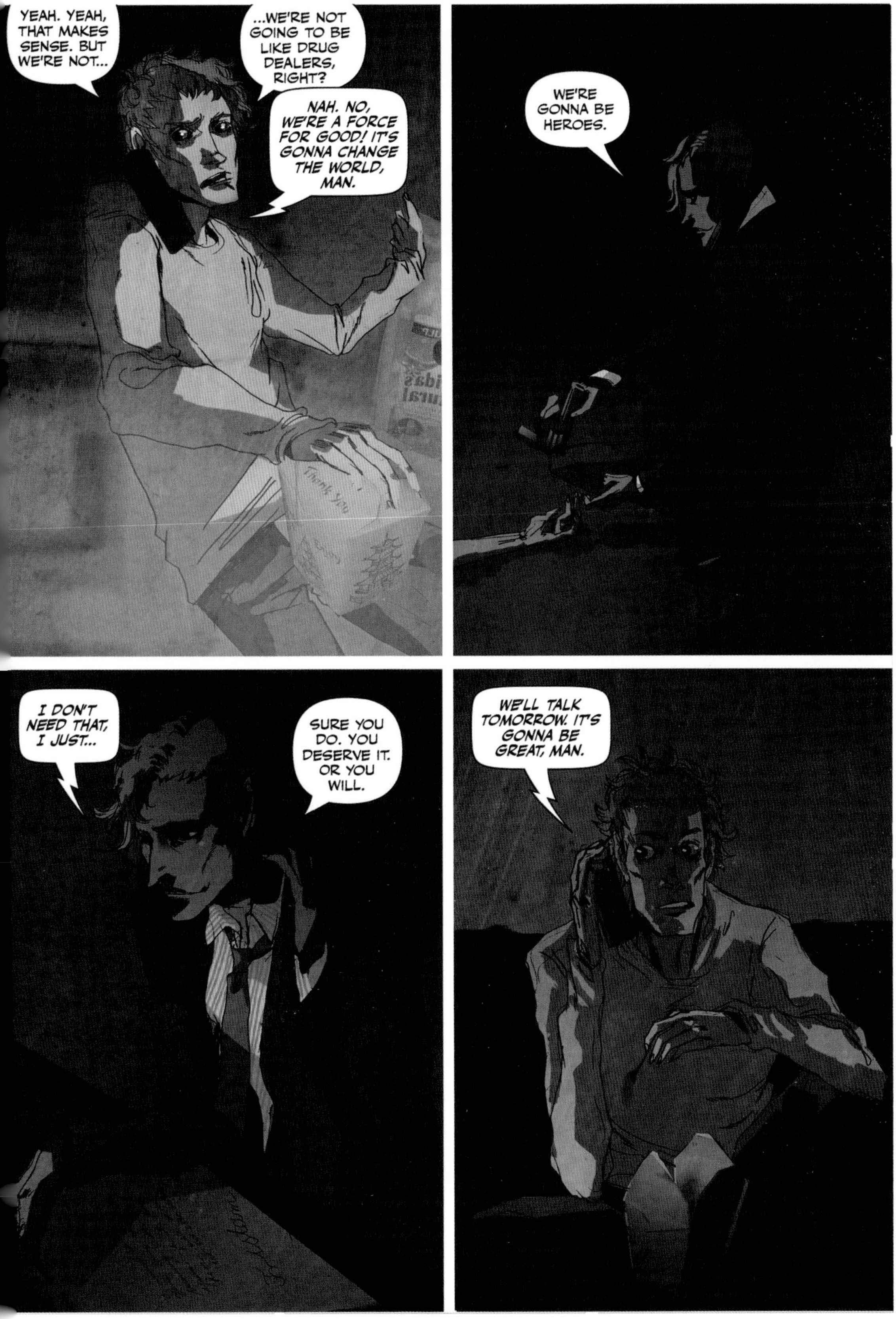
YEAH. YEAH, THAT MAKES SENSE. BUT WE'RE NOT...
...WE'RE NOT GOING TO BE LIKE DRUG DEALERS, RIGHT?
NAH. NO, WE'RE A FORCE FOR GOOD! IT'S GONNA CHANGE THE WORLD, MAN.
WE'RE GONNA BE HEROES.
I DON'T NEED THAT, I JUST...
SURE YOU DO. YOU DESERVE IT. OR YOU WILL.
WE'LL TALK TOMORROW. IT'S GONNA BE GREAT, MAN.

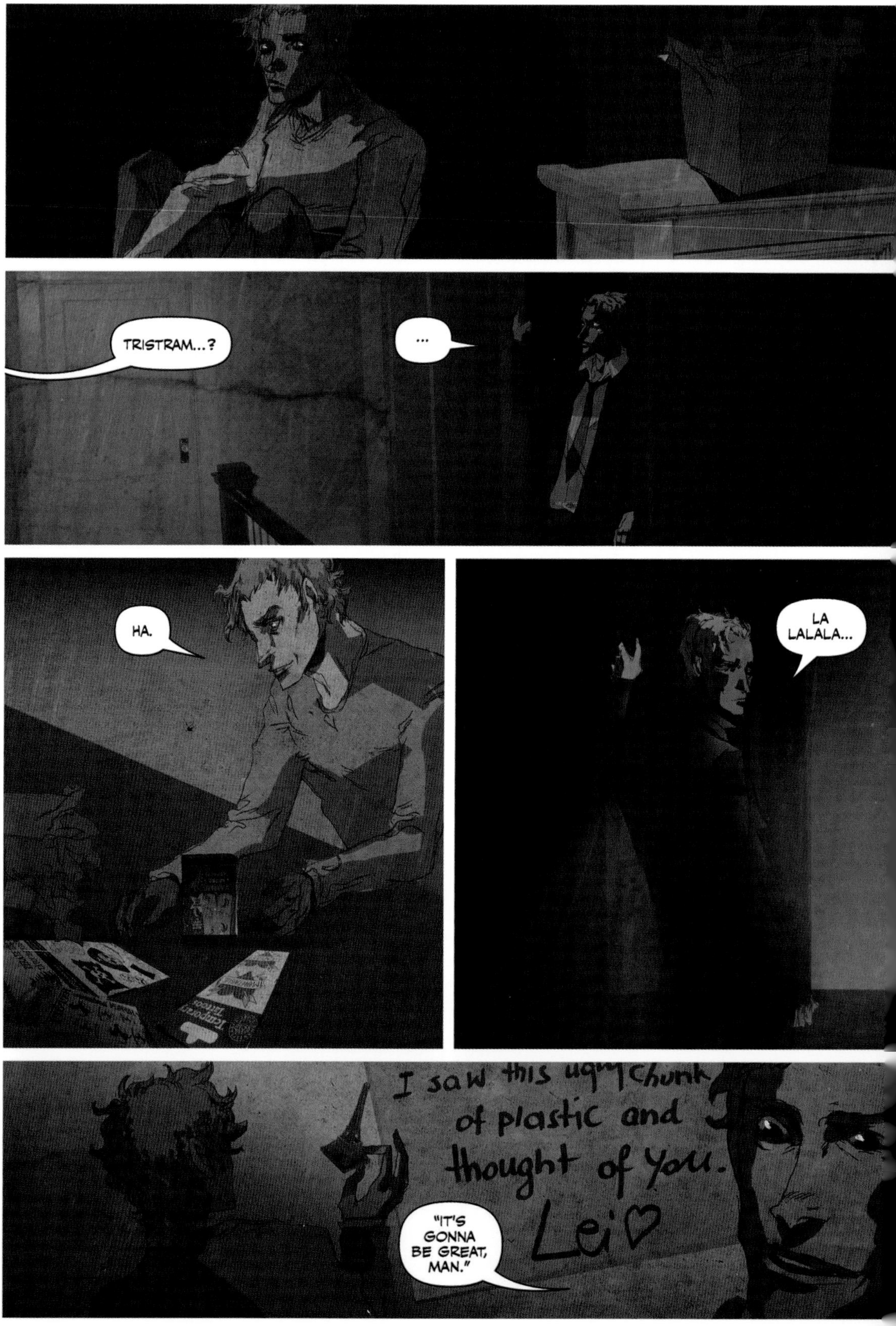
TRISTRAM...?
...
HA.
LA LALALA...
I saw this ugly chunk of plastic and thought of you.
Lei♡
"IT'S GONNA BE GREAT, MAN."

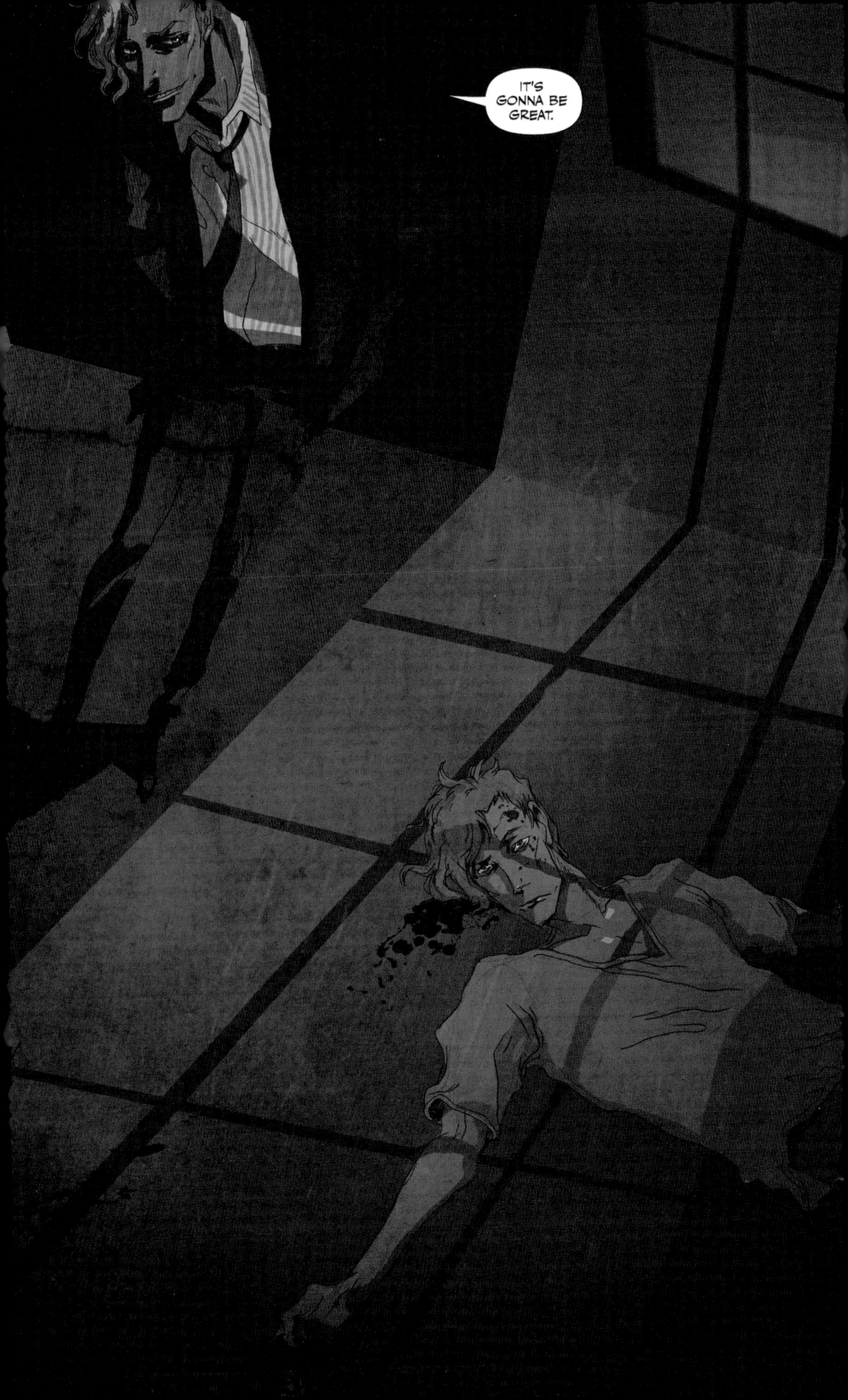
IT'S GONNA BE GREAT.

CHAPTER
TWO

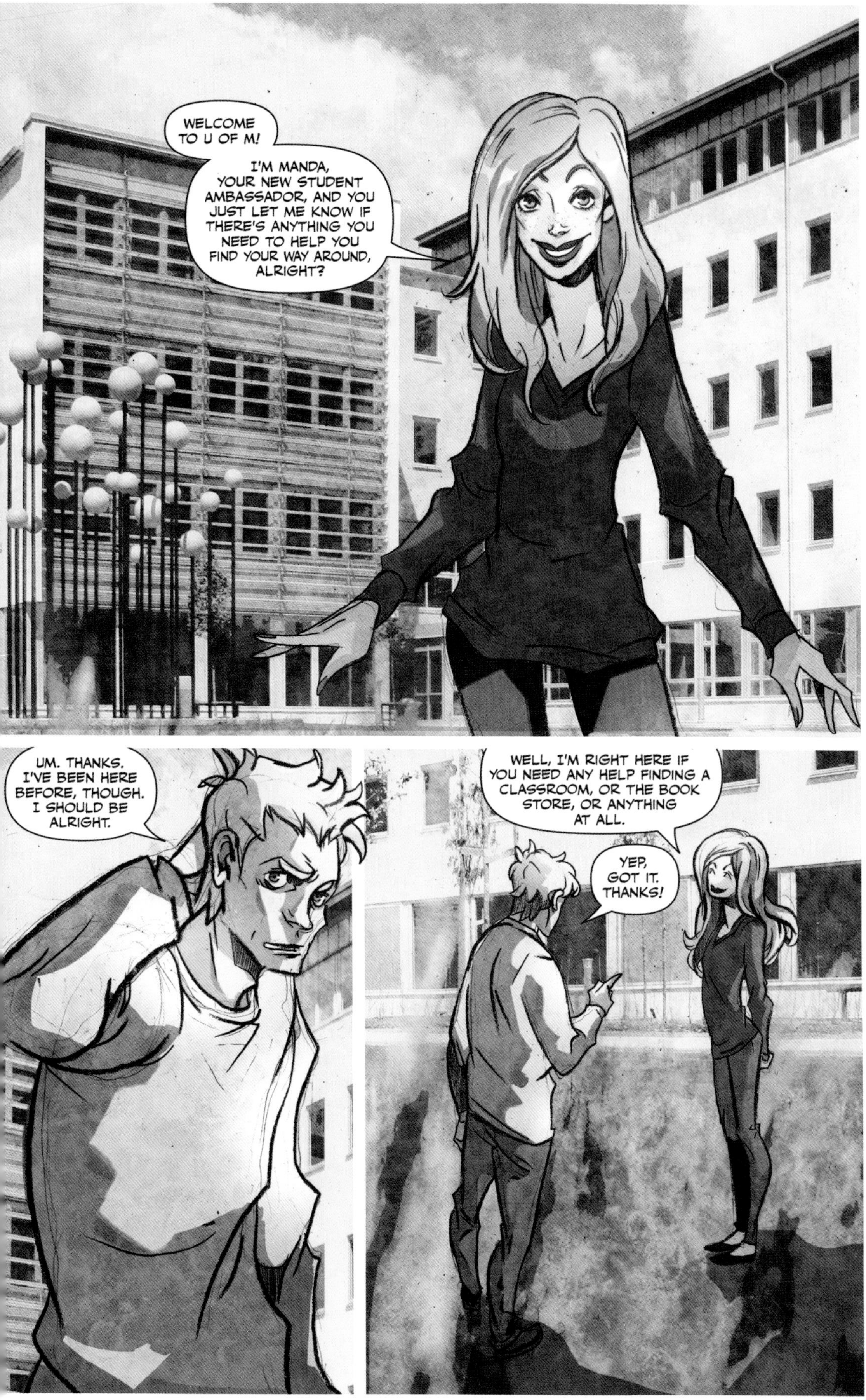
WELCOME TO U OF M!
I'M MANDA, YOUR NEW STUDENT AMBASSADOR, AND YOU JUST LET ME KNOW IF THERE'S ANYTHING YOU NEED TO HELP YOU FIND YOUR WAY AROUND, ALRIGHT?
UM. THANKS. I'VE BEEN HERE BEFORE, THOUGH. I SHOULD BE ALRIGHT.
WELL, I'M RIGHT HERE IF YOU NEED ANY HELP FINDING A CLASSROOM, OR THE BOOK STORE, OR ANYTHING AT ALL.
YEP, GOT IT. THANKS!

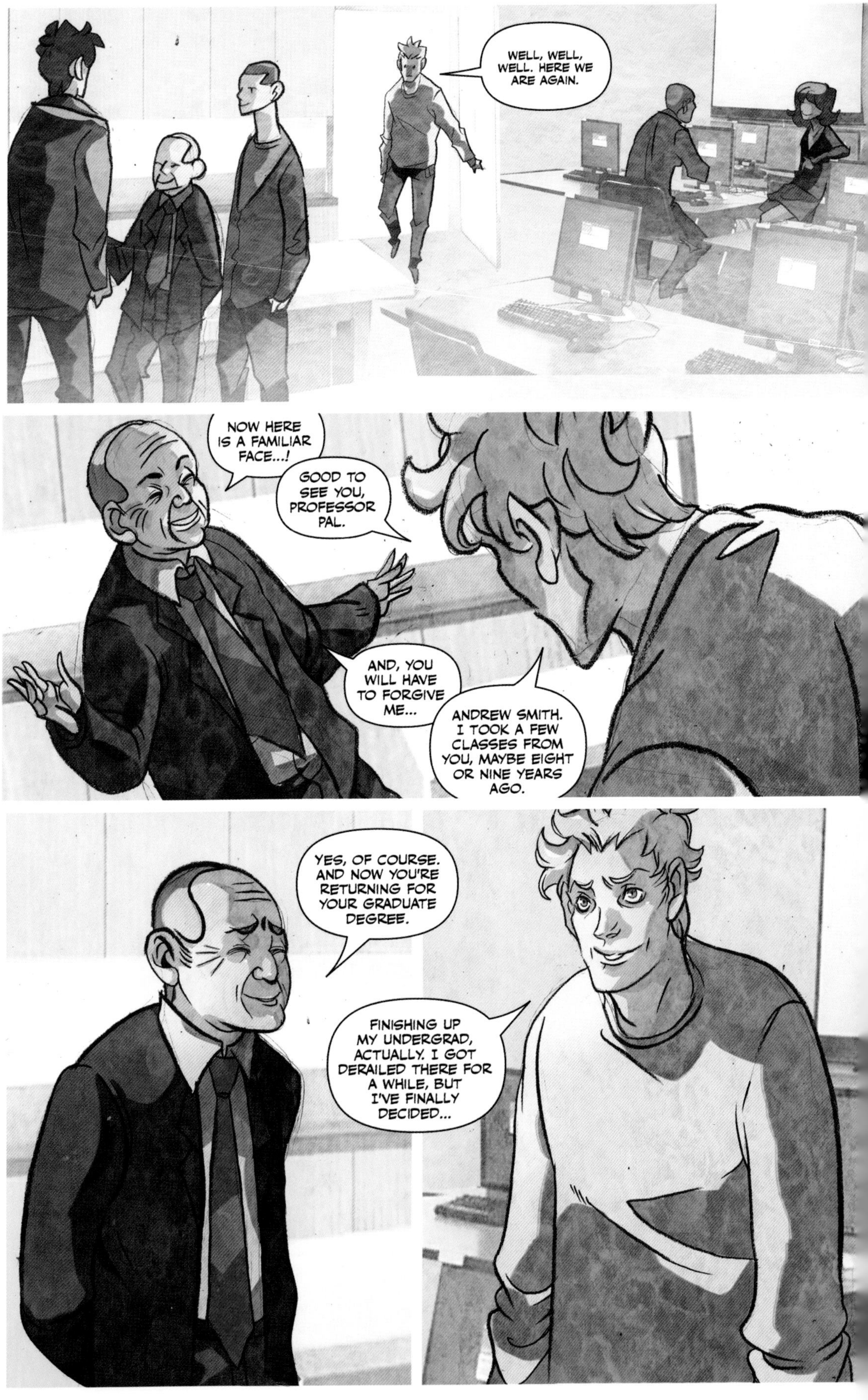
WELL, WELL, WELL. HERE WE ARE AGAIN.
NOW HERE IS A FAMILIAR FACE...!
GOOD TO SEE YOU, PROFESSOR PAL.
AND, YOU WILL HAVE TO FORGIVE ME...
ANDREW SMITH. I TOOK A FEW CLASSES FROM YOU, MAYBE EIGHT OR NINE YEARS AGO.
YES, OF COURSE. AND NOW YOU'RE RETURNING FOR YOUR GRADUATE DEGREE.
FINISHING UP MY UNDERGRAD, ACTUALLY. I GOT DERAILED THERE FOR A WHILE, BUT I'VE FINALLY DECIDED...

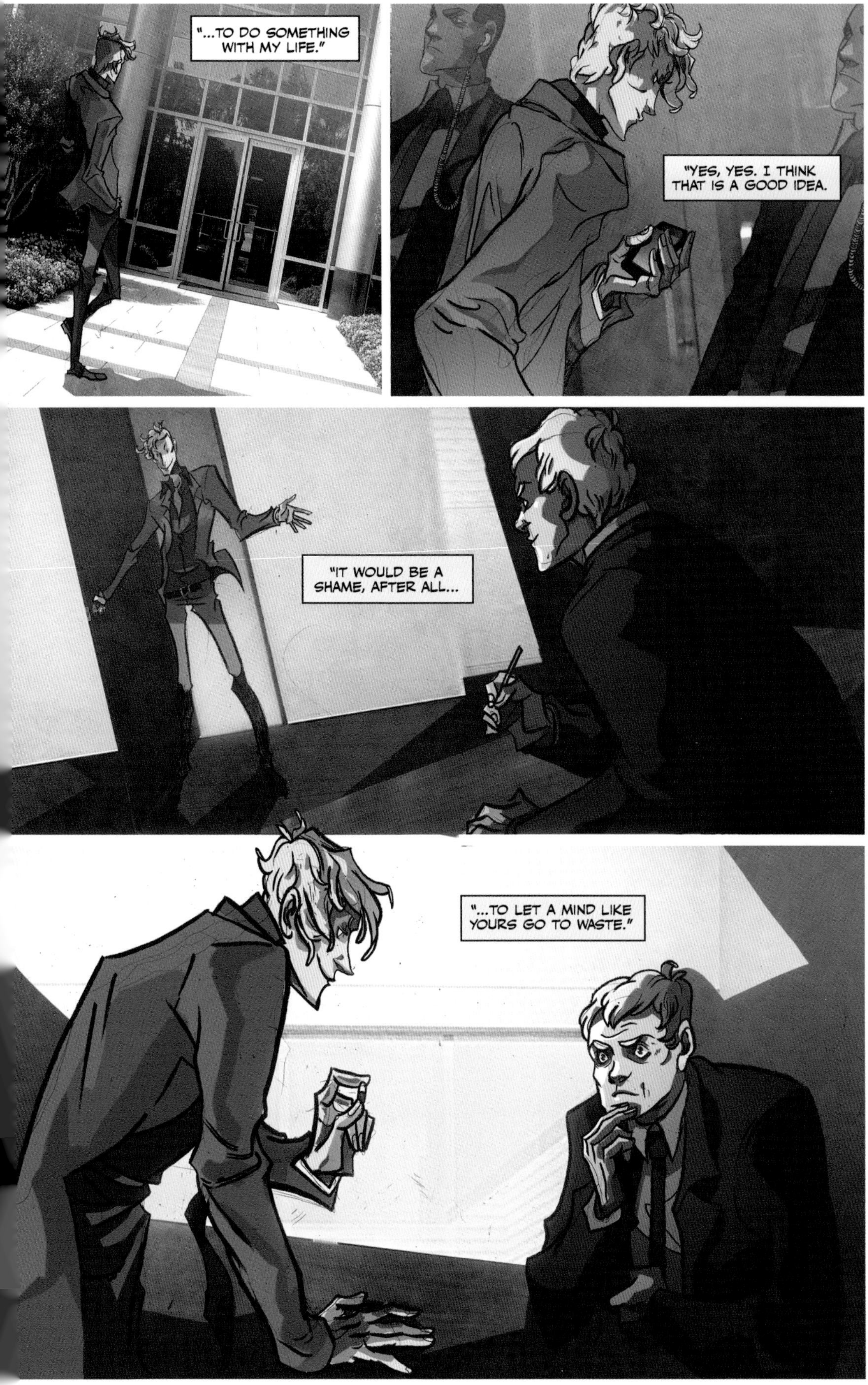
"...TO DO SOMETHING WITH MY LIFE."
"YES, YES. I THINK THAT IS A GOOD IDEA.
"IT WOULD BE A SHAME, AFTER ALL...
"...TO LET A MIND LIKE YOURS GO TO WASTE."

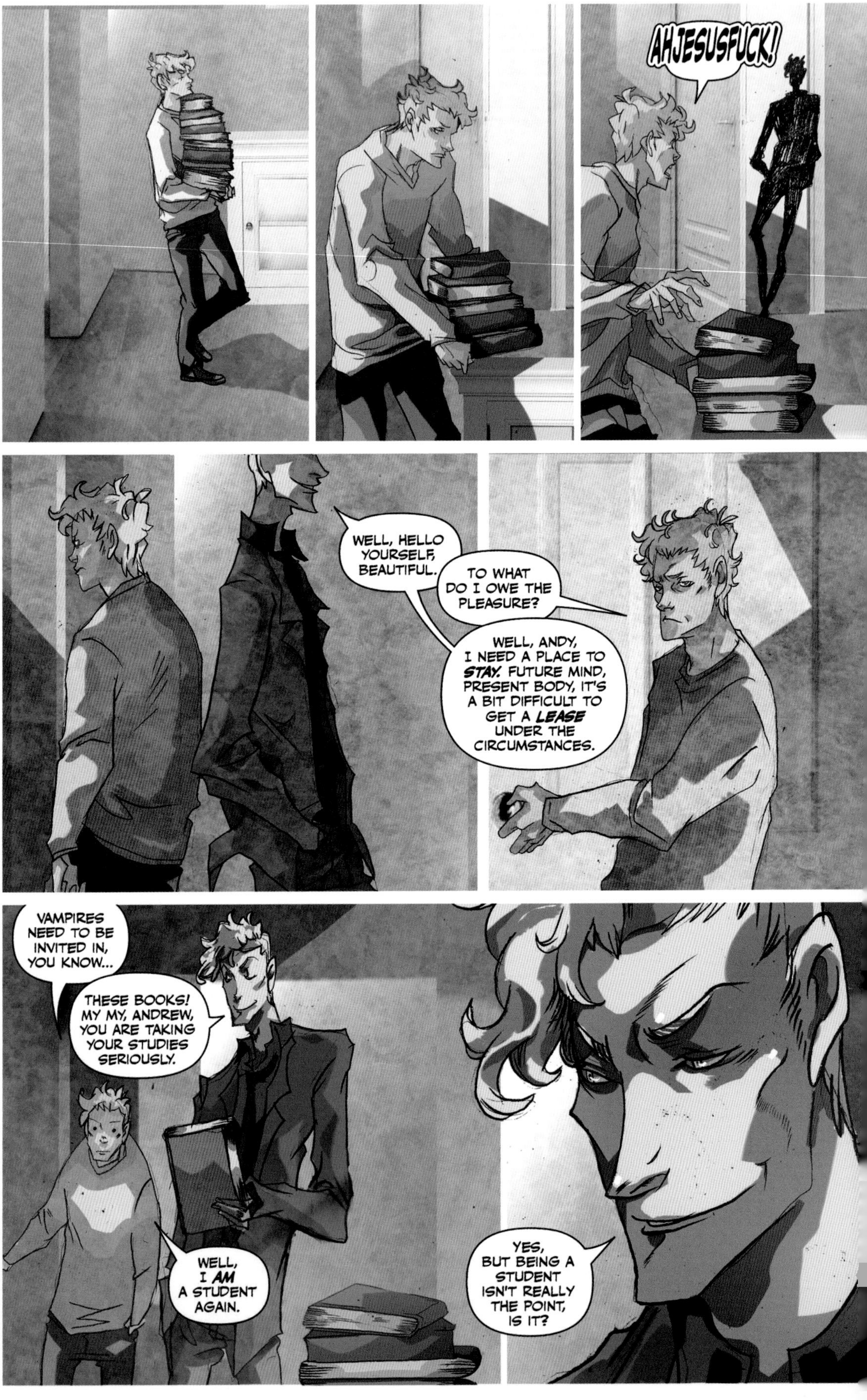
AHJESUSFUCK!
WELL, HELLO YOURSELF, BEAUTIFUL.
TO WHAT DO I OWE THE PLEASURE?
WELL, ANDY, I NEED A PLACE TO STAY. FUTURE MIND, PRESENT BODY, IT'S A BIT DIFFICULT TO GET A LEASE UNDER THE CIRCUMSTANCES.
VAMPIRES NEED TO BE INVITED IN, YOU KNOW...
THESE BOOKS! MY MY, ANDREW, YOU ARE TAKING YOUR STUDIES SERIOUSLY.
WELL, I AM A STUDENT AGAIN.
YES, BUT BEING A STUDENT ISN'T REALLY THE POINT, IS IT?

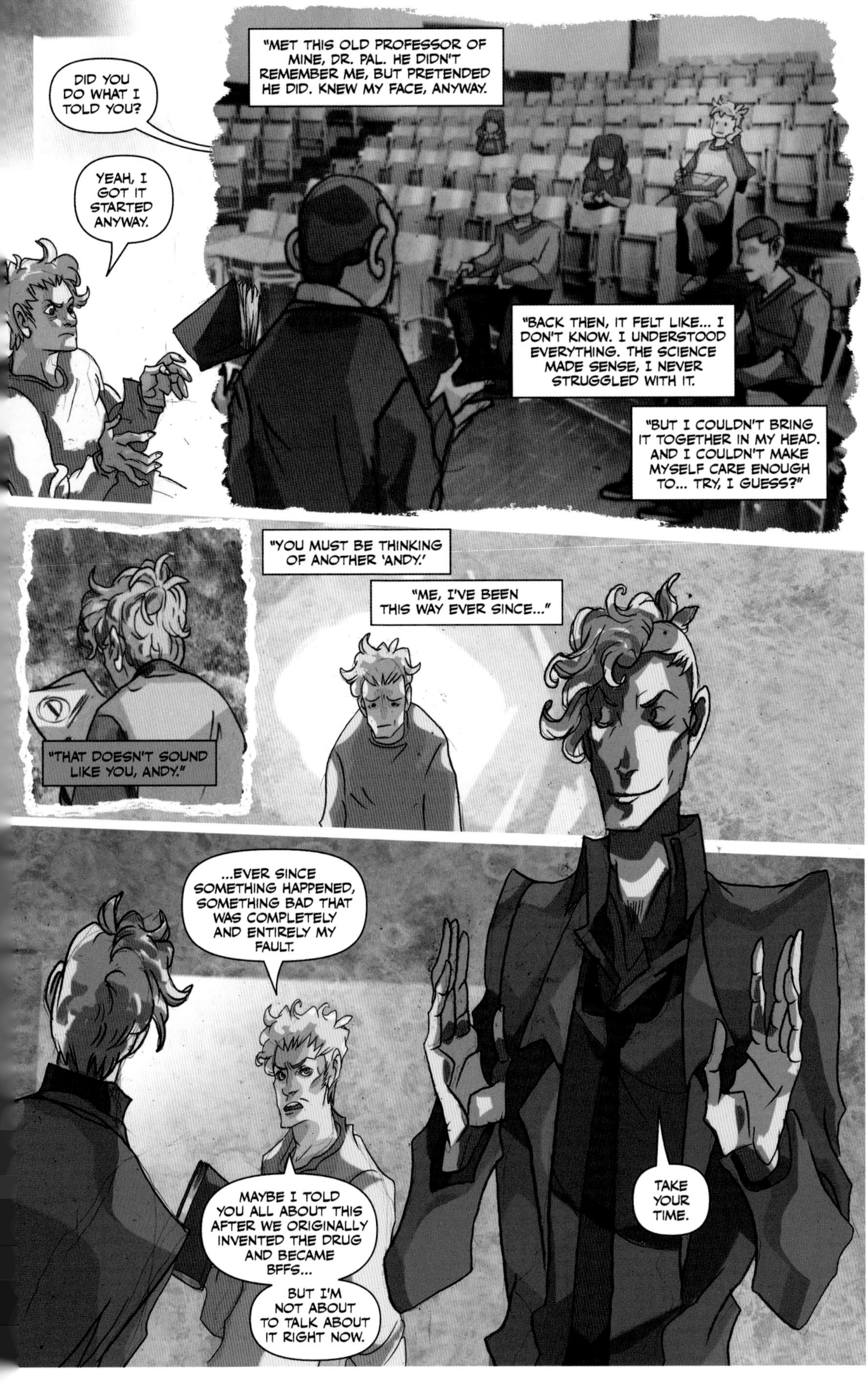
"MET THIS OLD PROFESSOR OF MINE, DR. PAL. HE DIDN'T REMEMBER ME, BUT PRETENDED HE DID. KNEW MY FACE, ANYWAY.
DID YOU DO WHAT I TOLD YOU?
YEAH, I GOT IT STARTED ANYWAY.
"BACK THEN, IT FELT LIKE... I DON'T KNOW. I UNDERSTOOD EVERYTHING. THE SCIENCE MADE SENSE, I NEVER STRUGGLED WITH IT.
"BUT I COULDN'T BRING IT TOGETHER IN MY HEAD. AND I COULDN'T MAKE MYSELF CARE ENOUGH TO... TRY, I GUESS?"
"THAT DOESN'T SOUND LIKE YOU, ANDY."
"YOU MUST BE THINKING OF ANOTHER 'ANDY.'
"ME, I'VE BEEN THIS WAY EVER SINCE..."
...EVER SINCE SOMETHING HAPPENED, SOMETHING BAD THAT WAS COMPLETELY AND ENTIRELY MY FAULT.
MAYBE I TOLD YOU ALL ABOUT THIS AFTER WE ORIGINALLY INVENTED THE DRUG AND BECAME BFFS...
BUT I'M NOT ABOUT TO TALK ABOUT IT RIGHT NOW.
TAKE YOUR TIME.

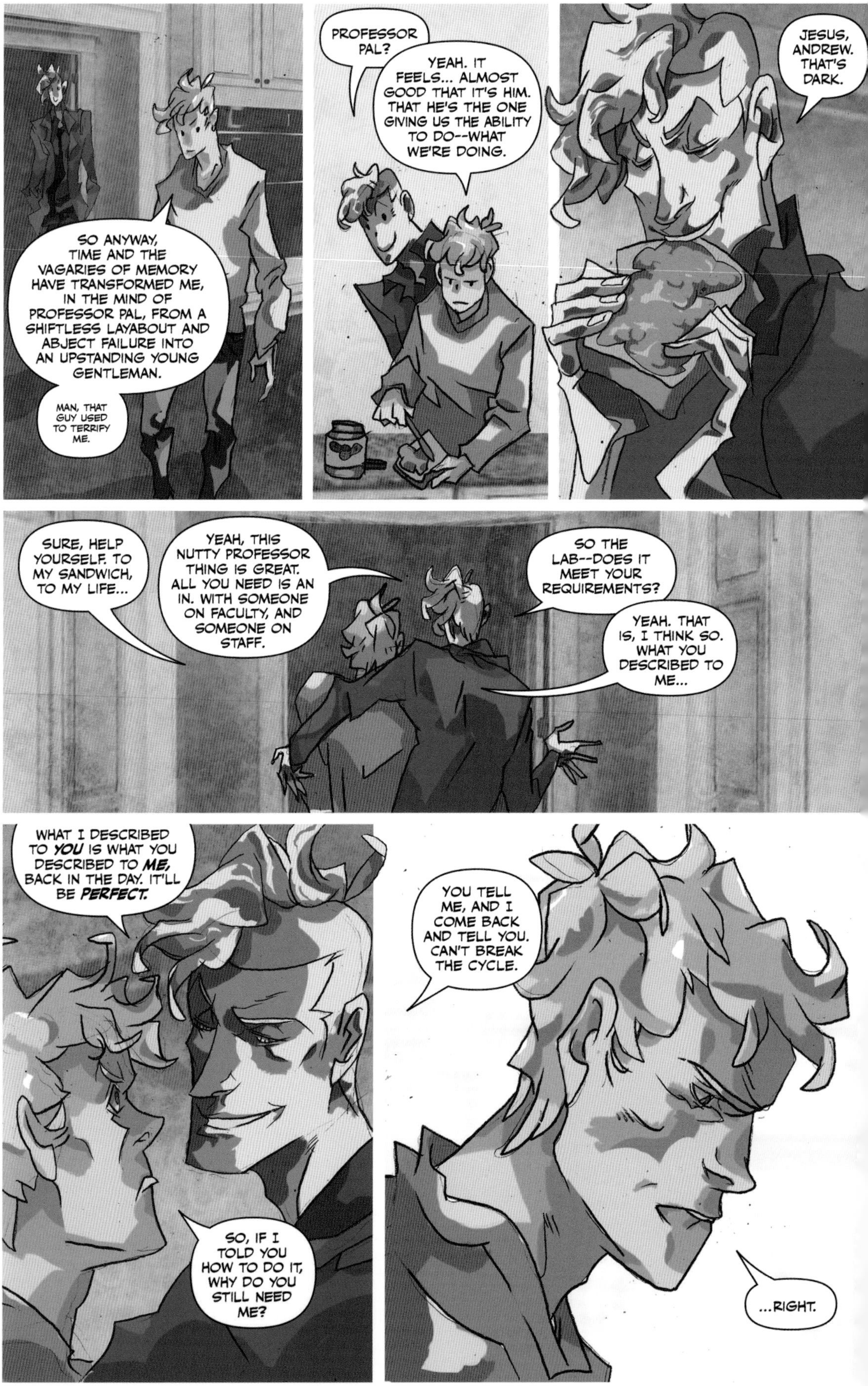
SO ANYWAY, TIME AND THE VAGARIES OF MEMORY HAVE TRANSFORMED ME, IN THE MIND OF PROFESSOR PAL, FROM A SHIFTLESS LAYABOUT AND ABJECT FAILURE INTO AN UPSTANDING YOUNG GENTLEMAN.
MAN, THAT GUY USED TO TERRIFY ME.
PROFESSOR PAL?
YEAH. IT FEELS... ALMOST GOOD THAT IT'S HIM. THAT HE'S THE ONE GIVING US THE ABILITY TO DO--WHAT WE'RE DOING.
JESUS, ANDREW. THAT'S DARK.
SURE, HELP YOURSELF. TO MY SANDWICH, TO MY LIFE...
YEAH, THIS NUTTY PROFESSOR THING IS GREAT. ALL YOU NEED IS AN IN. WITH SOMEONE ON FACULTY, AND SOMEONE ON STAFF.
SO THE LAB--DOES IT MEET YOUR REQUIREMENTS?
YEAH. THAT IS, I THINK SO. WHAT YOU DESCRIBED TO ME...
WHAT I DESCRIBED TO *YOU* IS WHAT YOU DESCRIBED TO ***ME,*** BACK IN THE DAY. IT'LL BE ***PERFECT.***
SO, IF I TOLD YOU HOW TO DO IT, WHY DO YOU STILL NEED ME?
YOU TELL ME, AND I COME BACK AND TELL YOU. CAN'T BREAK THE CYCLE.
...RIGHT.

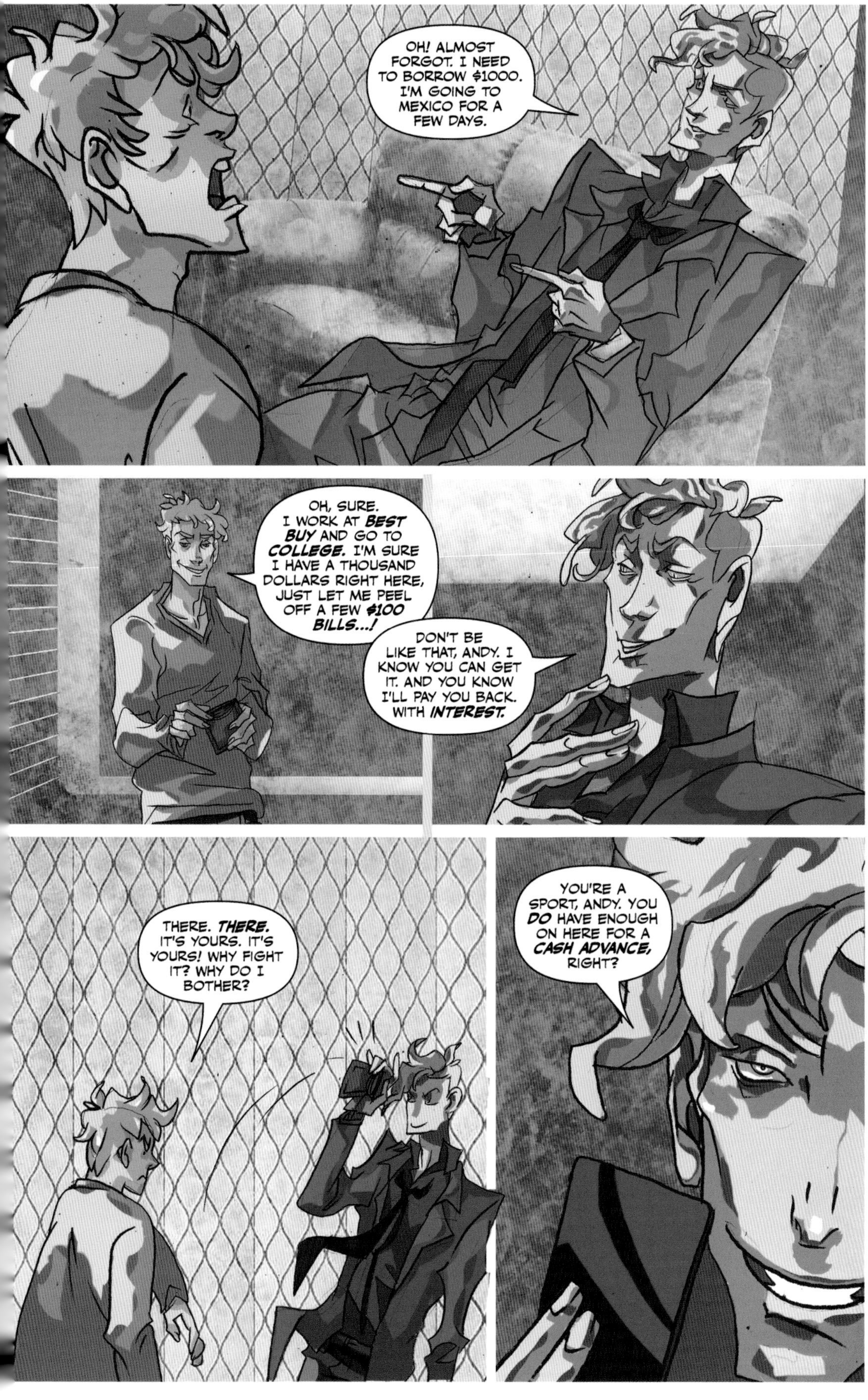
OH! ALMOST FORGOT. I NEED TO BORROW $1000. I'M GOING TO MEXICO FOR A FEW DAYS.
OH, SURE. I WORK AT BEST BUY AND GO TO COLLEGE. I'M SURE I HAVE A THOUSAND DOLLARS RIGHT HERE, JUST LET ME PEEL OFF A FEW $100 BILLS...!
DON'T BE LIKE THAT, ANDY. I KNOW YOU CAN GET IT. AND YOU KNOW I'LL PAY YOU BACK. WITH INTEREST.
THERE. THERE. IT'S YOURS. IT'S YOURS! WHY FIGHT IT? WHY DO I BOTHER?
YOU'RE A SPORT, ANDY. YOU DO HAVE ENOUGH ON HERE FOR A CASH ADVANCE, RIGHT?

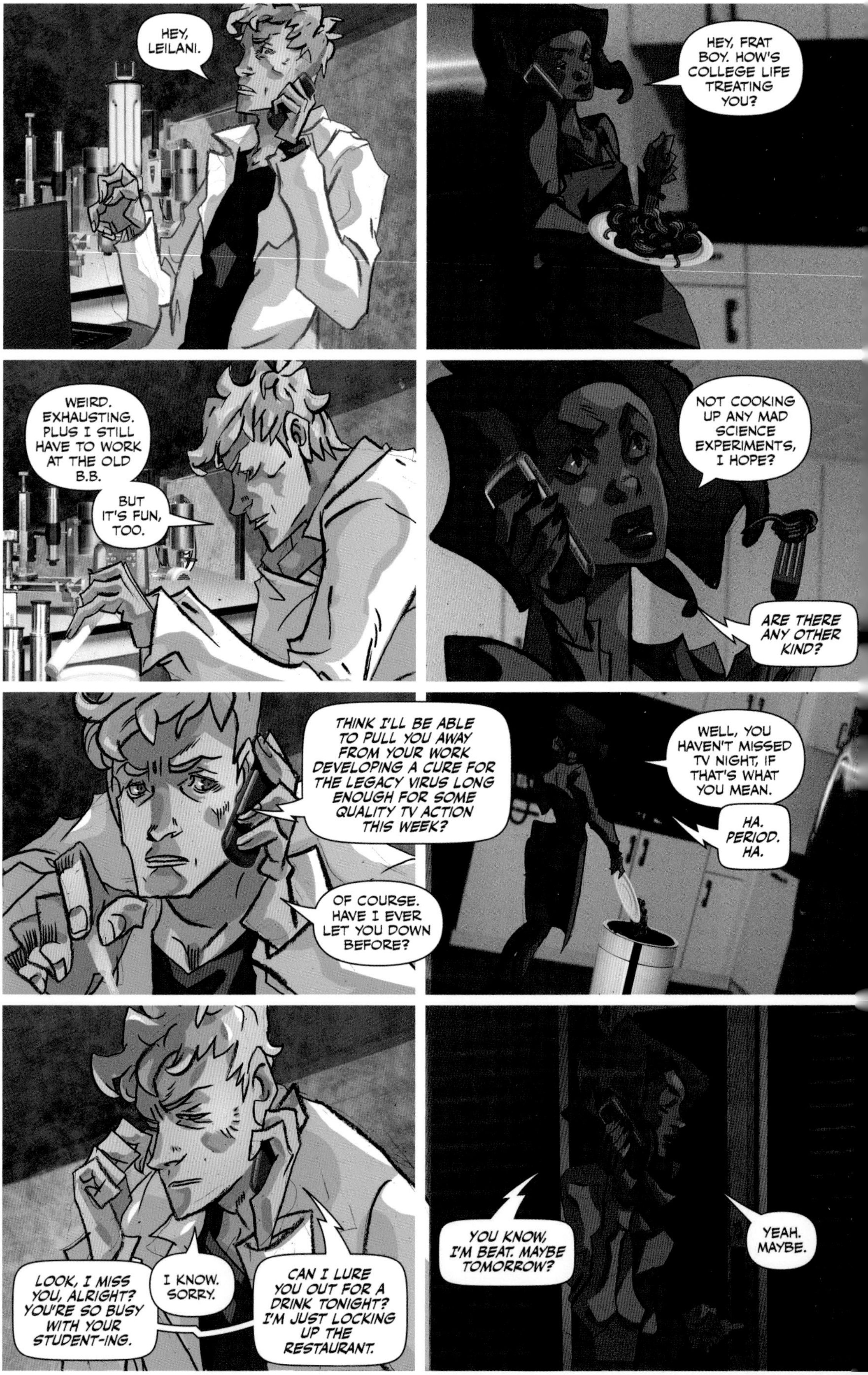
HEY, LEILANI.
HEY, FRAT BOY. HOW'S COLLEGE LIFE TREATING YOU?
WEIRD. EXHAUSTING. PLUS I STILL HAVE TO WORK AT THE OLD B.B.
BUT IT'S FUN, TOO.
NOT COOKING UP ANY MAD SCIENCE EXPERIMENTS, I HOPE?
ARE THERE ANY OTHER KIND?
THINK I'LL BE ABLE TO PULL YOU AWAY FROM YOUR WORK DEVELOPING A CURE FOR THE LEGACY VIRUS LONG ENOUGH FOR SOME QUALITY TV ACTION THIS WEEK?
OF COURSE. HAVE I EVER LET YOU DOWN BEFORE?
WELL, YOU HAVEN'T MISSED TV NIGHT, IF THAT'S WHAT YOU MEAN.
HA. PERIOD. HA.
LOOK, I MISS YOU, ALRIGHT? YOU'RE SO BUSY WITH YOUR STUDENT-ING.
I KNOW. SORRY.
CAN I LURE YOU OUT FOR A DRINK TONIGHT? I'M JUST LOCKING UP THE RESTAURANT.
YOU KNOW, I'M BEAT. MAYBE TOMORROW?
YEAH. MAYBE.

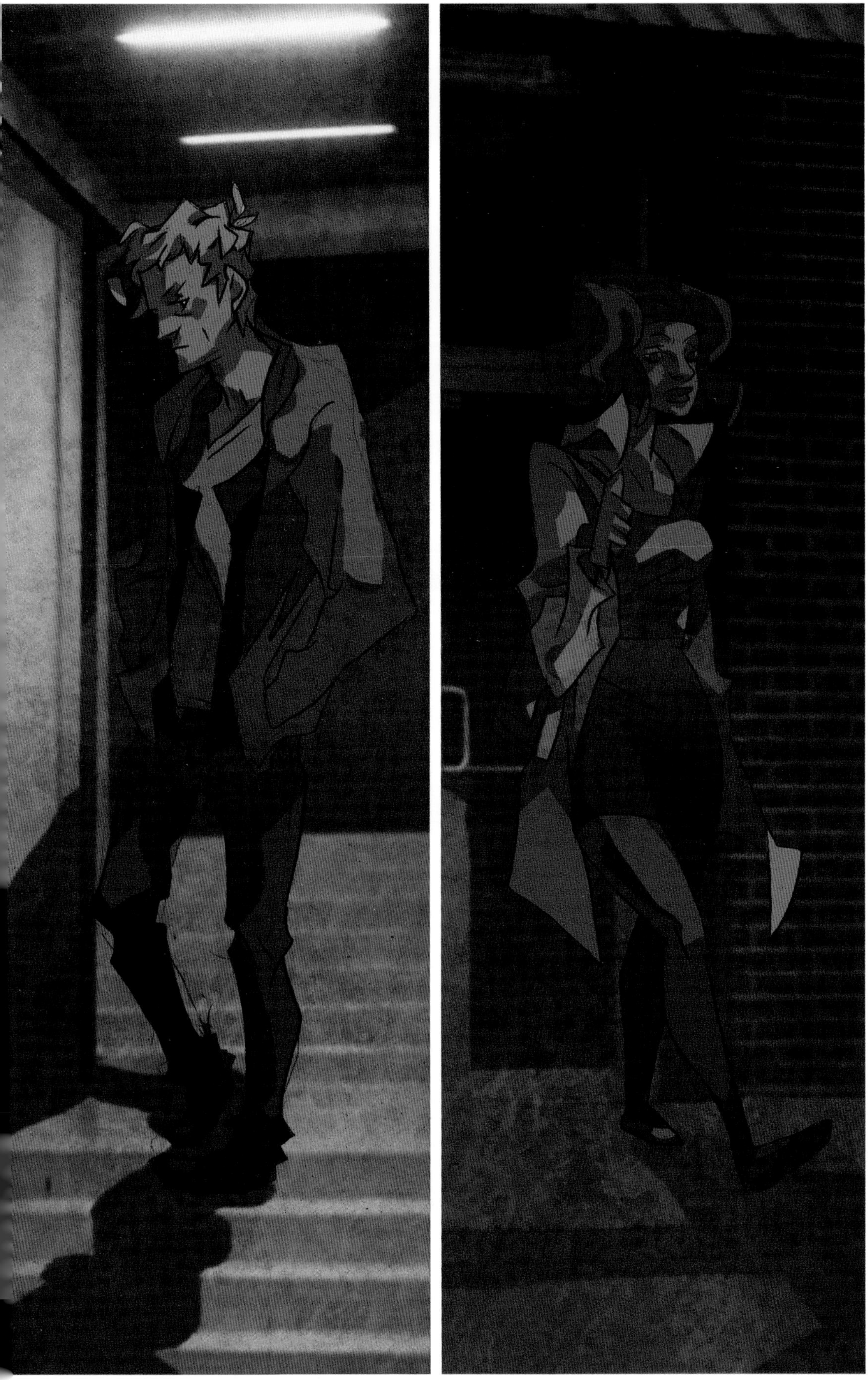

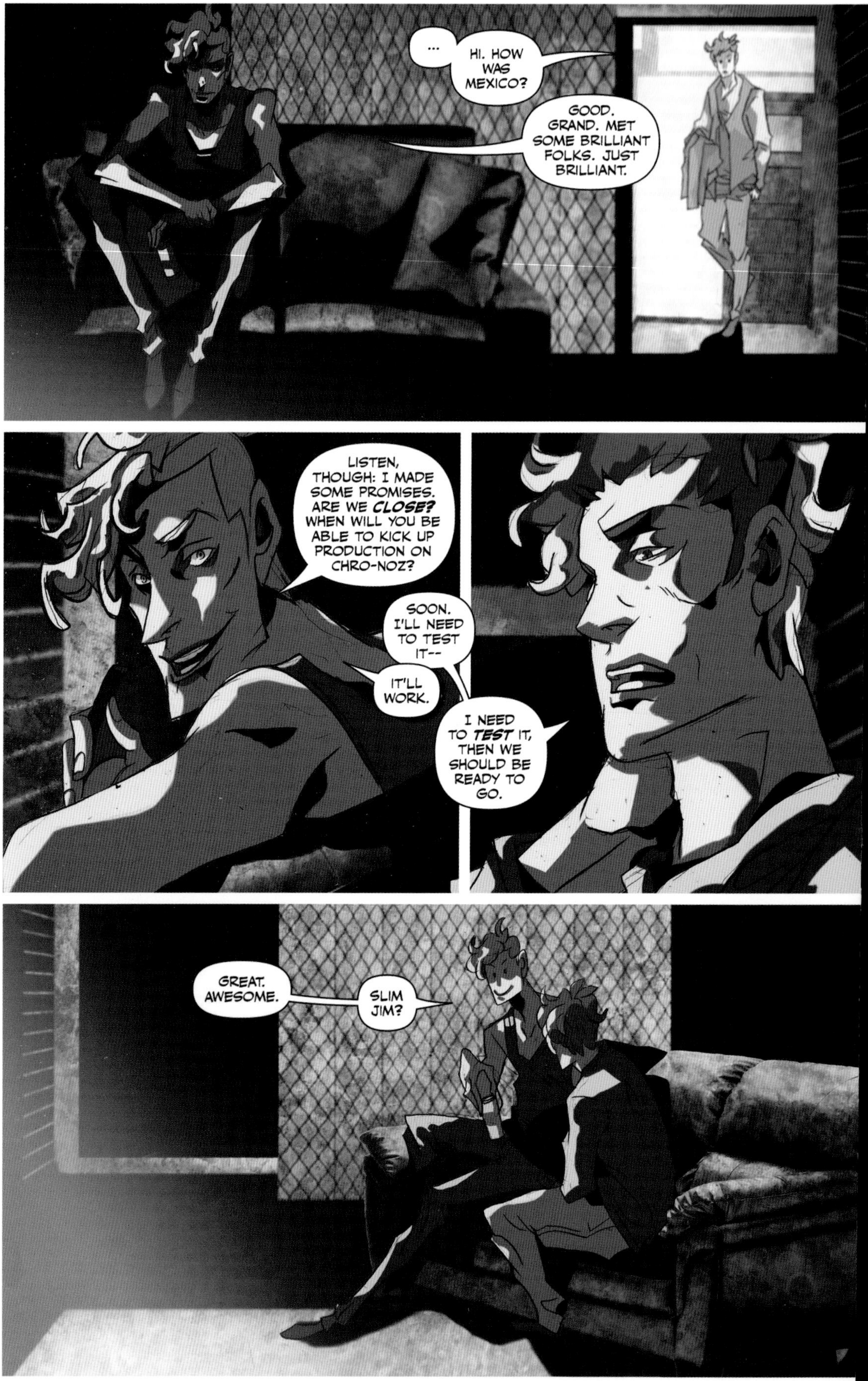
...
HI. HOW WAS MEXICO?
GOOD. GRAND. MET SOME BRILLIANT FOLKS. JUST BRILLIANT.
LISTEN, THOUGH: I MADE SOME PROMISES. ARE WE CLOSE? WHEN WILL YOU BE ABLE TO KICK UP PRODUCTION ON CHRO-NOZ?
SOON. I'LL NEED TO TEST IT--
IT'LL WORK.
I NEED TO TEST IT, THEN WE SHOULD BE READY TO GO.
GREAT. AWESOME.
SLIM JIM?

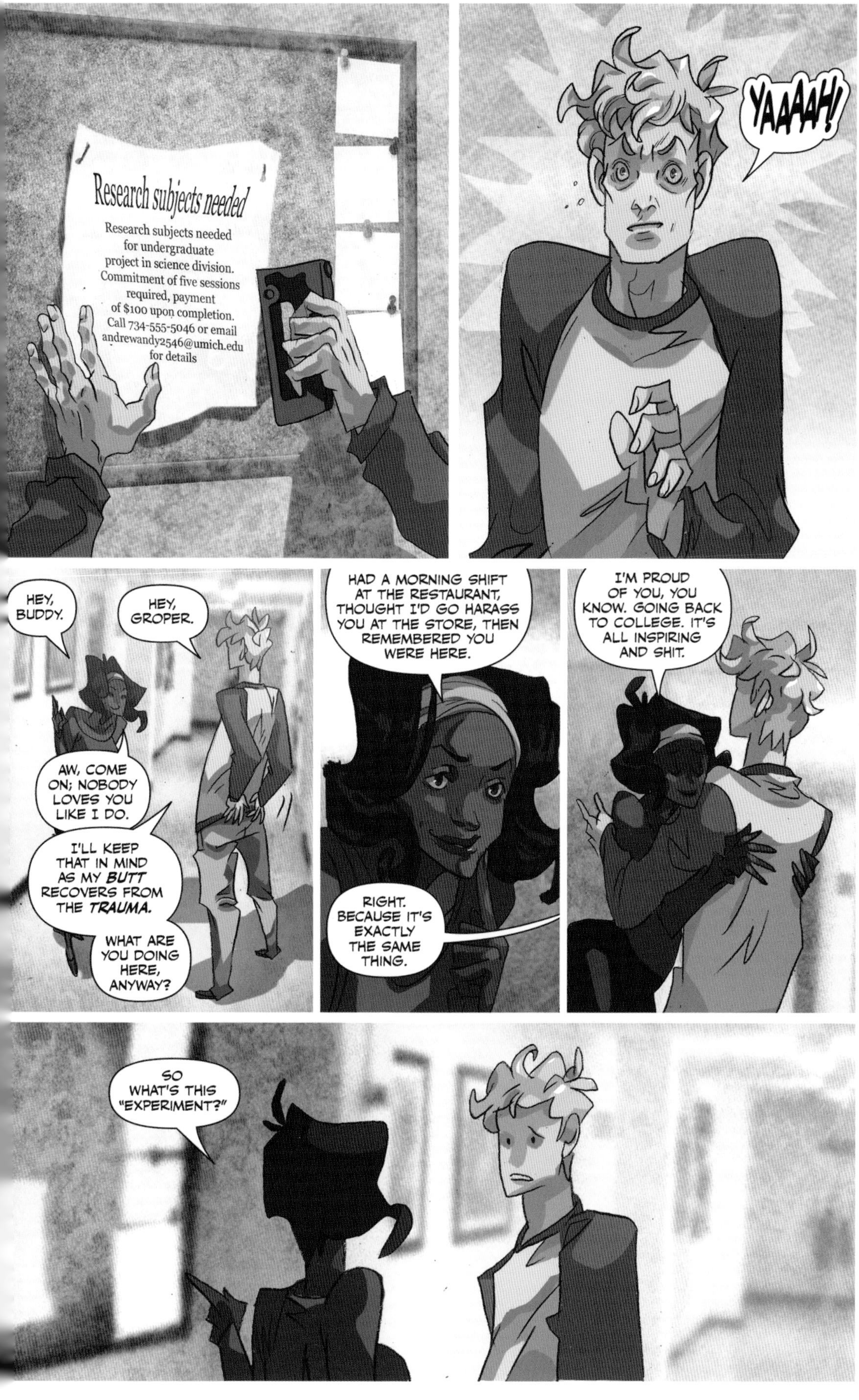
Research subjects needed
Research subjects needed for undergraduate project in science division. Commitment of five sessions required, payment of $100 upon completion. Call 734-555-5046 or email andrewandy2546@umich.edu for details
YAAAAH!
HEY, BUDDY.
HEY, GROPER.
AW, COME ON; NOBODY LOVES YOU LIKE I DO.
I'LL KEEP THAT IN MIND AS MY *BUTT* RECOVERS FROM THE *TRAUMA.*
WHAT ARE YOU DOING HERE, ANYWAY?
HAD A MORNING SHIFT AT THE RESTAURANT, THOUGHT I'D GO HARASS YOU AT THE STORE, THEN REMEMBERED YOU WERE HERE.
RIGHT. BECAUSE IT'S EXACTLY THE SAME THING.
I'M PROUD OF YOU, YOU KNOW. GOING BACK TO COLLEGE. IT'S ALL INSPIRING AND SHIT.
SO WHAT'S THIS "EXPERIMENT?"

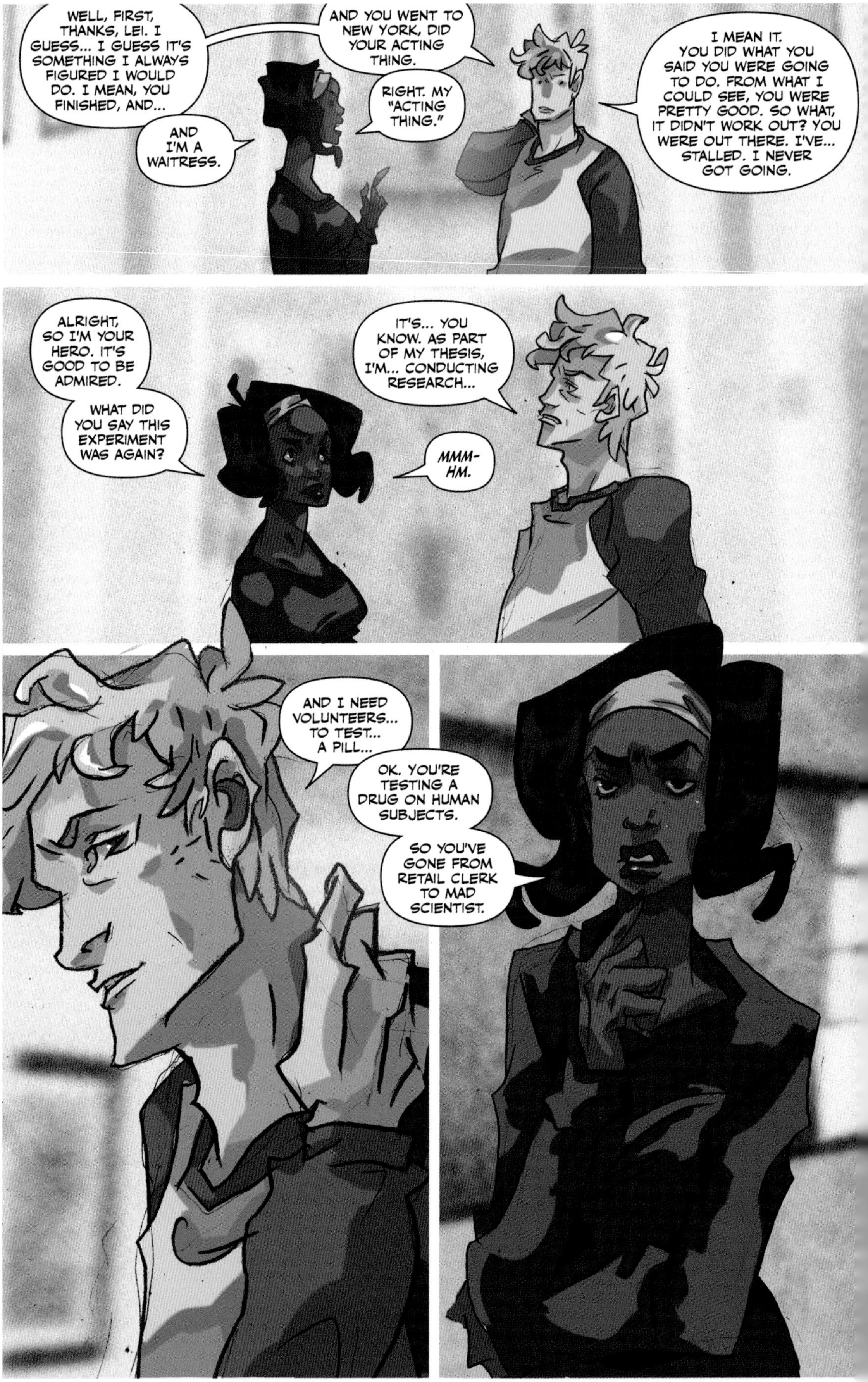
WELL, FIRST, THANKS, LEI. I GUESS... I GUESS IT'S SOMETHING I ALWAYS FIGURED I WOULD DO. I MEAN, YOU FINISHED, AND...
AND YOU WENT TO NEW YORK, DID YOUR ACTING THING.
AND I'M A WAITRESS.
RIGHT. MY "ACTING THING."
I MEAN IT. YOU DID WHAT YOU SAID YOU WERE GOING TO DO. FROM WHAT I COULD SEE, YOU WERE PRETTY GOOD. SO WHAT, IT DIDN'T WORK OUT? YOU WERE OUT THERE. I'VE... STALLED. I NEVER GOT GOING.
ALRIGHT, SO I'M YOUR HERO. IT'S GOOD TO BE ADMIRED.
WHAT DID YOU SAY THIS EXPERIMENT WAS AGAIN?
IT'S... YOU KNOW. AS PART OF MY THESIS, I'M... CONDUCTING RESEARCH...
MMM-HM.
AND I NEED VOLUNTEERS... TO TEST... A PILL...
OK. YOU'RE TESTING A DRUG ON HUMAN SUBJECTS.
SO YOU'VE GONE FROM RETAIL CLERK TO MAD SCIENTIST.

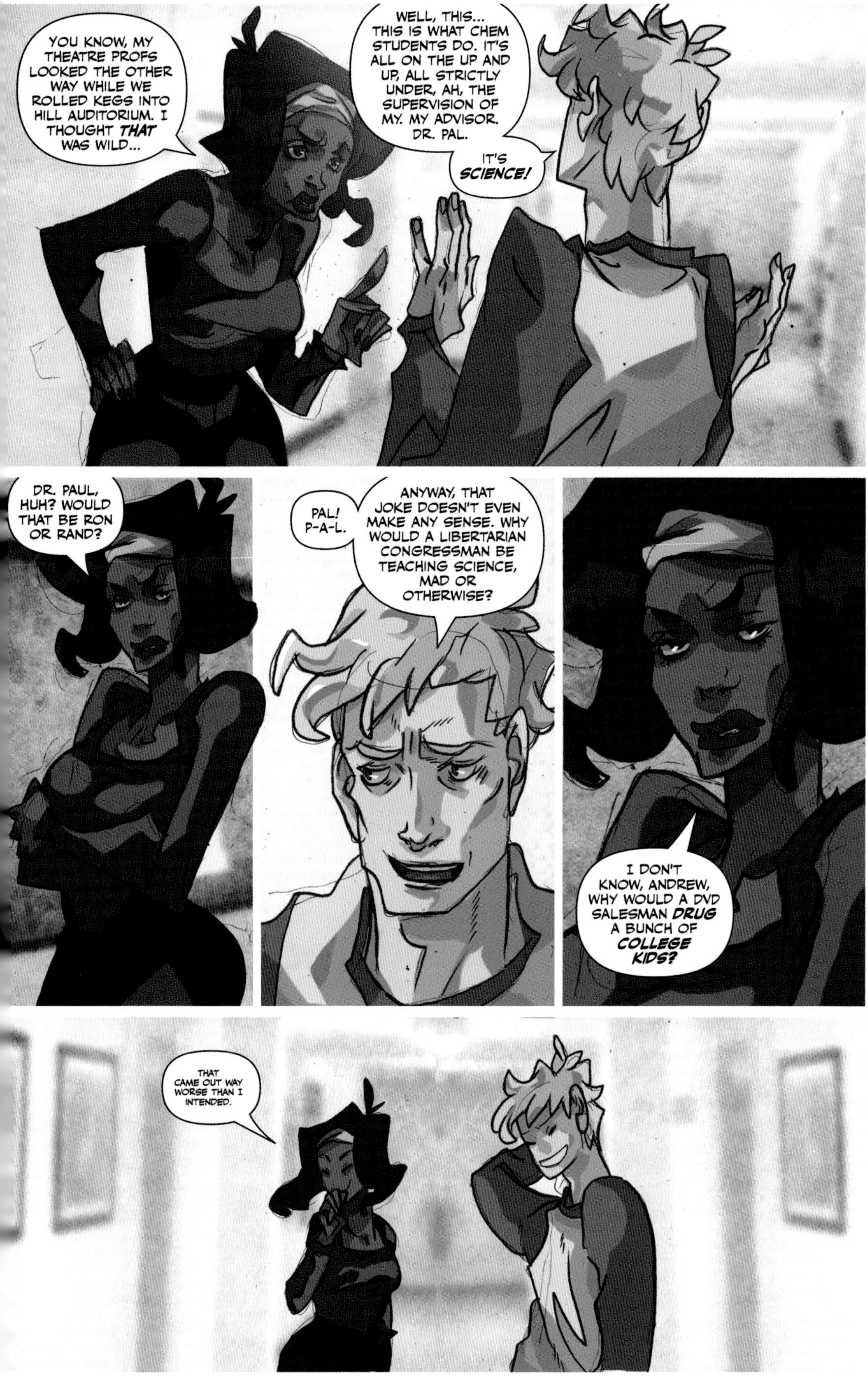
YOU KNOW, MY THEATRE PROFS LOOKED THE OTHER WAY WHILE WE ROLLED KEGS INTO HILL AUDITORIUM. I THOUGHT ***THAT*** WAS WILD...
WELL, THIS... THIS IS WHAT CHEM STUDENTS DO. IT'S ALL ON THE UP AND UP, ALL STRICTLY UNDER, AH, THE SUPERVISION OF MY. MY ADVISOR. DR. PAL.
IT'S ***SCIENCE!***
DR. PAUL, HUH? WOULD THAT BE RON OR RAND?
PAL! P-A-L.
ANYWAY, THAT JOKE DOESN'T EVEN MAKE ANY SENSE. WHY WOULD A LIBERTARIAN CONGRESSMAN BE TEACHING SCIENCE, MAD OR OTHERWISE?
I DON'T KNOW, ANDREW, WHY WOULD A DVD SALESMAN ***DRUG*** A BUNCH OF ***COLLEGE KIDS?***
THAT CAME OUT WAY WORSE THAN I INTENDED.

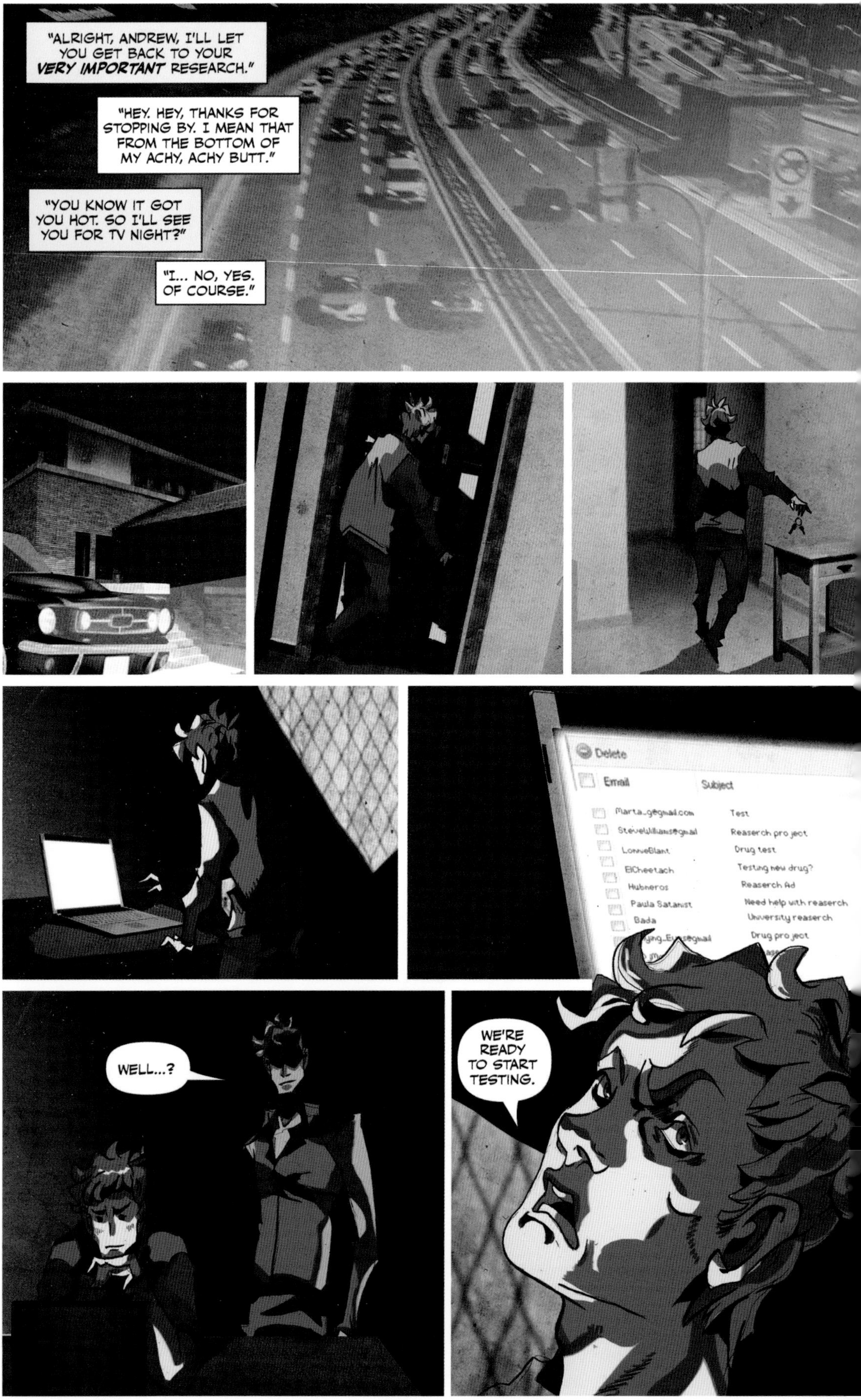
"ALRIGHT, ANDREW, I'LL LET YOU GET BACK TO YOUR VERY IMPORTANT RESEARCH."
"HEY. HEY, THANKS FOR STOPPING BY. I MEAN THAT FROM THE BOTTOM OF MY ACHY, ACHY BUTT."
"YOU KNOW IT GOT YOU HOT. SO I'LL SEE YOU FOR TV NIGHT?"
"I... NO, YES. OF COURSE."
Delete
Email
Subject
Marta_g@gmail.com
Test
SteveWilliams@gmail
Reaserch project
LonnieBlant
Drug test
ElCheetach
Testing new drug?
Hubneros
Reaserch Ad
Paula Satanist
Need help with reaserch
Bada
University reaserch
Drug project
WELL...?
WE'RE READY TO START TESTING.

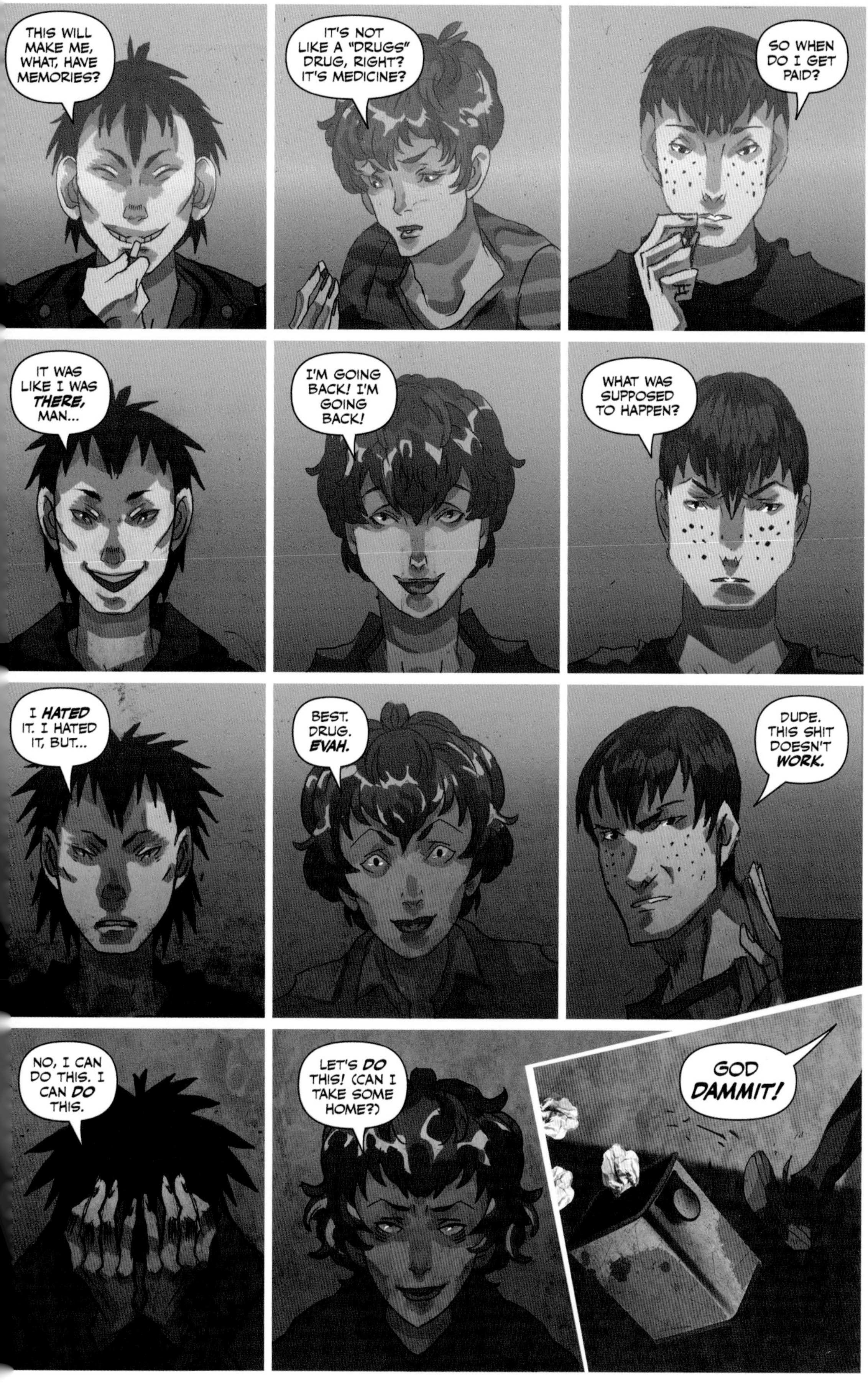
THIS WILL MAKE ME, WHAT, HAVE MEMORIES?
IT'S NOT LIKE A "DRUGS" DRUG, RIGHT? IT'S MEDICINE?
SO WHEN DO I GET PAID?
IT WAS LIKE I WAS *THERE,* MAN...
I'M GOING BACK! I'M GOING BACK!
WHAT WAS SUPPOSED TO HAPPEN?
I *HATED* IT. I HATED IT, BUT...
BEST. DRUG. *EVAH.*
DUDE. THIS SHIT DOESN'T *WORK.*
NO, I CAN DO THIS. I CAN *DO* THIS.
LET'S *DO* THIS! (CAN I TAKE SOME HOME?)
GOD *DAMMIT!*

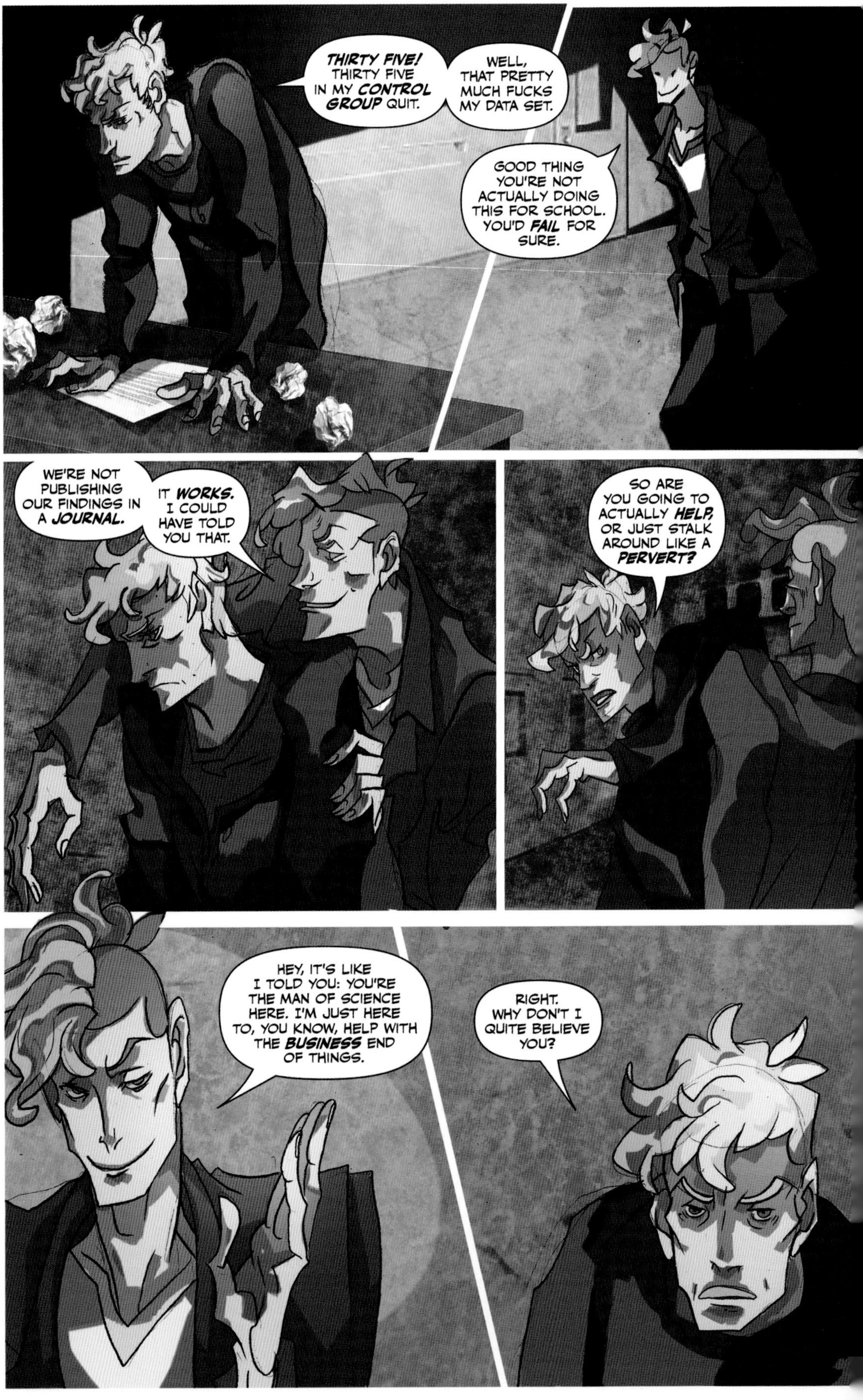
THIRTY FIVE! THIRTY FIVE IN MY CONTROL GROUP QUIT.
WELL, THAT PRETTY MUCH FUCKS MY DATA SET.
GOOD THING YOU'RE NOT ACTUALLY DOING THIS FOR SCHOOL. YOU'D FAIL FOR SURE.
WE'RE NOT PUBLISHING OUR FINDINGS IN A JOURNAL.
IT WORKS. I COULD HAVE TOLD YOU THAT.
SO ARE YOU GOING TO ACTUALLY HELP, OR JUST STALK AROUND LIKE A PERVERT?
HEY, IT'S LIKE I TOLD YOU: YOU'RE THE MAN OF SCIENCE HERE. I'M JUST HERE TO, YOU KNOW, HELP WITH THE BUSINESS END OF THINGS.
RIGHT. WHY DON'T I QUITE BELIEVE YOU?

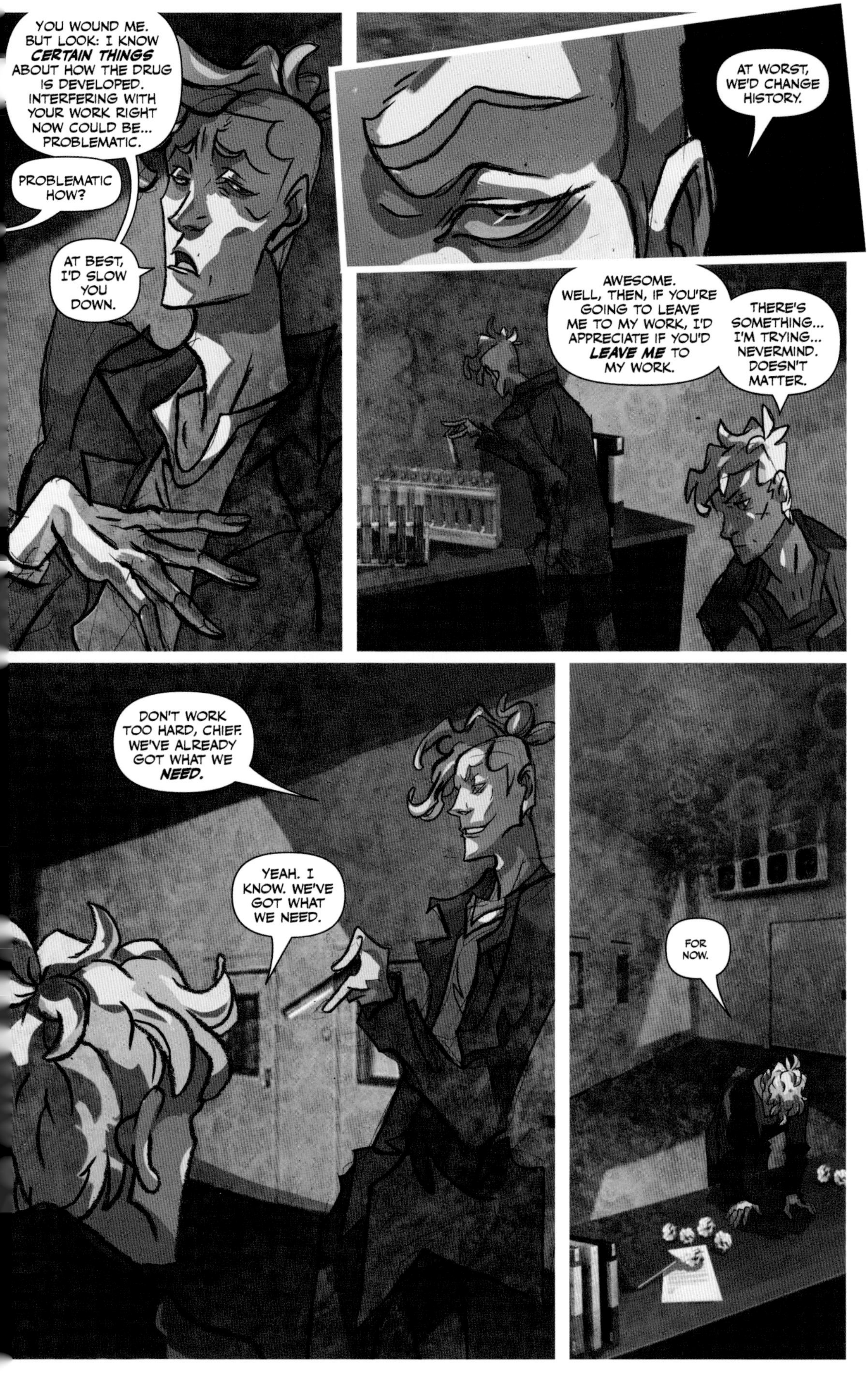
YOU WOUND ME. BUT LOOK: I KNOW CERTAIN THINGS ABOUT HOW THE DRUG IS DEVELOPED. INTERFERING WITH YOUR WORK RIGHT NOW COULD BE... PROBLEMATIC.
PROBLEMATIC HOW?
AT BEST, I'D SLOW YOU DOWN.
AT WORST, WE'D CHANGE HISTORY.
AWESOME. WELL, THEN, IF YOU'RE GOING TO LEAVE ME TO MY WORK, I'D APPRECIATE IF YOU'D LEAVE ME TO MY WORK.
THERE'S SOMETHING... I'M TRYING... NEVERMIND. DOESN'T MATTER.
DON'T WORK TOO HARD, CHIEF. WE'VE ALREADY GOT WHAT WE NEED.
YEAH. I KNOW. WE'VE GOT WHAT WE NEED.
FOR NOW.

CHAPTER
THREE

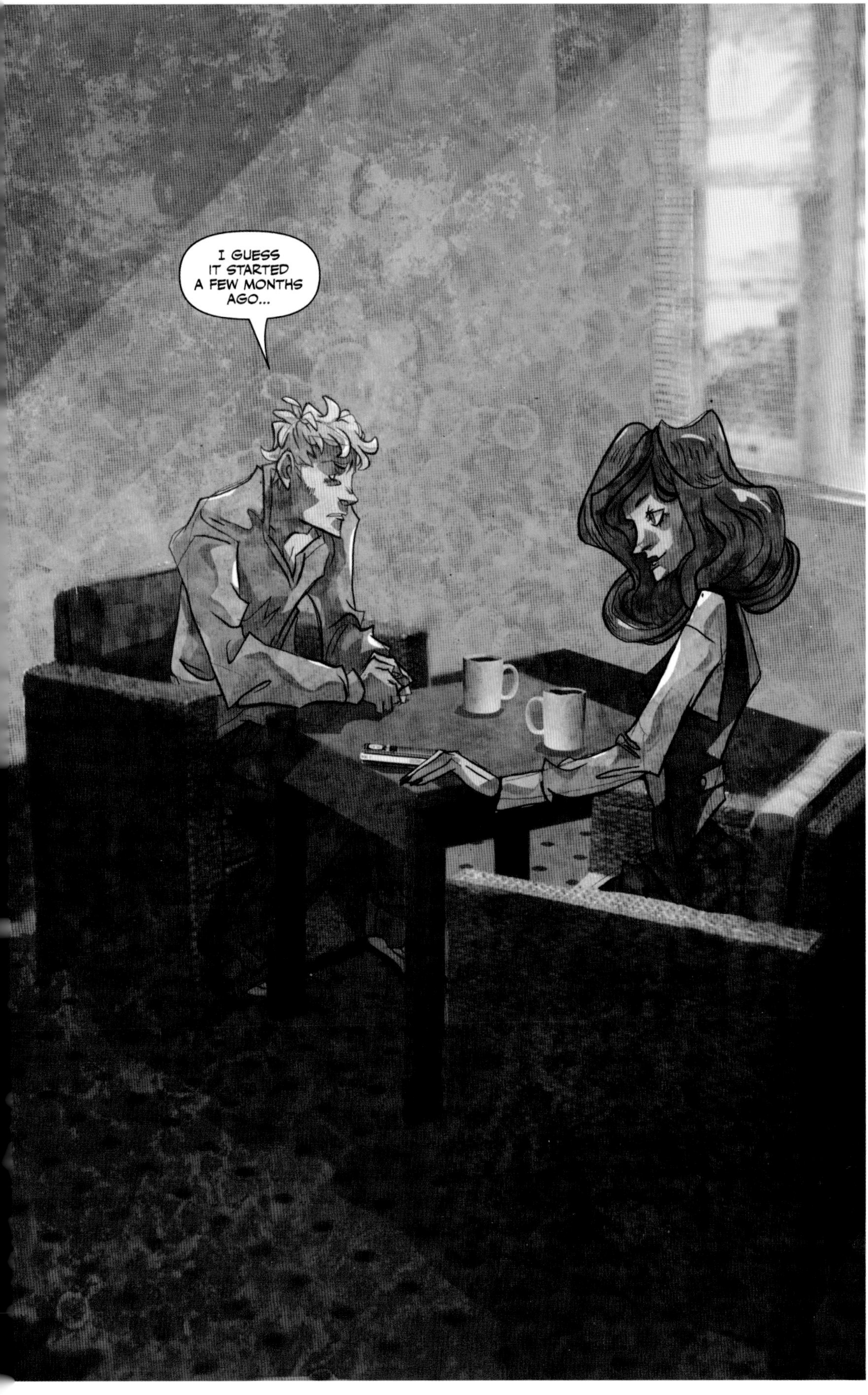
I GUESS IT STARTED A FEW MONTHS AGO...

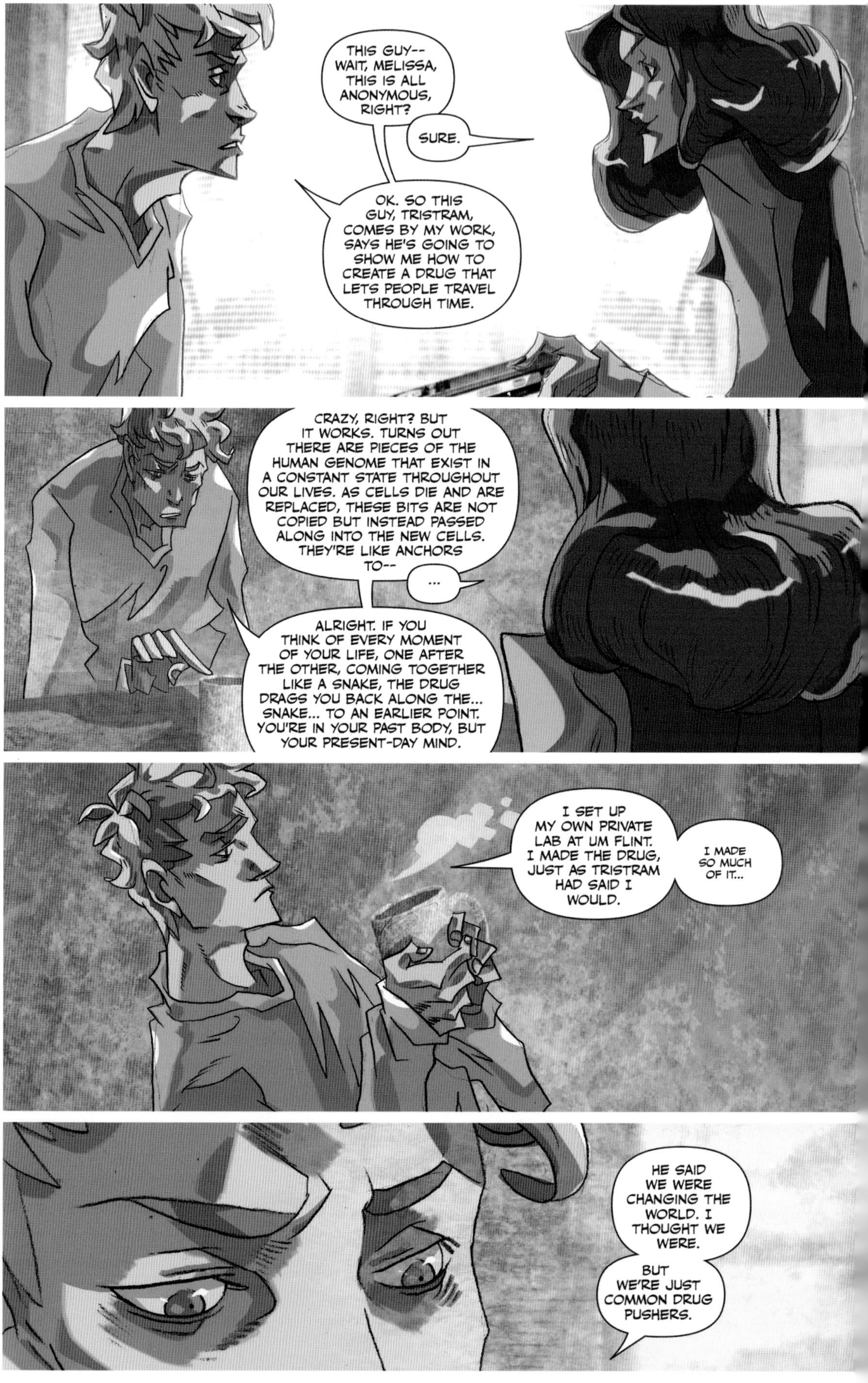
THIS GUY-- WAIT, MELISSA, THIS IS ALL ANONYMOUS, RIGHT?
SURE.
OK. SO THIS GUY, TRISTRAM, COMES BY MY WORK, SAYS HE'S GOING TO SHOW ME HOW TO CREATE A DRUG THAT LETS PEOPLE TRAVEL THROUGH TIME.
CRAZY, RIGHT? BUT IT WORKS. TURNS OUT THERE ARE PIECES OF THE HUMAN GENOME THAT EXIST IN A CONSTANT STATE THROUGHOUT OUR LIVES. AS CELLS DIE AND ARE REPLACED, THESE BITS ARE NOT COPIED BUT INSTEAD PASSED ALONG INTO THE NEW CELLS. THEY'RE LIKE ANCHORS TO--
...
ALRIGHT. IF YOU THINK OF EVERY MOMENT OF YOUR LIFE, ONE AFTER THE OTHER, COMING TOGETHER LIKE A SNAKE, THE DRUG DRAGS YOU BACK ALONG THE... SNAKE... TO AN EARLIER POINT. YOU'RE IN YOUR PAST BODY, BUT YOUR PRESENT-DAY MIND.
I SET UP MY OWN PRIVATE LAB AT UM FLINT. I MADE THE DRUG, JUST AS TRISTRAM HAD SAID I WOULD.
I MADE SO MUCH OF IT...
HE SAID WE WERE CHANGING THE WORLD. I THOUGHT WE WERE.
BUT WE'RE JUST COMMON DRUG PUSHERS.

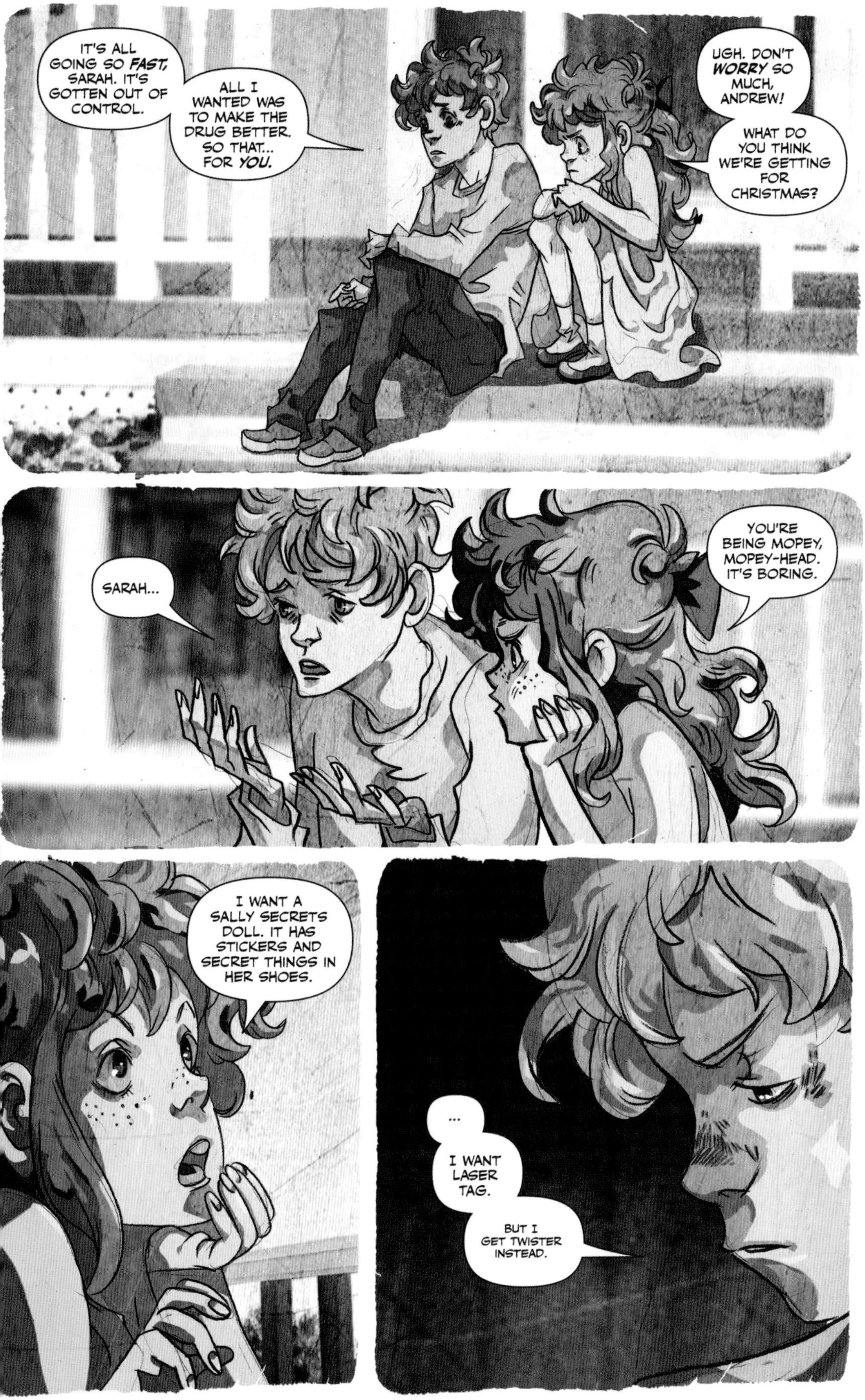
IT'S ALL GOING SO FAST, SARAH. IT'S GOTTEN OUT OF CONTROL.
ALL I WANTED WAS TO MAKE THE DRUG BETTER. SO THAT... FOR YOU.
UGH. DON'T WORRY SO MUCH, ANDREW!
WHAT DO YOU THINK WE'RE GETTING FOR CHRISTMAS?
SARAH...
YOU'RE BEING MOPEY, MOPEY-HEAD. IT'S BORING.
I WANT A SALLY SECRETS DOLL. IT HAS STICKERS AND SECRET THINGS IN HER SHOES.
...
I WANT LASER TAG.
BUT I GET TWISTER INSTEAD.

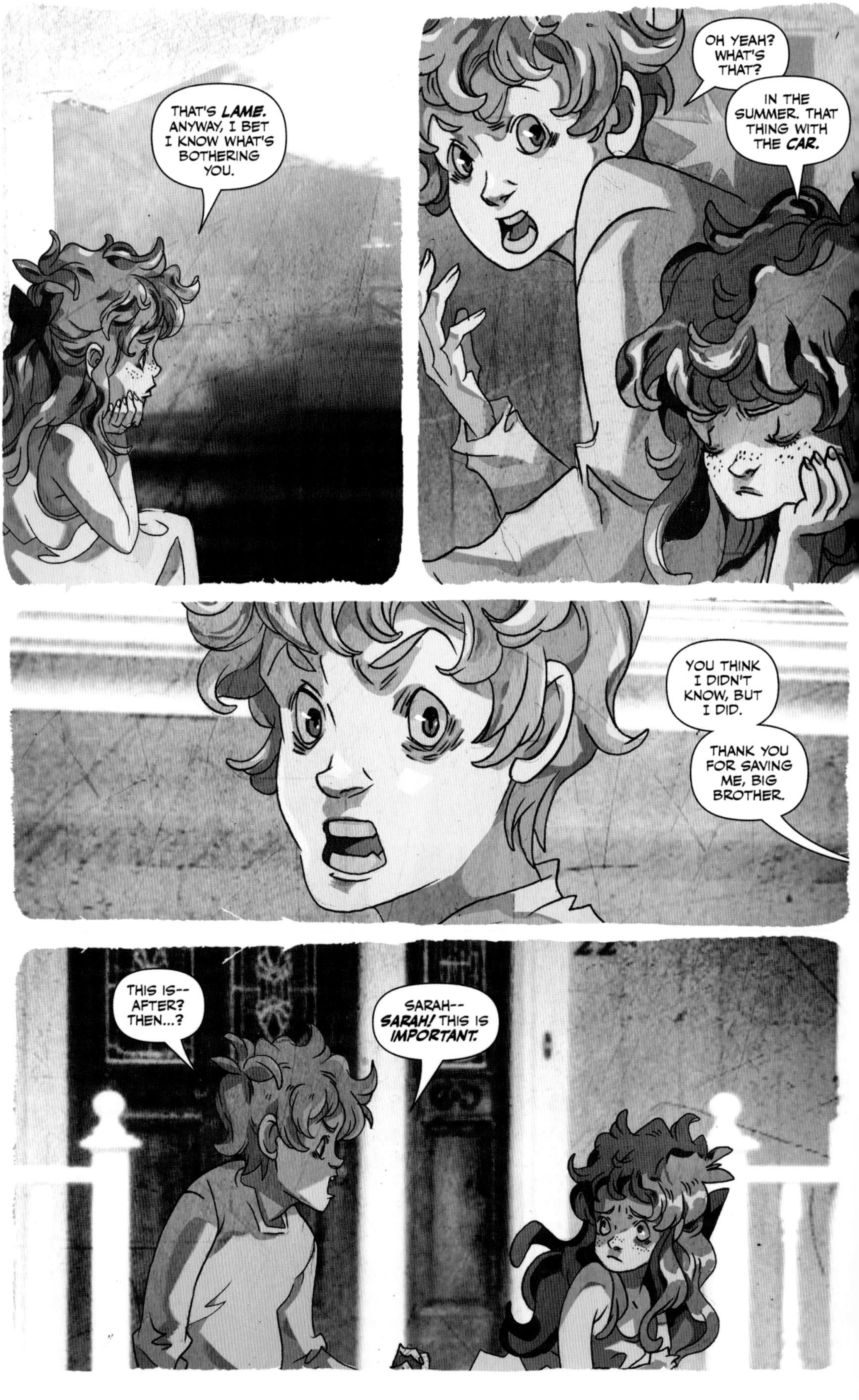
THAT'S **LAME.** ANYWAY, I BET I KNOW WHAT'S BOTHERING YOU.
OH YEAH? WHAT'S THAT?
IN THE SUMMER. THAT THING WITH THE **CAR.**
YOU THINK I DIDN'T KNOW, BUT I DID.
THANK YOU FOR SAVING ME, BIG BROTHER.
THIS IS-- AFTER? THEN...?
SARAH-- **SARAH!** THIS IS **IMPORTANT.**

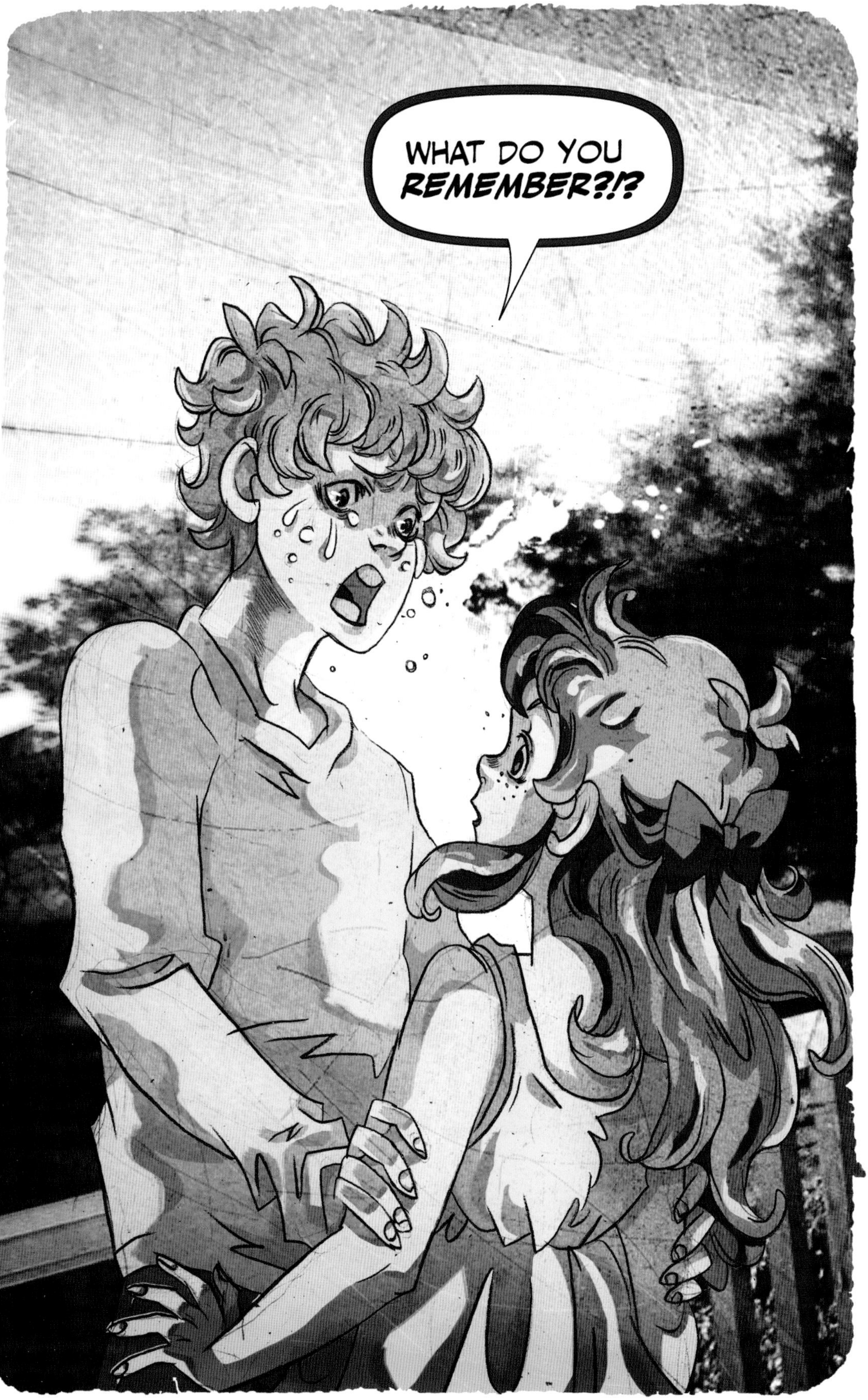
WHAT DO YOU REMEMBER?!?

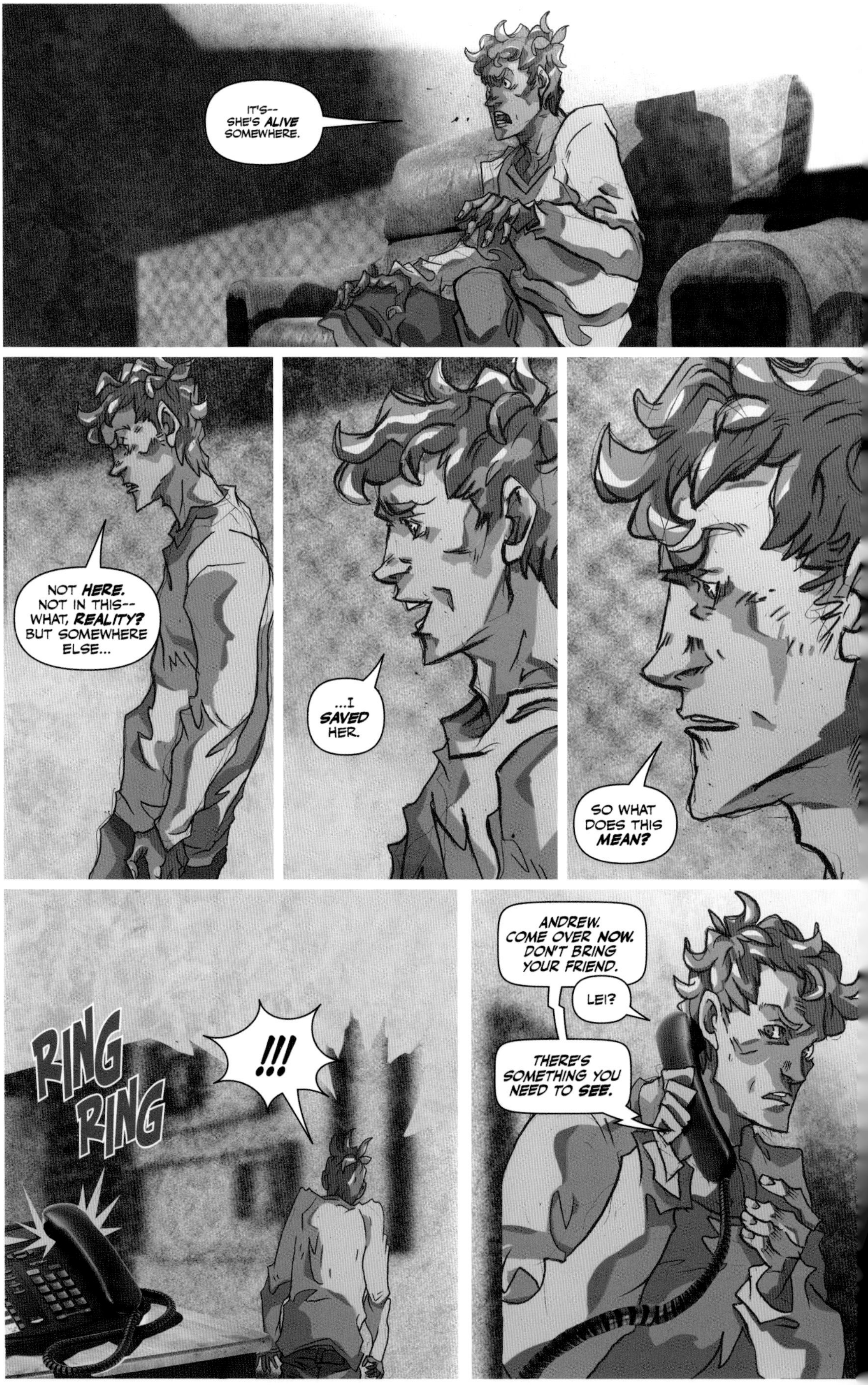
IT'S-- SHE'S ALIVE SOMEWHERE.
NOT HERE. NOT IN THIS-- WHAT, REALITY? BUT SOMEWHERE ELSE...
...I SAVED HER.
SO WHAT DOES THIS MEAN?
RING RING
!!!
ANDREW. COME OVER NOW. DON'T BRING YOUR FRIEND.
LEI?
THERE'S SOMETHING YOU NEED TO SEE.

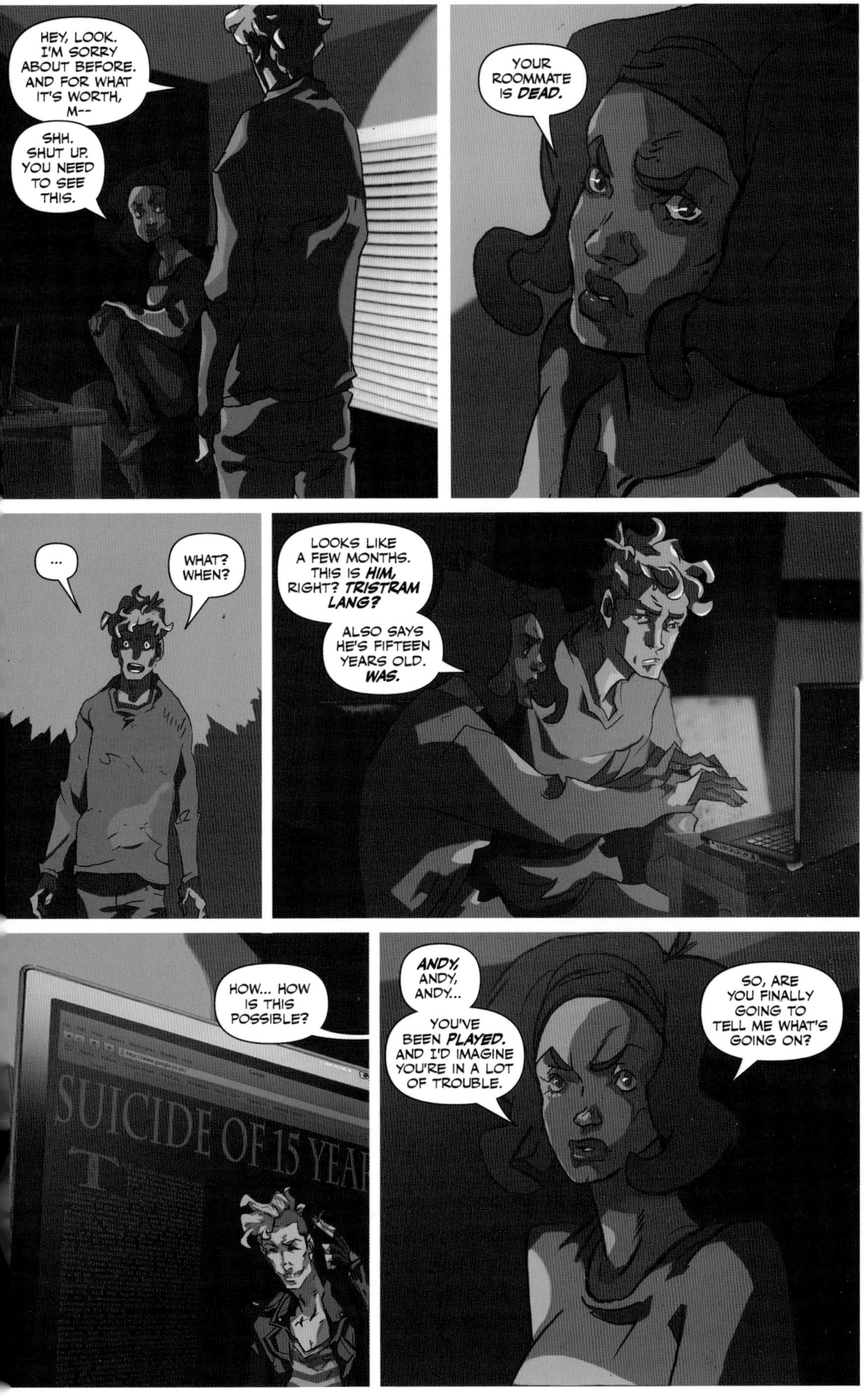
HEY, LOOK. I'M SORRY ABOUT BEFORE. AND FOR WHAT IT'S WORTH, M--
SHH. SHUT UP. YOU NEED TO SEE THIS.
YOUR ROOMMATE IS DEAD.
...
WHAT? WHEN?
LOOKS LIKE A FEW MONTHS. THIS IS HIM, RIGHT? TRISTRAM LANG?
ALSO SAYS HE'S FIFTEEN YEARS OLD. WAS.
HOW... HOW IS THIS POSSIBLE?
SUICIDE OF 15 YEAR
ANDY, ANDY, ANDY...
YOU'VE BEEN PLAYED. AND I'D IMAGINE YOU'RE IN A LOT OF TROUBLE.
SO, ARE YOU FINALLY GOING TO TELL ME WHAT'S GOING ON?

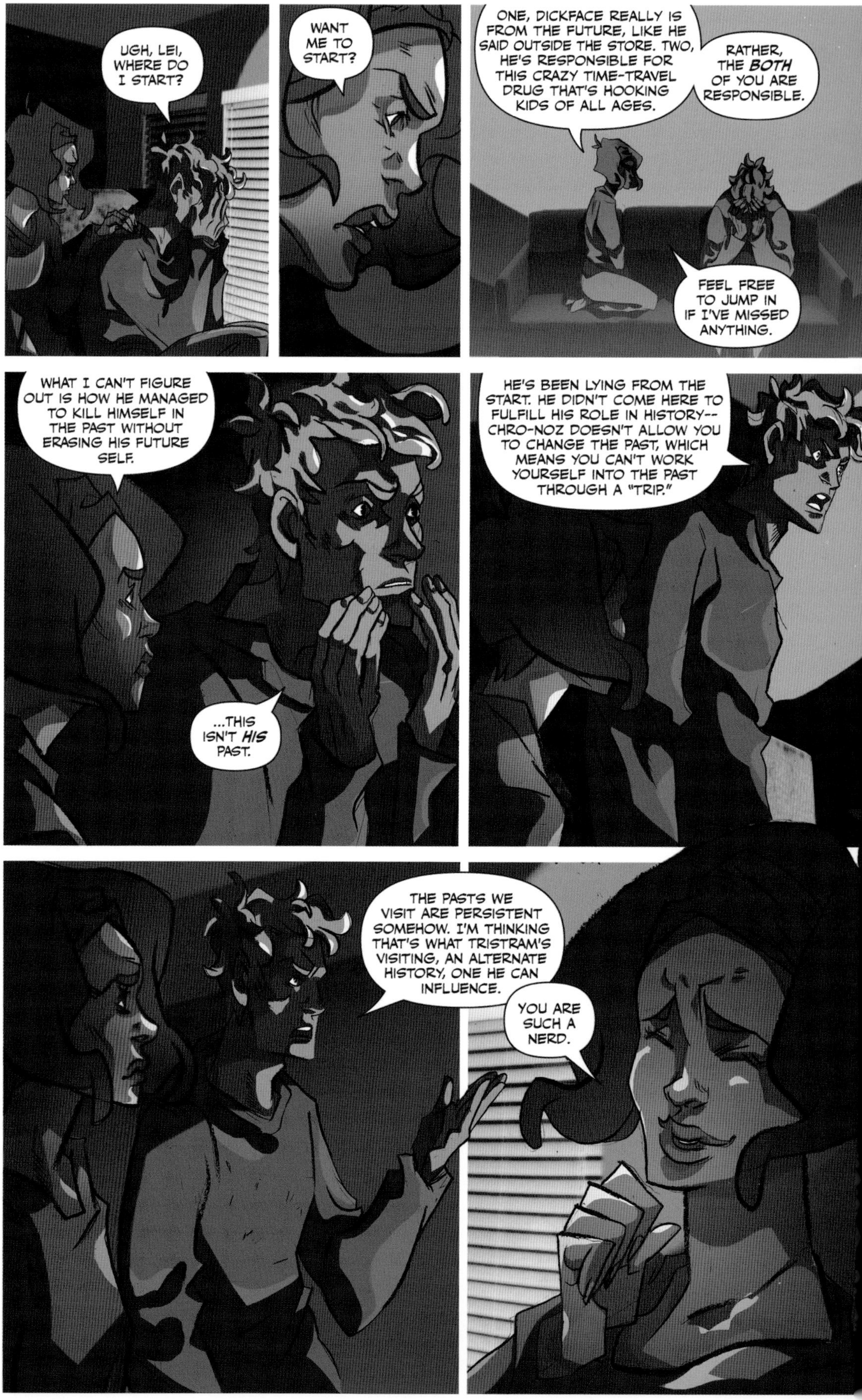
UGH, LEI, WHERE DO I START?
WANT ME TO START?
ONE, DICKFACE REALLY IS FROM THE FUTURE, LIKE HE SAID OUTSIDE THE STORE. TWO, HE'S RESPONSIBLE FOR THIS CRAZY TIME-TRAVEL DRUG THAT'S HOOKING KIDS OF ALL AGES.
RATHER, THE BOTH OF YOU ARE RESPONSIBLE.
FEEL FREE TO JUMP IN IF I'VE MISSED ANYTHING.
WHAT I CAN'T FIGURE OUT IS HOW HE MANAGED TO KILL HIMSELF IN THE PAST WITHOUT ERASING HIS FUTURE SELF.
...THIS ISN'T HIS PAST.
HE'S BEEN LYING FROM THE START. HE DIDN'T COME HERE TO FULFILL HIS ROLE IN HISTORY-- CHRO-NOZ DOESN'T ALLOW YOU TO CHANGE THE PAST, WHICH MEANS YOU CAN'T WORK YOURSELF INTO THE PAST THROUGH A "TRIP."
THE PASTS WE VISIT ARE PERSISTENT SOMEHOW. I'M THINKING THAT'S WHAT TRISTRAM'S VISITING, AN ALTERNATE HISTORY, ONE HE CAN INFLUENCE.
YOU ARE SUCH A NERD.

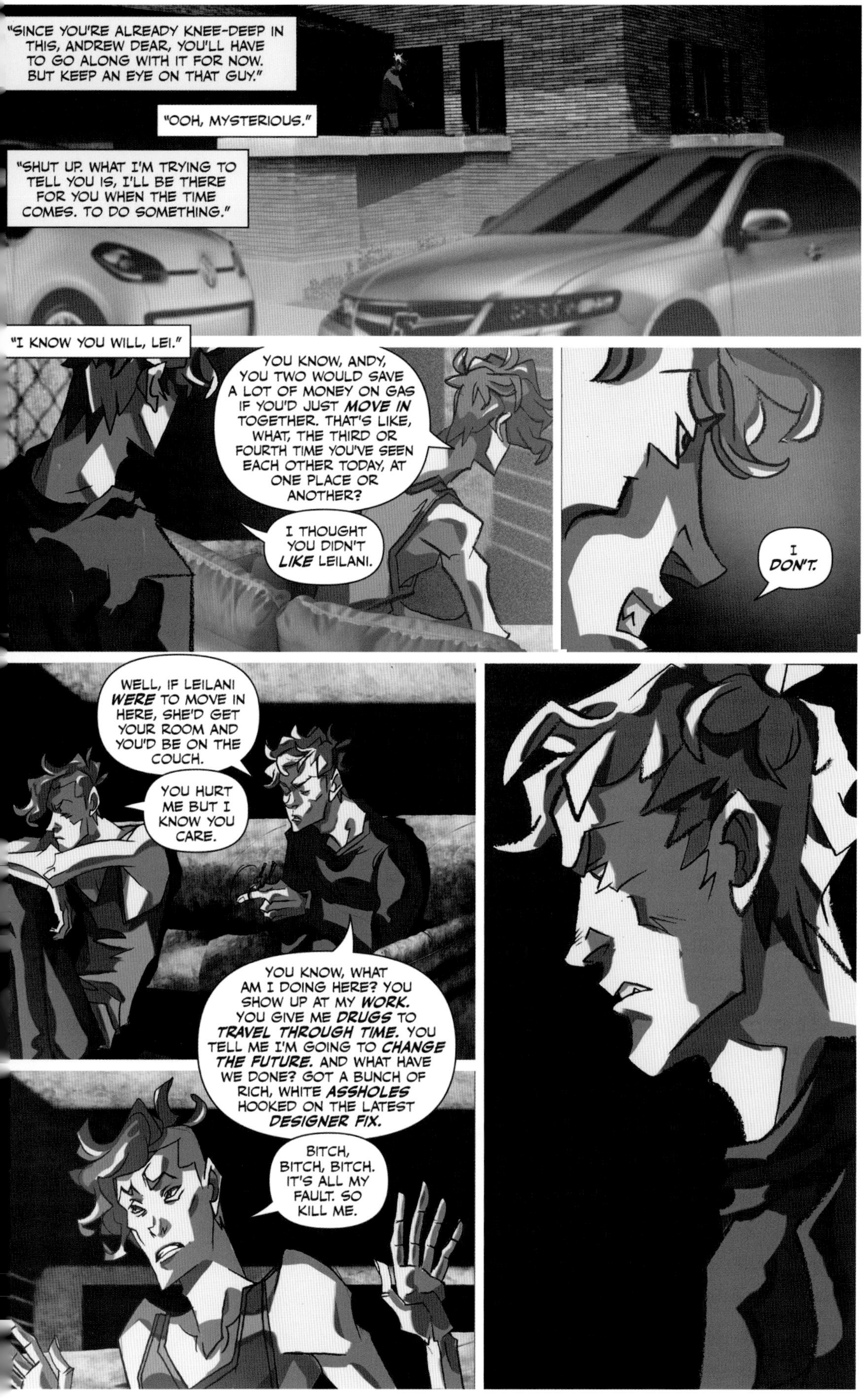
"SINCE YOU'RE ALREADY KNEE-DEEP IN THIS, ANDREW DEAR, YOU'LL HAVE TO GO ALONG WITH IT FOR NOW. BUT KEEP AN EYE ON THAT GUY."
"OOH, MYSTERIOUS."
"SHUT UP. WHAT I'M TRYING TO TELL YOU IS, I'LL BE THERE FOR YOU WHEN THE TIME COMES. TO DO SOMETHING."
"I KNOW YOU WILL, LEI."
YOU KNOW, ANDY, YOU TWO WOULD SAVE A LOT OF MONEY ON GAS IF YOU'D JUST MOVE IN TOGETHER. THAT'S LIKE, WHAT, THE THIRD OR FOURTH TIME YOU'VE SEEN EACH OTHER TODAY, AT ONE PLACE OR ANOTHER?
I THOUGHT YOU DIDN'T LIKE LEILANI.
I DON'T.
WELL, IF LEILANI WERE TO MOVE IN HERE, SHE'D GET YOUR ROOM AND YOU'D BE ON THE COUCH.
YOU HURT ME BUT I KNOW YOU CARE.
YOU KNOW, WHAT AM I DOING HERE? YOU SHOW UP AT MY WORK. YOU GIVE ME DRUGS TO TRAVEL THROUGH TIME. YOU TELL ME I'M GOING TO CHANGE THE FUTURE. AND WHAT HAVE WE DONE? GOT A BUNCH OF RICH, WHITE ASSHOLES HOOKED ON THE LATEST DESIGNER FIX.
BITCH, BITCH, BITCH. IT'S ALL MY FAULT. SO KILL ME.

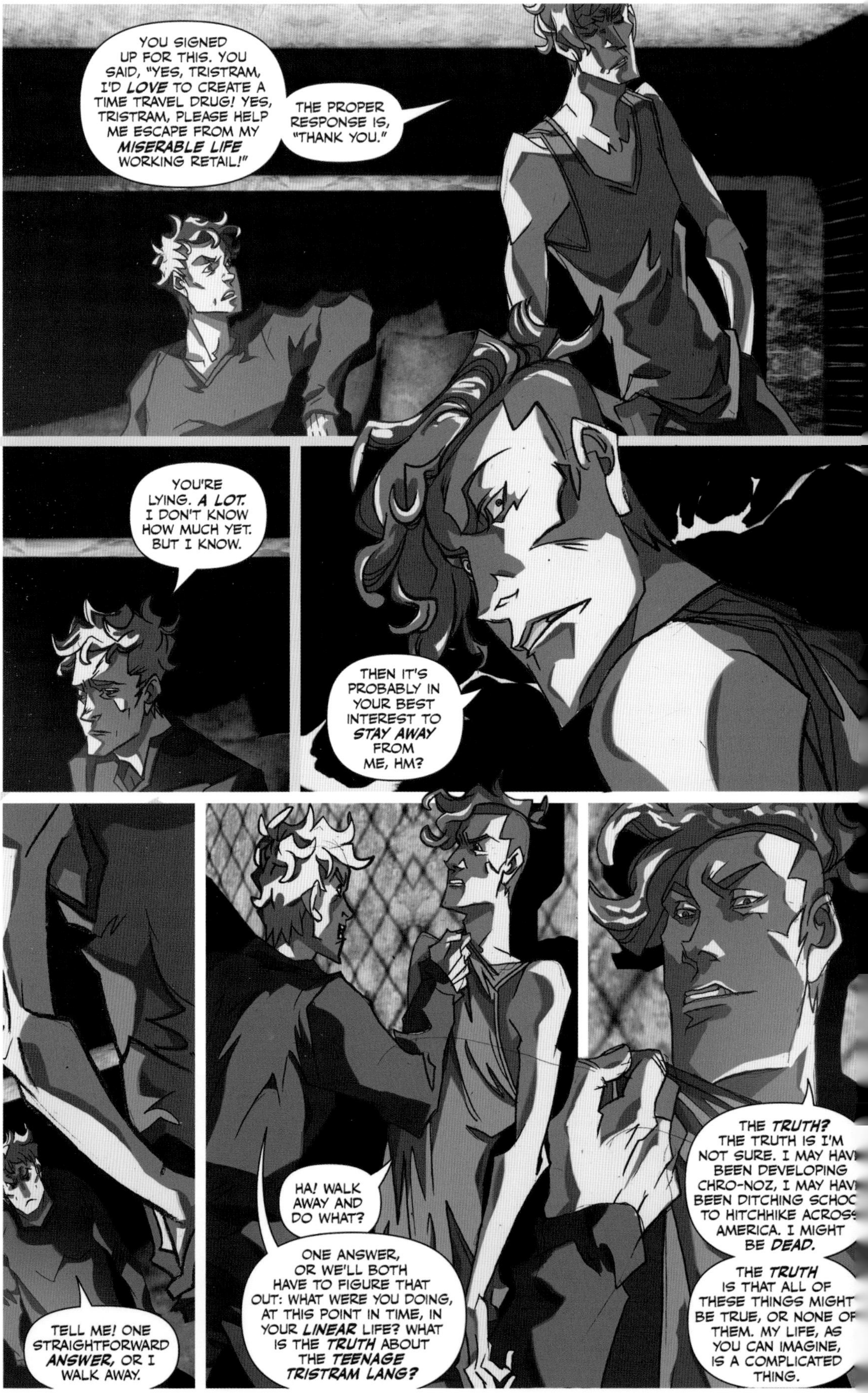
YOU SIGNED UP FOR THIS. YOU SAID, "YES, TRISTRAM, I'D *LOVE* TO CREATE A TIME TRAVEL DRUG! YES, TRISTRAM, PLEASE HELP ME ESCAPE FROM MY *MISERABLE LIFE* WORKING RETAIL!"
THE PROPER RESPONSE IS, "THANK YOU."
YOU'RE LYING. *A LOT.* I DON'T KNOW HOW MUCH YET. BUT I KNOW.
THEN IT'S PROBABLY IN YOUR BEST INTEREST TO *STAY AWAY* FROM ME, HM?
TELL ME! ONE STRAIGHTFORWARD *ANSWER,* OR I WALK AWAY.
HA! WALK AWAY AND DO WHAT?
ONE ANSWER, OR WE'LL BOTH HAVE TO FIGURE THAT OUT: WHAT WERE YOU DOING, AT THIS POINT IN TIME, IN YOUR *LINEAR* LIFE? WHAT IS THE *TRUTH* ABOUT THE *TEENAGE TRISTRAM LANG?*
THE *TRUTH?* THE TRUTH IS I'M NOT SURE. I MAY HAV BEEN DEVELOPING CHRO-NOZ, I MAY HAV BEEN DITCHING SCHOC TO HITCHHIKE ACROSS AMERICA. I MIGHT BE *DEAD.*
THE *TRUTH* IS THAT ALL OF THESE THINGS MIGHT BE TRUE, OR NONE OF THEM. MY LIFE, AS YOU CAN IMAGINE, IS A COMPLICATED THING.

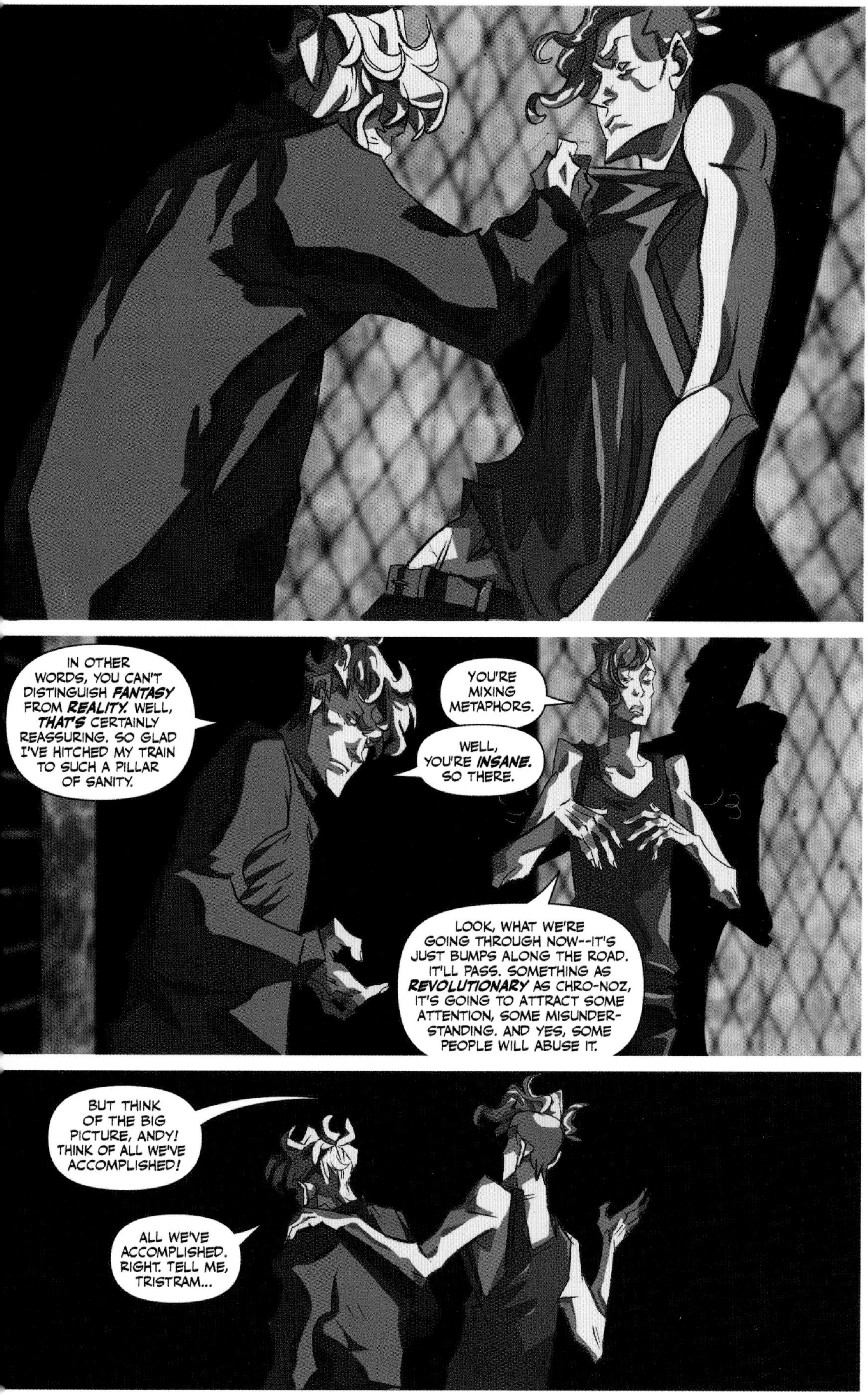
IN OTHER WORDS, YOU CAN'T DISTINGUISH FANTASY FROM REALITY. WELL, THAT'S CERTAINLY REASSURING. SO GLAD I'VE HITCHED MY TRAIN TO SUCH A PILLAR OF SANITY.
YOU'RE MIXING METAPHORS.
WELL, YOU'RE INSANE. SO THERE.
LOOK, WHAT WE'RE GOING THROUGH NOW--IT'S JUST BUMPS ALONG THE ROAD. IT'LL PASS. SOMETHING AS REVOLUTIONARY AS CHRO-NOZ, IT'S GOING TO ATTRACT SOME ATTENTION, SOME MISUNDER-STANDING. AND YES, SOME PEOPLE WILL ABUSE IT.
BUT THINK OF THE BIG PICTURE, ANDY! THINK OF ALL WE'VE ACCOMPLISHED!
ALL WE'VE ACCOMPLISHED. RIGHT. TELL ME, TRISTRAM...

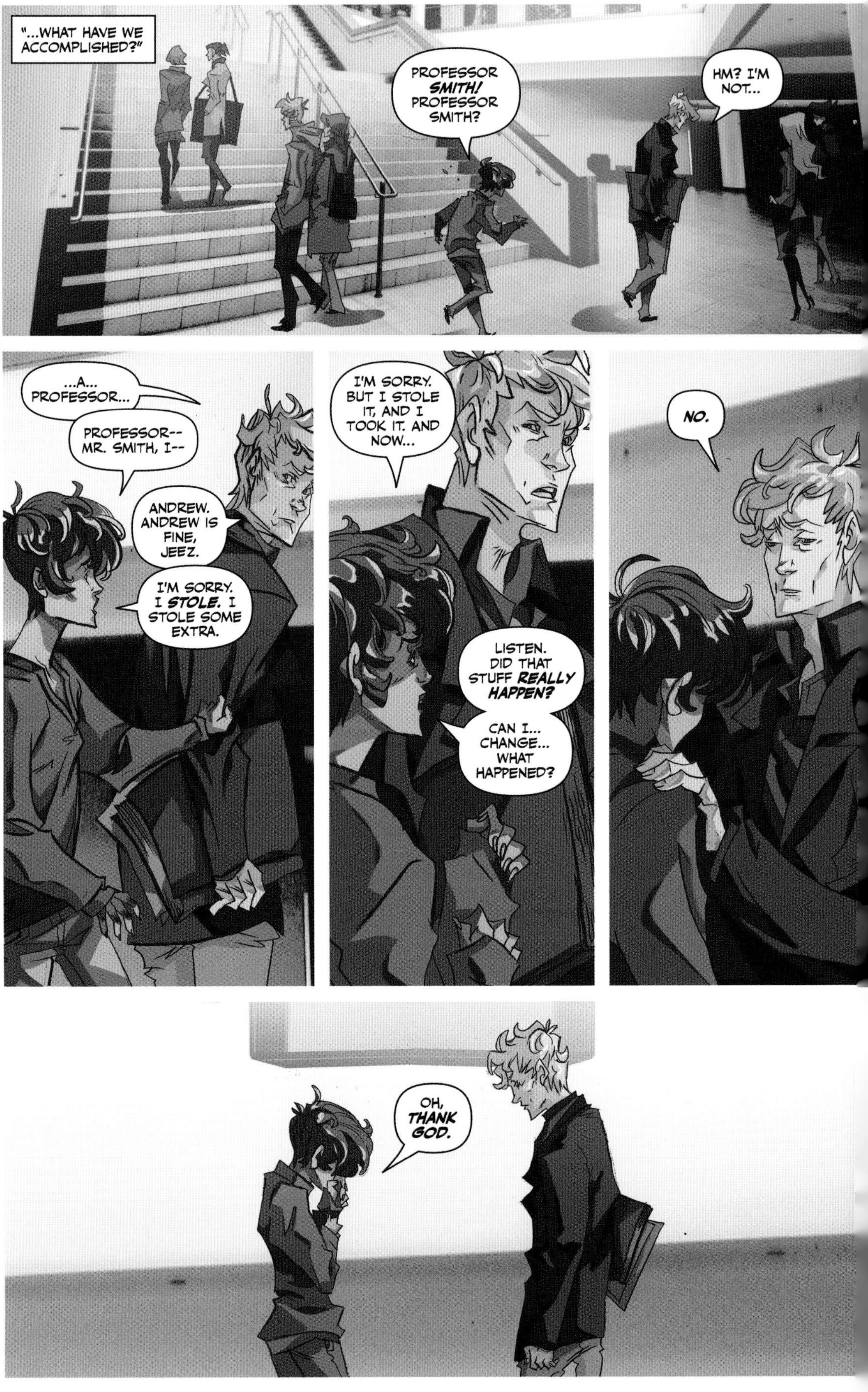
"...WHAT HAVE WE ACCOMPLISHED?"
PROFESSOR SMITH! PROFESSOR SMITH?
HM? I'M NOT...
...A... PROFESSOR...
PROFESSOR-- MR. SMITH, I--
ANDREW. ANDREW IS FINE, JEEZ.
I'M SORRY. I STOLE. I STOLE SOME EXTRA.
I'M SORRY. BUT I STOLE IT, AND I TOOK IT. AND NOW...
LISTEN. DID THAT STUFF REALLY HAPPEN?
CAN I... CHANGE... WHAT HAPPENED?
NO.
OH, THANK GOD.

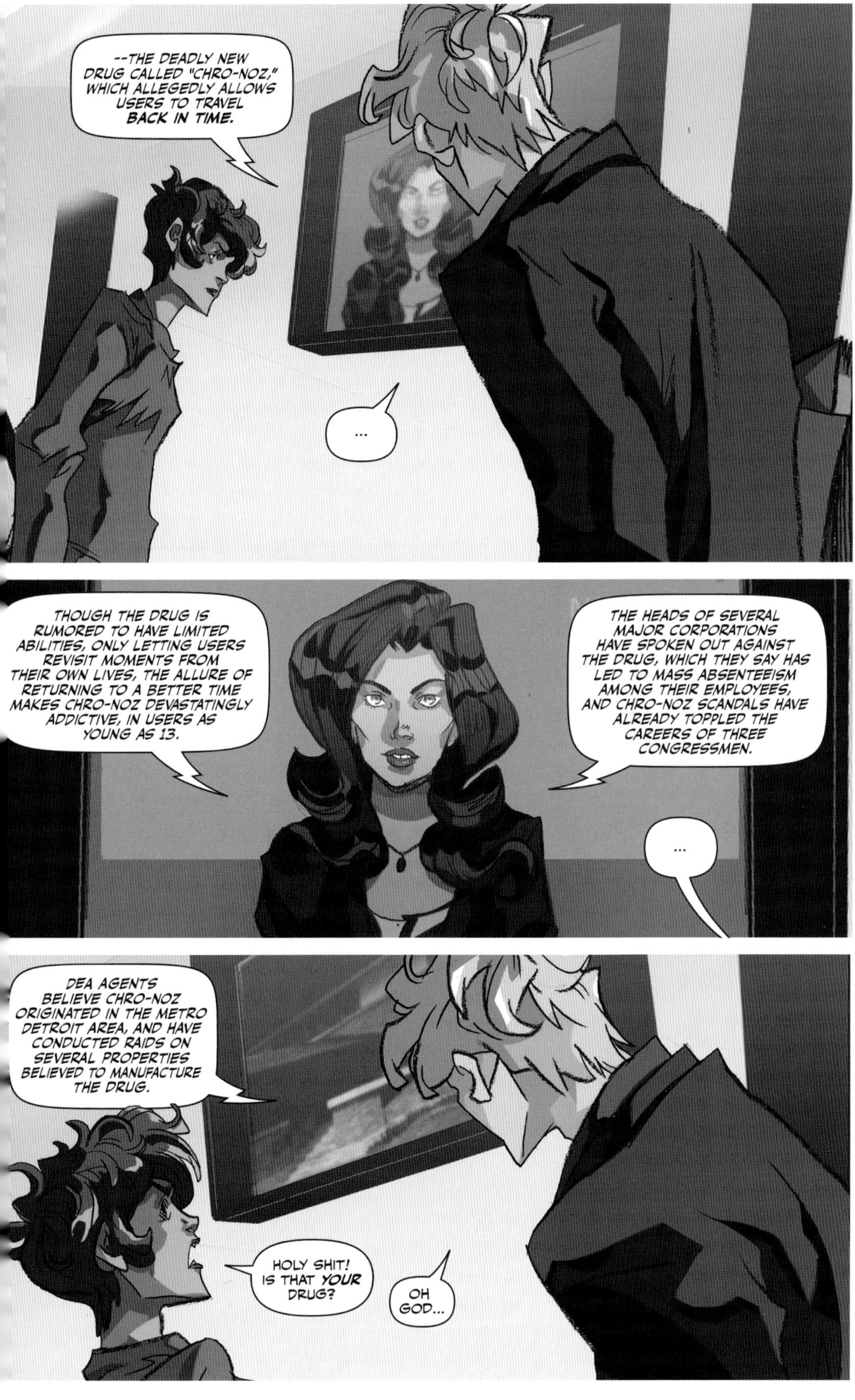
--THE DEADLY NEW DRUG CALLED "CHRO-NOZ," WHICH ALLEGEDLY ALLOWS USERS TO TRAVEL **BACK IN TIME.**
...
THOUGH THE DRUG IS RUMORED TO HAVE LIMITED ABILITIES, ONLY LETTING USERS REVISIT MOMENTS FROM THEIR OWN LIVES, THE ALLURE OF RETURNING TO A BETTER TIME MAKES CHRO-NOZ DEVASTATINGLY ADDICTIVE, IN USERS AS YOUNG AS 13.
THE HEADS OF SEVERAL MAJOR CORPORATIONS HAVE SPOKEN OUT AGAINST THE DRUG, WHICH THEY SAY HAS LED TO MASS ABSENTEEISM AMONG THEIR EMPLOYEES, AND CHRO-NOZ SCANDALS HAVE ALREADY TOPPLED THE CAREERS OF THREE CONGRESSMEN.
...
DEA AGENTS BELIEVE CHRO-NOZ ORIGINATED IN THE METRO DETROIT AREA, AND HAVE CONDUCTED RAIDS ON SEVERAL PROPERTIES BELIEVED TO MANUFACTURE THE DRUG.
HOLY SHIT! IS THAT ***YOUR*** DRUG?
OH GOD...

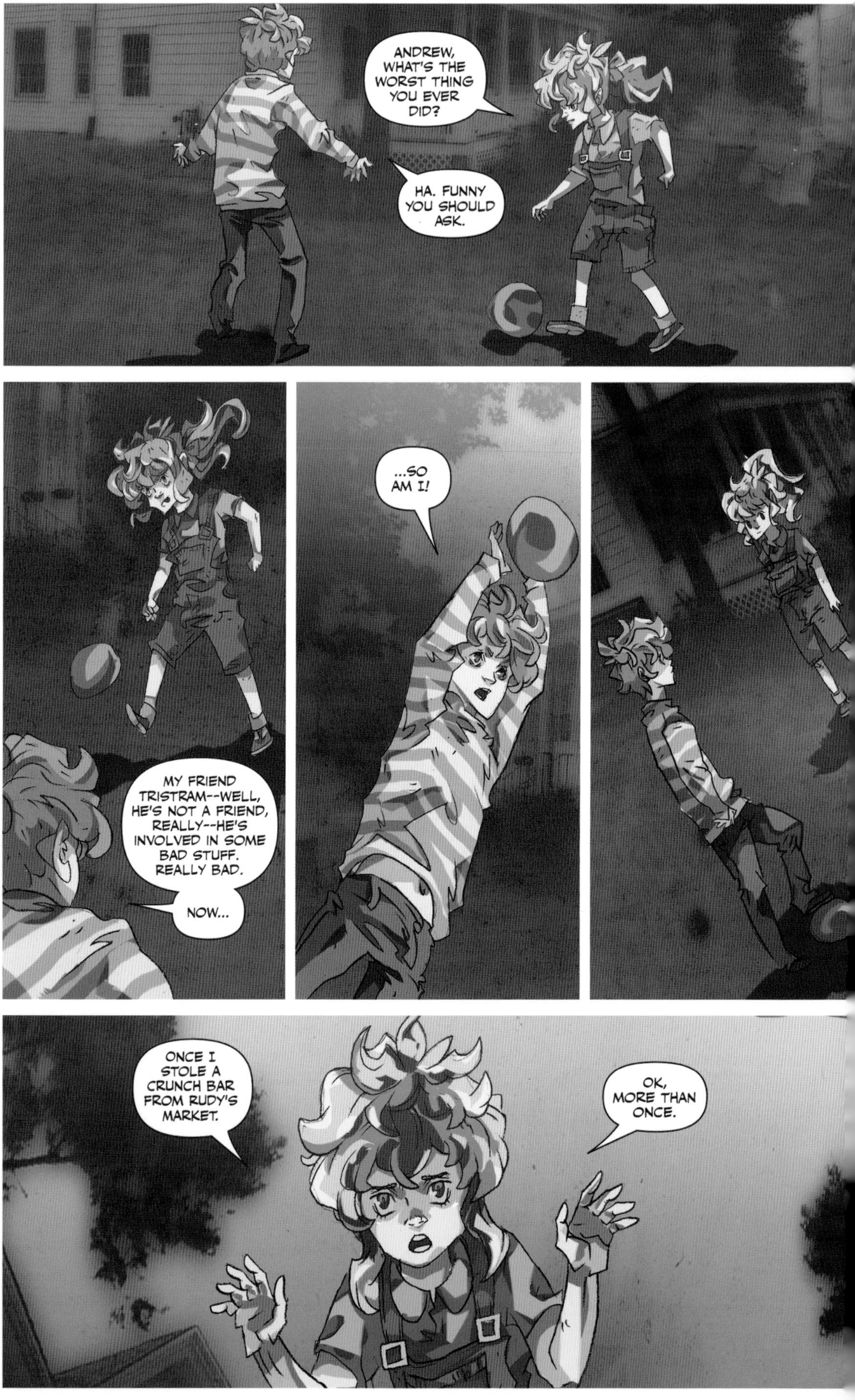
ANDREW, WHAT'S THE WORST THING YOU EVER DID?
HA. FUNNY YOU SHOULD ASK.
MY FRIEND TRISTRAM--WELL, HE'S NOT A FRIEND, REALLY--HE'S INVOLVED IN SOME BAD STUFF. REALLY BAD.
NOW...
...SO AM I!
ONCE I STOLE A CRUNCH BAR FROM RUDY'S MARKET.
OK, MORE THAN ONCE.

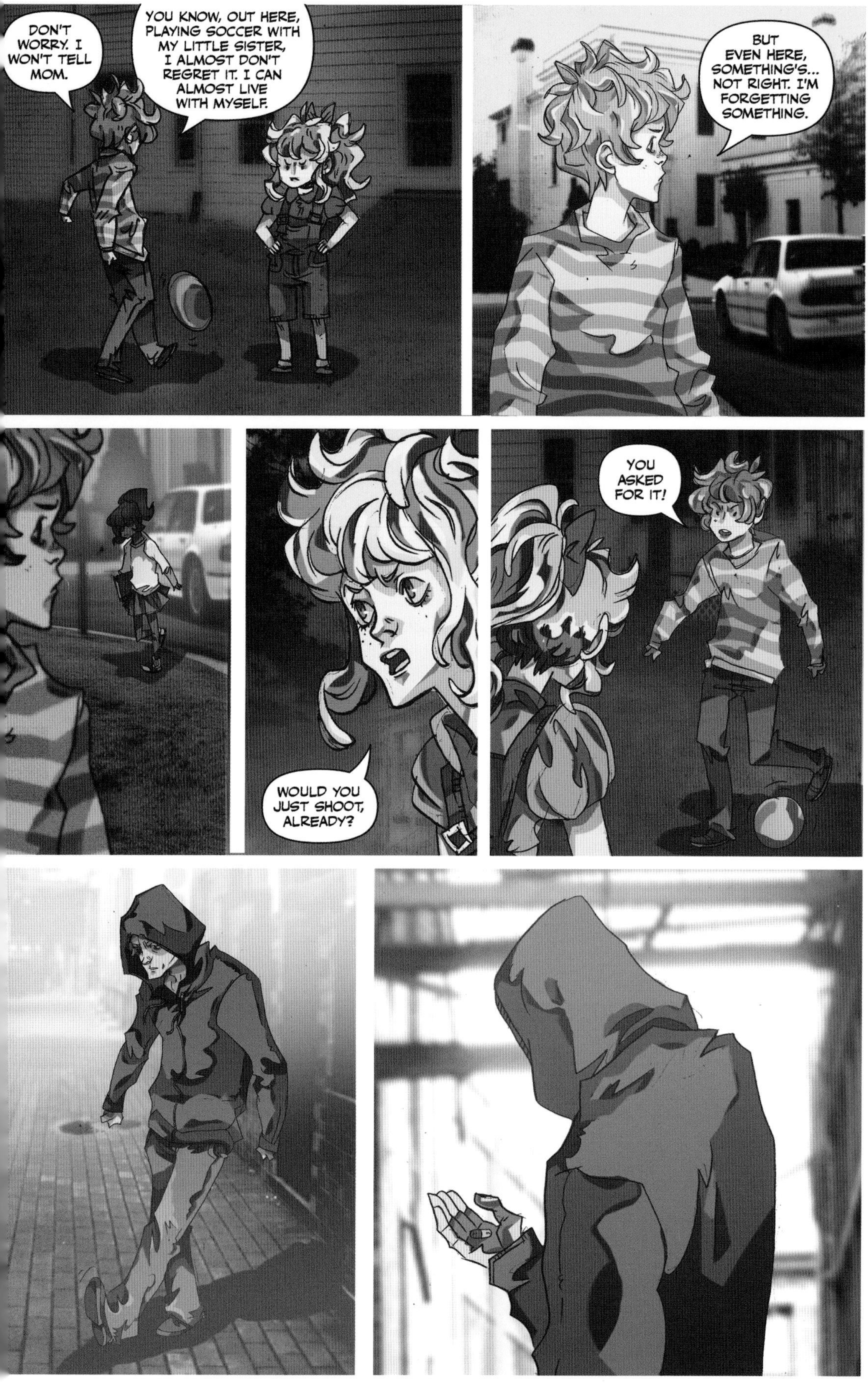
DON'T WORRY. I WON'T TELL MOM.
YOU KNOW, OUT HERE, PLAYING SOCCER WITH MY LITTLE SISTER, I ALMOST DON'T REGRET IT. I CAN ALMOST LIVE WITH MYSELF.
BUT EVEN HERE, SOMETHING'S... NOT RIGHT. I'M FORGETTING SOMETHING.
WOULD YOU JUST SHOOT, ALREADY?
YOU ASKED FOR IT!

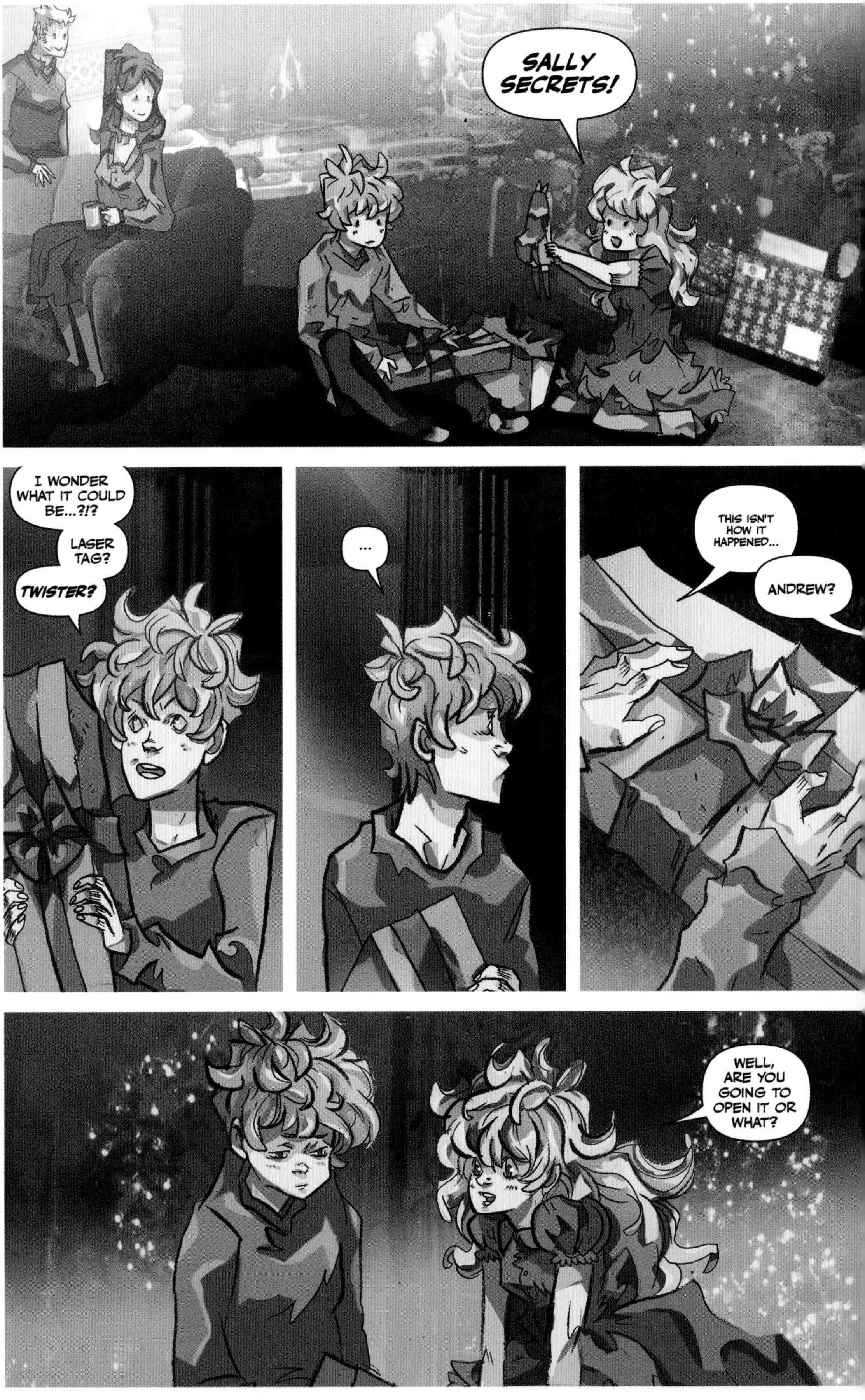
SALLY SECRETS!
I WONDER WHAT IT COULD BE...?!?
LASER TAG?
TWISTER?
...
THIS ISN'T HOW IT HAPPENED...
ANDREW?
WELL, ARE YOU GOING TO OPEN IT OR WHAT?

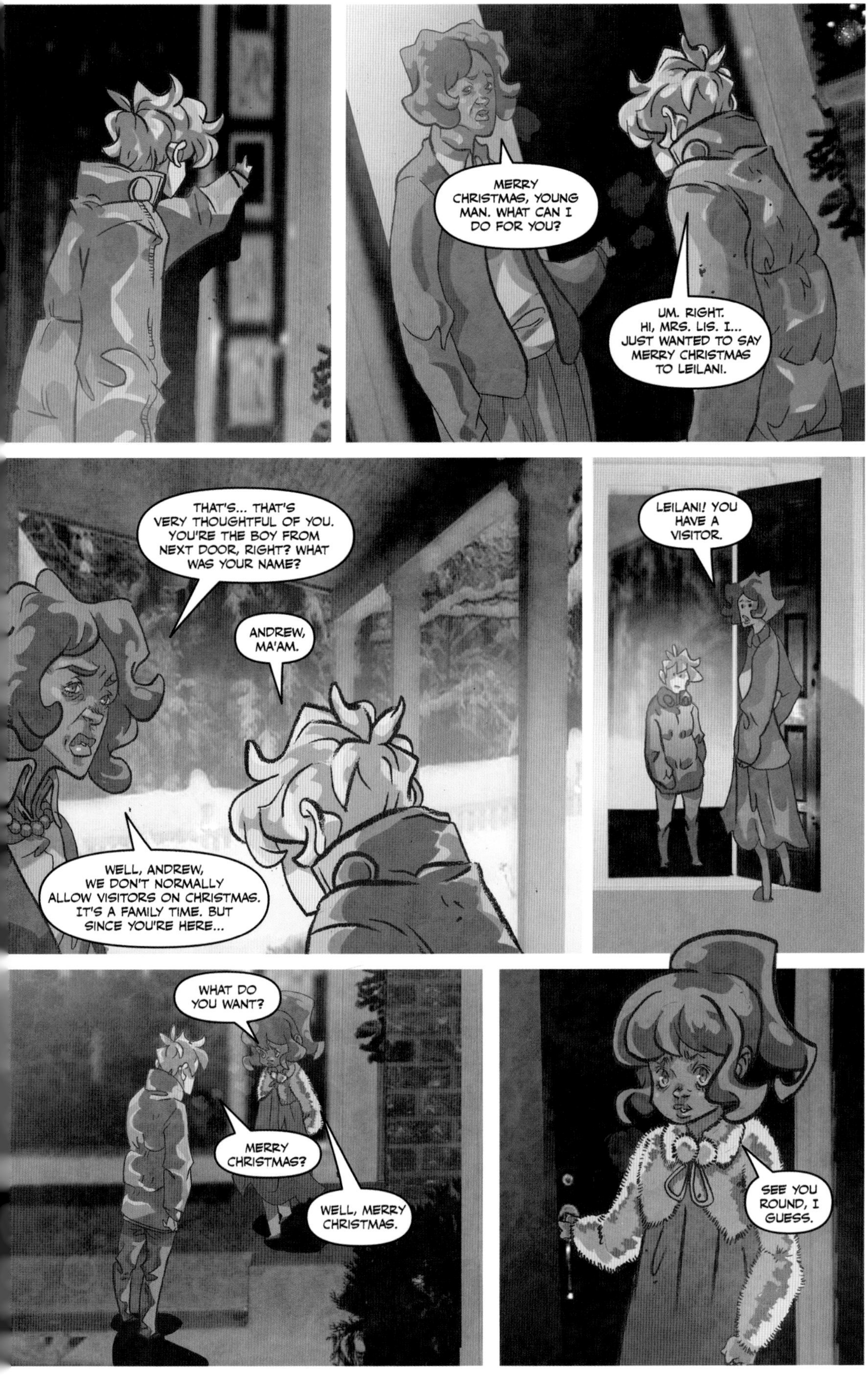
MERRY CHRISTMAS, YOUNG MAN. WHAT CAN I DO FOR YOU?
UM. RIGHT. HI, MRS. LIS. I... JUST WANTED TO SAY MERRY CHRISTMAS TO LEILANI.
THAT'S... THAT'S VERY THOUGHTFUL OF YOU. YOU'RE THE BOY FROM NEXT DOOR, RIGHT? WHAT WAS YOUR NAME?
ANDREW, MA'AM.
WELL, ANDREW, WE DON'T NORMALLY ALLOW VISITORS ON CHRISTMAS. IT'S A FAMILY TIME. BUT SINCE YOU'RE HERE...
LEILANI! YOU HAVE A VISITOR.
WHAT DO YOU WANT?
MERRY CHRISTMAS?
WELL, MERRY CHRISTMAS.
SEE YOU ROUND, I GUESS.

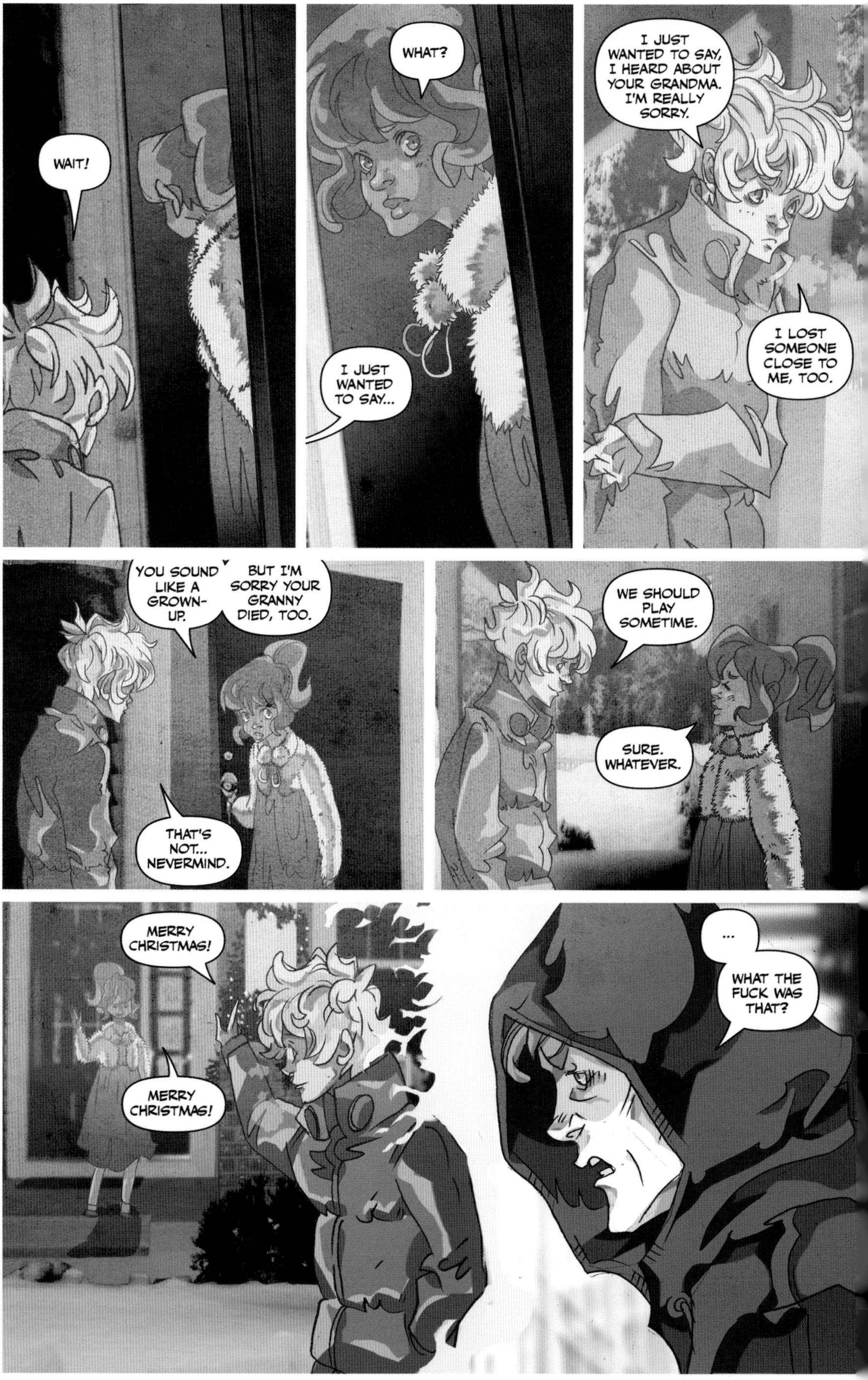
WAIT!
WHAT?
I JUST WANTED TO SAY...
I JUST WANTED TO SAY, I HEARD ABOUT YOUR GRANDMA. I'M REALLY SORRY.
I LOST SOMEONE CLOSE TO ME, TOO.
YOU SOUND LIKE A GROWN-UP.
BUT I'M SORRY YOUR GRANNY DIED, TOO.
THAT'S NOT... NEVERMIND.
WE SHOULD PLAY SOMETIME.
SURE. WHATEVER.
MERRY CHRISTMAS!
MERRY CHRISTMAS!
...
WHAT THE FUCK WAS THAT?

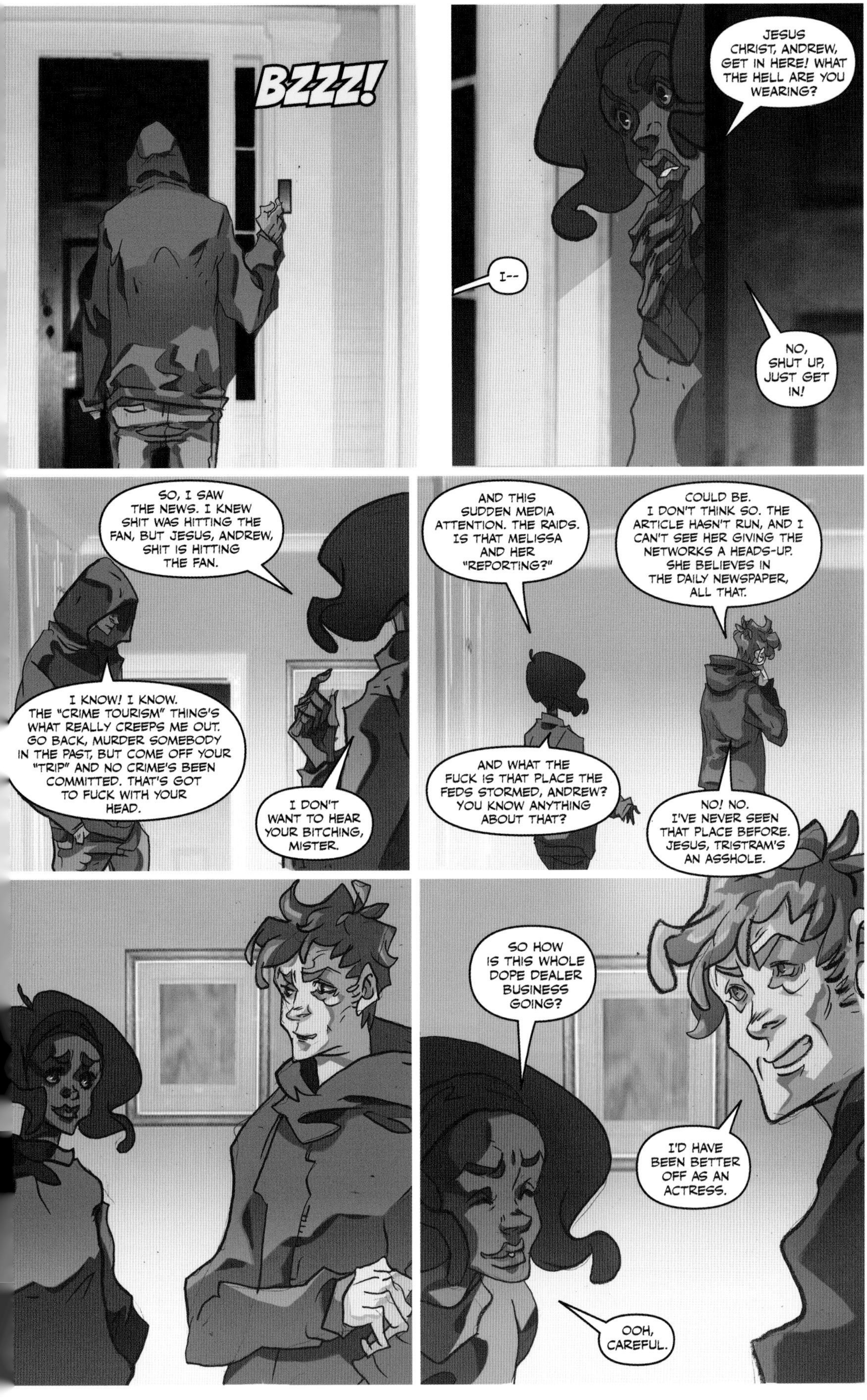
BZZZ!
JESUS CHRIST, ANDREW, GET IN HERE! WHAT THE HELL ARE YOU WEARING?
I--
NO, SHUT UP, JUST GET IN!
SO, I SAW THE NEWS. I KNEW SHIT WAS HITTING THE FAN, BUT JESUS, ANDREW, SHIT IS HITTING THE FAN.
I KNOW! I KNOW. THE "CRIME TOURISM" THING'S WHAT REALLY CREEPS ME OUT. GO BACK, MURDER SOMEBODY IN THE PAST, BUT COME OFF YOUR "TRIP" AND NO CRIME'S BEEN COMMITTED. THAT'S GOT TO FUCK WITH YOUR HEAD.
I DON'T WANT TO HEAR YOUR BITCHING, MISTER.
AND THIS SUDDEN MEDIA ATTENTION. THE RAIDS. IS THAT MELISSA AND HER "REPORTING?"
COULD BE. I DON'T THINK SO. THE ARTICLE HASN'T RUN, AND I CAN'T SEE HER GIVING THE NETWORKS A HEADS-UP. SHE BELIEVES IN THE DAILY NEWSPAPER, ALL THAT.
AND WHAT THE FUCK IS THAT PLACE THE FEDS STORMED, ANDREW? YOU KNOW ANYTHING ABOUT THAT?
NO! NO. I'VE NEVER SEEN THAT PLACE BEFORE. JESUS, TRISTRAM'S AN ASSHOLE.
SO HOW IS THIS WHOLE DOPE DEALER BUSINESS GOING?
I'D HAVE BEEN BETTER OFF AS AN ACTRESS.
OOH, CAREFUL.

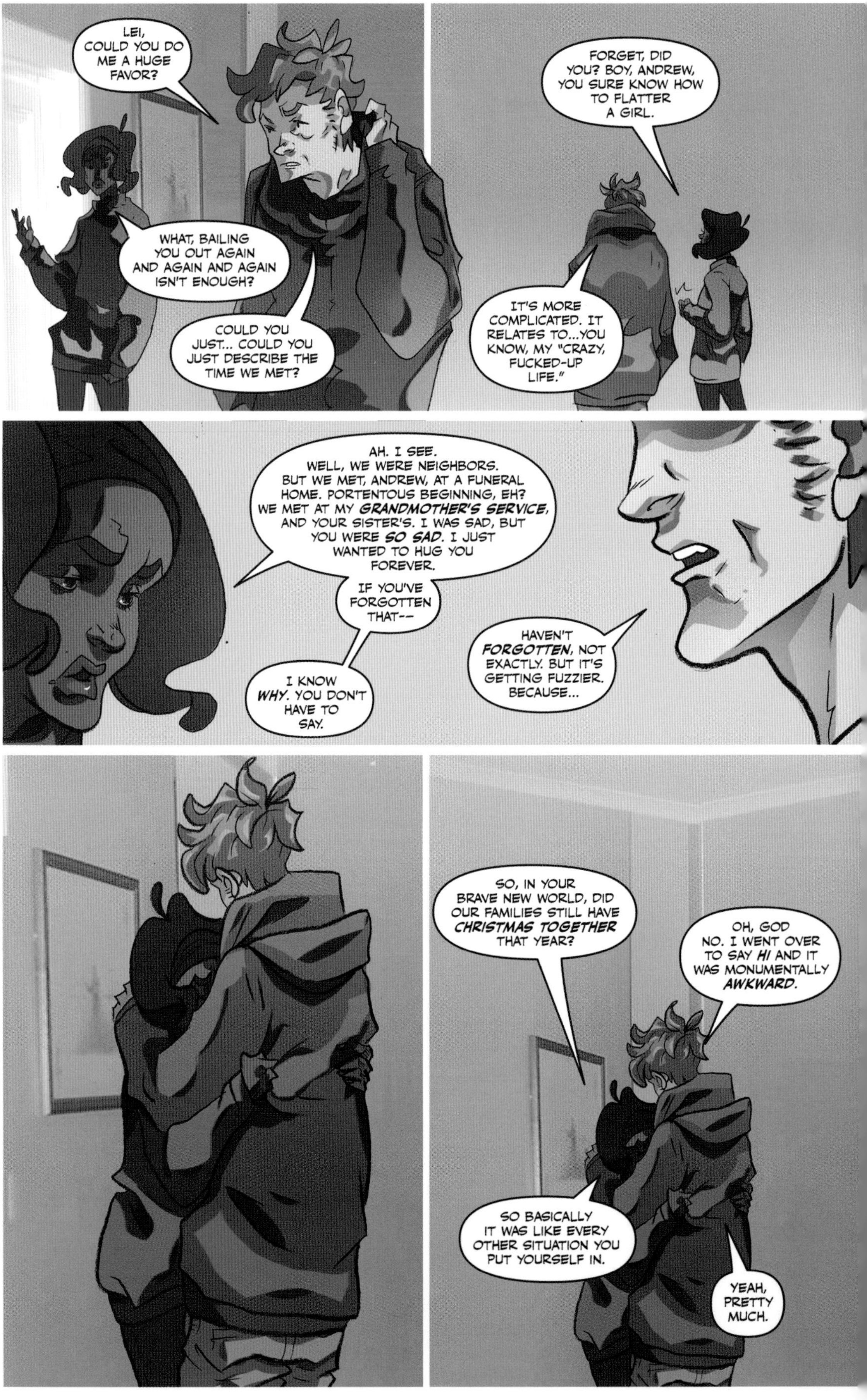
LEI, COULD YOU DO ME A HUGE FAVOR?
WHAT, BAILING YOU OUT AGAIN AND AGAIN AND AGAIN ISN'T ENOUGH?
COULD YOU JUST... COULD YOU JUST DESCRIBE THE TIME WE MET?
FORGET, DID YOU? BOY, ANDREW, YOU SURE KNOW HOW TO FLATTER A GIRL.
IT'S MORE COMPLICATED. IT RELATES TO...YOU KNOW, MY "CRAZY, FUCKED-UP LIFE."
AH. I SEE. WELL, WE WERE NEIGHBORS. BUT WE MET, ANDREW, AT A FUNERAL HOME. PORTENTOUS BEGINNING, EH? WE MET AT MY ***GRANDMOTHER'S SERVICE***, AND YOUR SISTER'S. I WAS SAD, BUT YOU WERE ***SO SAD***. I JUST WANTED TO HUG YOU FOREVER.
IF YOU'VE FORGOTTEN THAT--
HAVEN'T ***FORGOTTEN***, NOT EXACTLY. BUT IT'S GETTING FUZZIER. BECAUSE...
I KNOW ***WHY***. YOU DON'T HAVE TO SAY.
SO, IN YOUR BRAVE NEW WORLD, DID OUR FAMILIES STILL HAVE ***CHRISTMAS TOGETHER*** THAT YEAR?
OH, GOD NO. I WENT OVER TO SAY ***HI*** AND IT WAS MONUMENTALLY ***AWKWARD***.
SO BASICALLY IT WAS LIKE EVERY OTHER SITUATION YOU PUT YOURSELF IN.
YEAH, PRETTY MUCH.

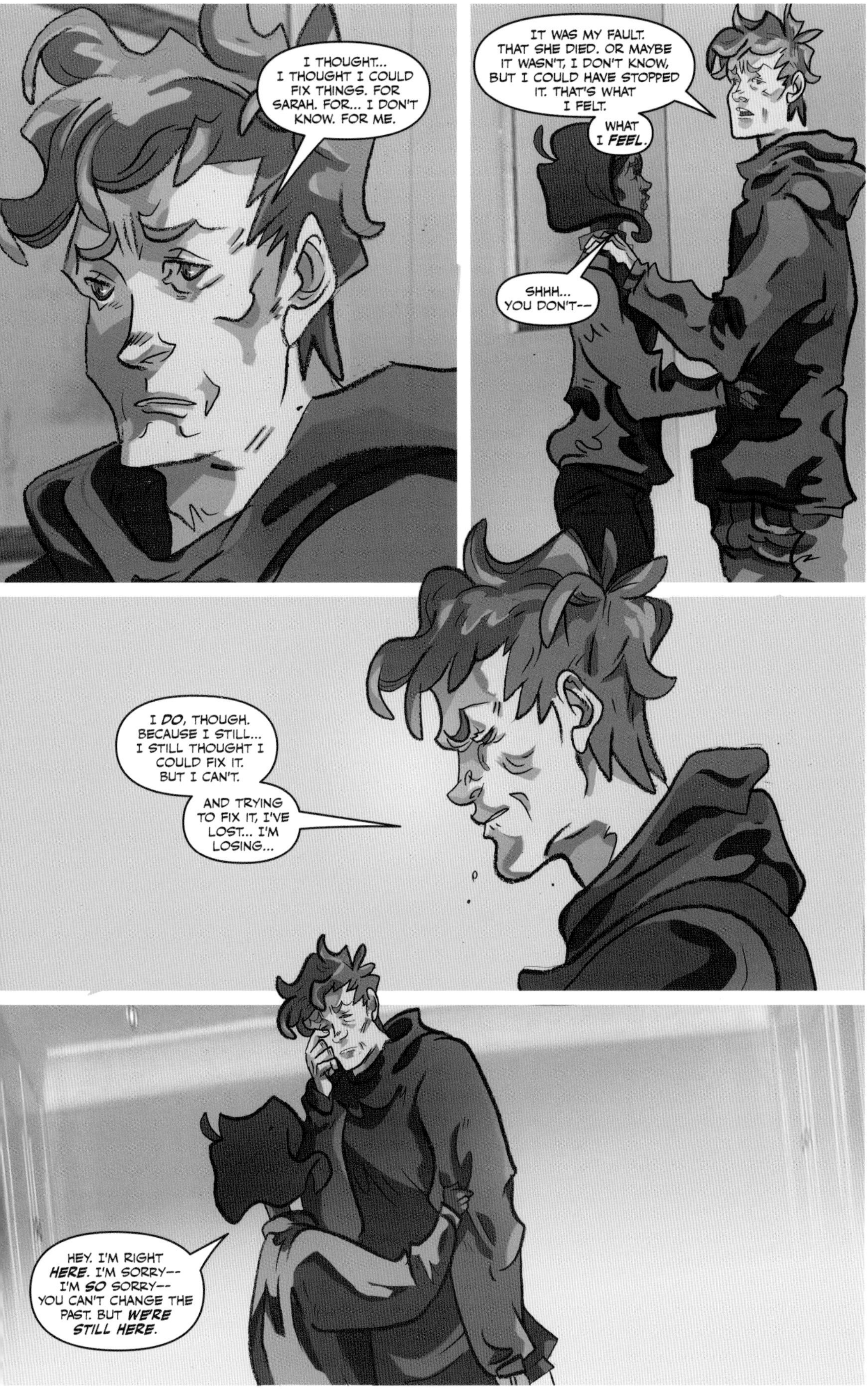
I THOUGHT... I THOUGHT I COULD FIX THINGS. FOR SARAH. FOR... I DON'T KNOW. FOR ME.
IT WAS MY FAULT. THAT SHE DIED. OR MAYBE IT WASN'T, I DON'T KNOW, BUT I COULD HAVE STOPPED IT. THAT'S WHAT I FELT.
WHAT I FEEL.
SHHH... YOU DON'T--
I DO, THOUGH. BECAUSE I STILL... I STILL THOUGHT I COULD FIX IT. BUT I CAN'T.
AND TRYING TO FIX IT, I'VE LOST... I'M LOSING...
HEY. I'M RIGHT HERE. I'M SORRY-- I'M SO SORRY-- YOU CAN'T CHANGE THE PAST. BUT WE'RE STILL HERE.

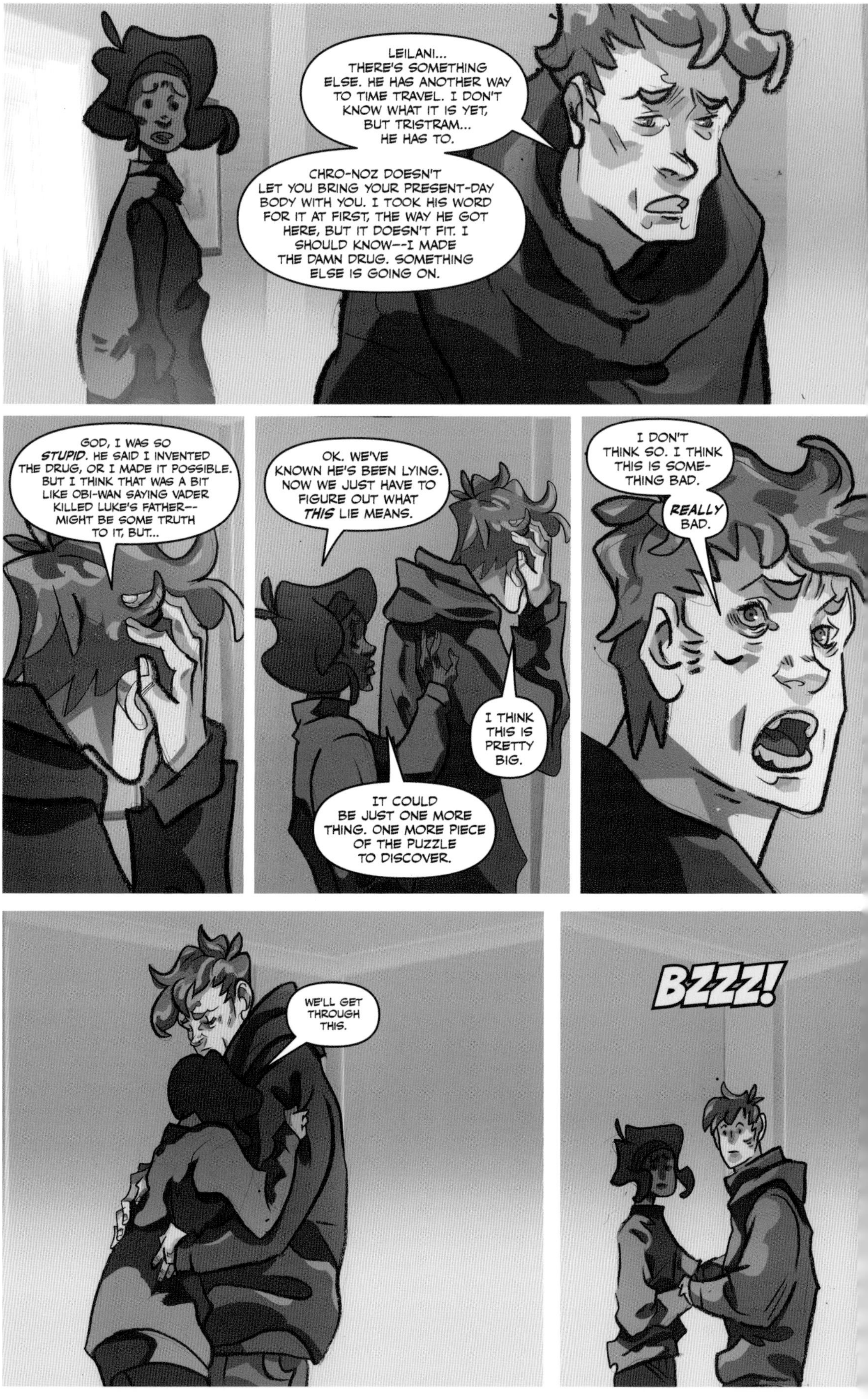
LEILANI... THERE'S SOMETHING ELSE. HE HAS ANOTHER WAY TO TIME TRAVEL. I DON'T KNOW WHAT IT IS YET, BUT TRISTRAM... HE HAS TO.
CHRO-NOZ DOESN'T LET YOU BRING YOUR PRESENT-DAY BODY WITH YOU. I TOOK HIS WORD FOR IT AT FIRST, THE WAY HE GOT HERE, BUT IT DOESN'T FIT. I SHOULD KNOW--I MADE THE DAMN DRUG. SOMETHING ELSE IS GOING ON.
GOD, I WAS SO *STUPID*. HE SAID I INVENTED THE DRUG, OR I MADE IT POSSIBLE. BUT I THINK THAT WAS A BIT LIKE OBI-WAN SAYING VADER KILLED LUKE'S FATHER-- MIGHT BE SOME TRUTH TO IT, BUT...
OK. WE'VE KNOWN HE'S BEEN LYING. NOW WE JUST HAVE TO FIGURE OUT WHAT *THIS* LIE MEANS.
I THINK THIS IS PRETTY BIG.
IT COULD BE JUST ONE MORE THING. ONE MORE PIECE OF THE PUZZLE TO DISCOVER.
I DON'T THINK SO. I THINK THIS IS SOME-THING BAD.
*REALLY* BAD.
WE'LL GET THROUGH THIS.
BZZZ!

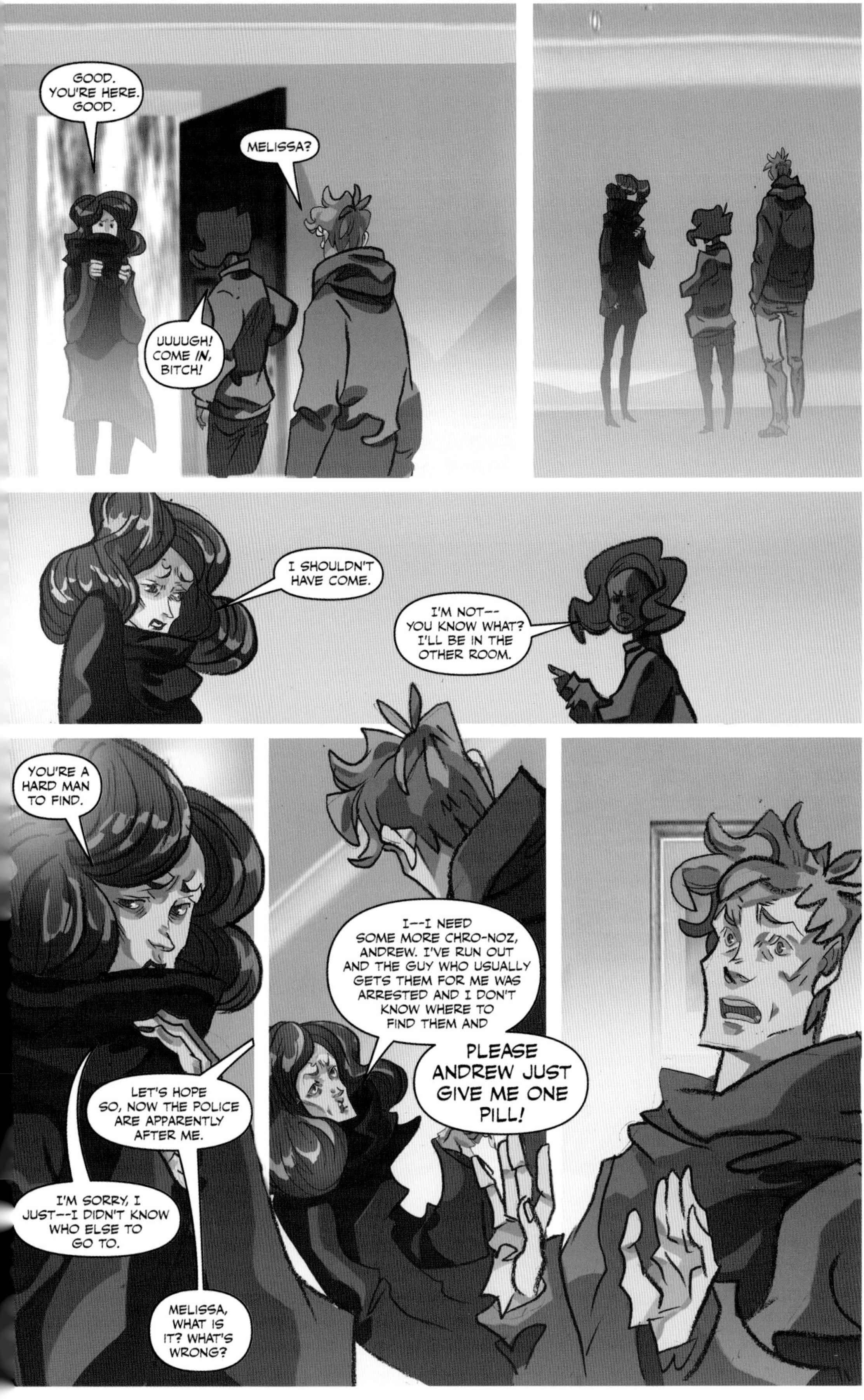
GOOD. YOU'RE HERE. GOOD.
MELISSA?
UUUUGH! COME *IN*, BITCH!
I SHOULDN'T HAVE COME.
I'M NOT-- YOU KNOW WHAT? I'LL BE IN THE OTHER ROOM.
YOU'RE A HARD MAN TO FIND.
LET'S HOPE SO, NOW THE POLICE ARE APPARENTLY AFTER ME.
I'M SORRY, I JUST--I DIDN'T KNOW WHO ELSE TO GO TO.
MELISSA, WHAT IS IT? WHAT'S WRONG?
I--I NEED SOME MORE CHRO-NOZ, ANDREW. I'VE RUN OUT AND THE GUY WHO USUALLY GETS THEM FOR ME WAS ARRESTED AND I DON'T KNOW WHERE TO FIND THEM AND
PLEASE ANDREW JUST GIVE ME ONE PILL!

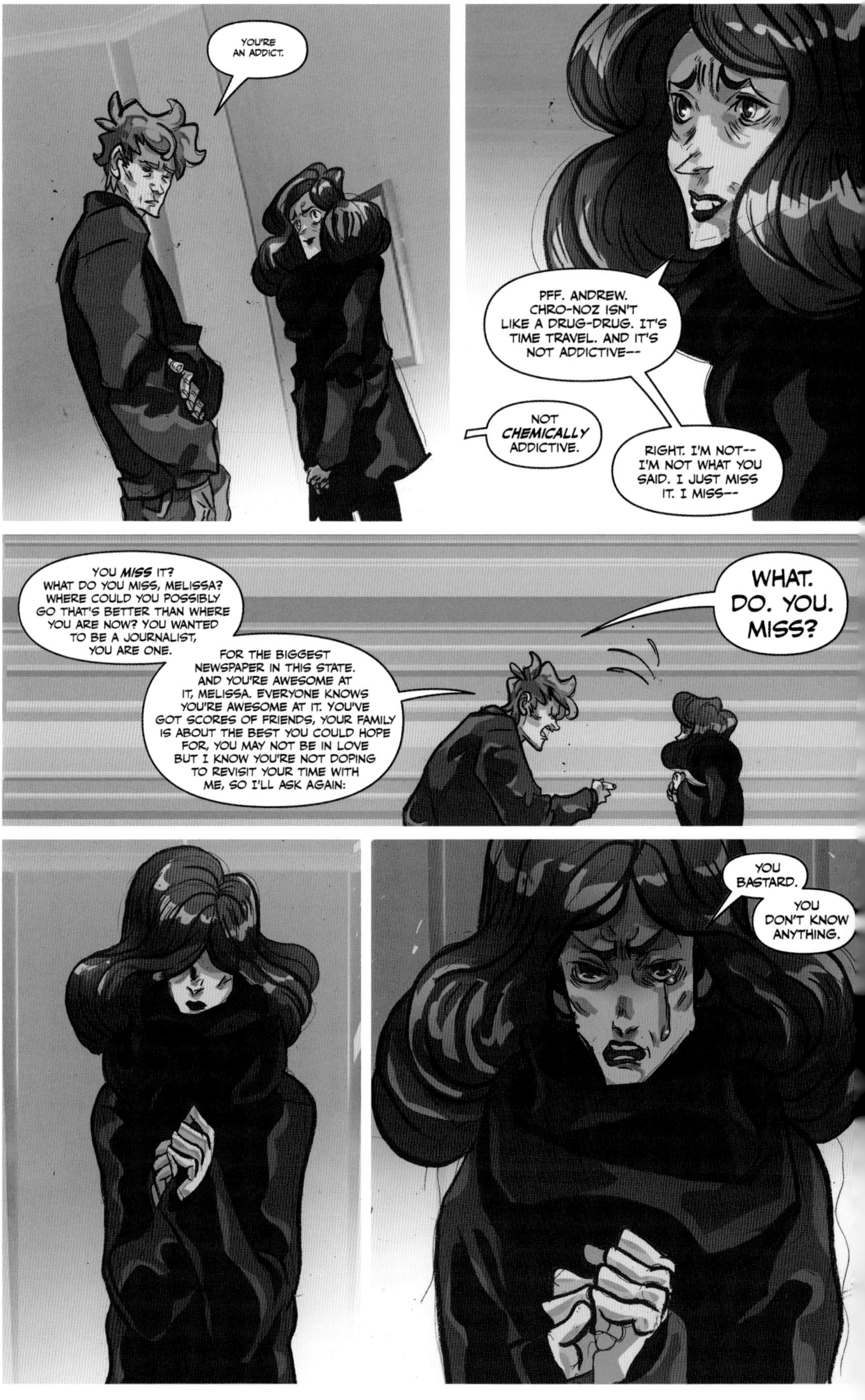
YOU'RE AN ADDICT.
PFF. ANDREW. CHRO-NOZ ISN'T LIKE A DRUG-DRUG. IT'S TIME TRAVEL. AND IT'S NOT ADDICTIVE--
NOT *CHEMICALLY* ADDICTIVE.
RIGHT. I'M NOT-- I'M NOT WHAT YOU SAID. I JUST MISS IT. I MISS--
YOU *MISS* IT? WHAT DO YOU MISS, MELISSA? WHERE COULD YOU POSSIBLY GO THAT'S BETTER THAN WHERE YOU ARE NOW? YOU WANTED TO BE A JOURNALIST, YOU ARE ONE.
FOR THE BIGGEST NEWSPAPER IN THIS STATE. AND YOU'RE AWESOME AT IT, MELISSA. EVERYONE KNOWS YOU'RE AWESOME AT IT. YOU'VE GOT SCORES OF FRIENDS, YOUR FAMILY IS ABOUT THE BEST YOU COULD HOPE FOR, YOU MAY NOT BE IN LOVE BUT I KNOW YOU'RE NOT DOPING TO REVISIT YOUR TIME WITH ME, SO I'LL ASK AGAIN:
WHAT. DO. YOU. MISS?
YOU BASTARD.
YOU DON'T KNOW ANYTHING.

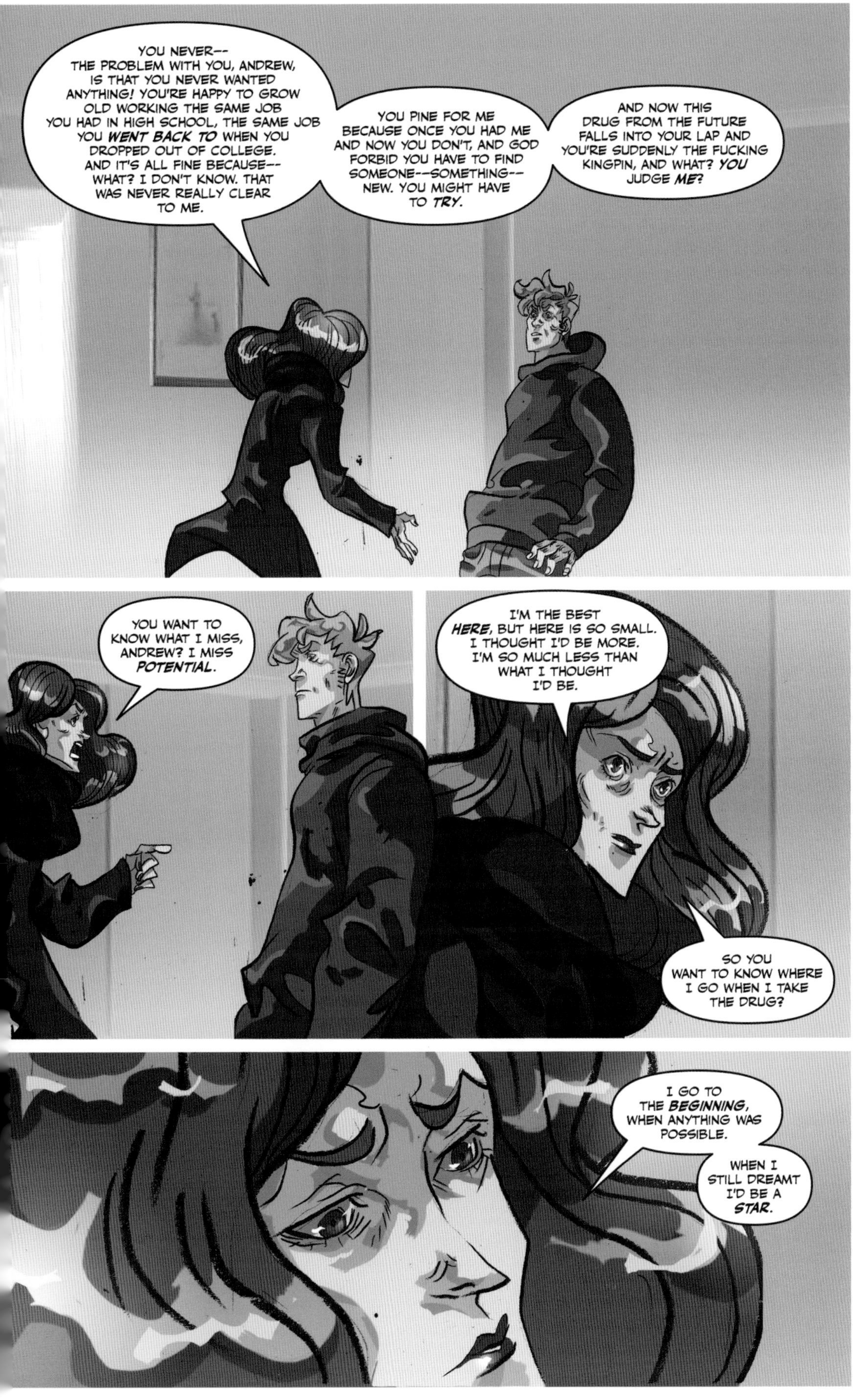
YOU NEVER-- THE PROBLEM WITH YOU, ANDREW, IS THAT YOU NEVER WANTED ANYTHING! YOU'RE HAPPY TO GROW OLD WORKING THE SAME JOB YOU HAD IN HIGH SCHOOL, THE SAME JOB YOU **WENT BACK TO** WHEN YOU DROPPED OUT OF COLLEGE. AND IT'S ALL FINE BECAUSE-- WHAT? I DON'T KNOW. THAT WAS NEVER REALLY CLEAR TO ME.
YOU PINE FOR ME BECAUSE ONCE YOU HAD ME AND NOW YOU DON'T, AND GOD FORBID YOU HAVE TO FIND SOMEONE--SOMETHING-- NEW. YOU MIGHT HAVE TO **TRY.**
AND NOW THIS DRUG FROM THE FUTURE FALLS INTO YOUR LAP AND YOU'RE SUDDENLY THE FUCKING KINGPIN, AND WHAT? **YOU** JUDGE **ME?**
YOU WANT TO KNOW WHAT I MISS, ANDREW? I MISS **POTENTIAL.**
I'M THE BEST **HERE,** BUT HERE IS SO SMALL. I THOUGHT I'D BE MORE. I'M SO MUCH LESS THAN WHAT I THOUGHT I'D BE.
SO YOU WANT TO KNOW WHERE I GO WHEN I TAKE THE DRUG?
I GO TO THE **BEGINNING,** WHEN ANYTHING WAS POSSIBLE.
WHEN I STILL DREAMT I'D BE A **STAR.**

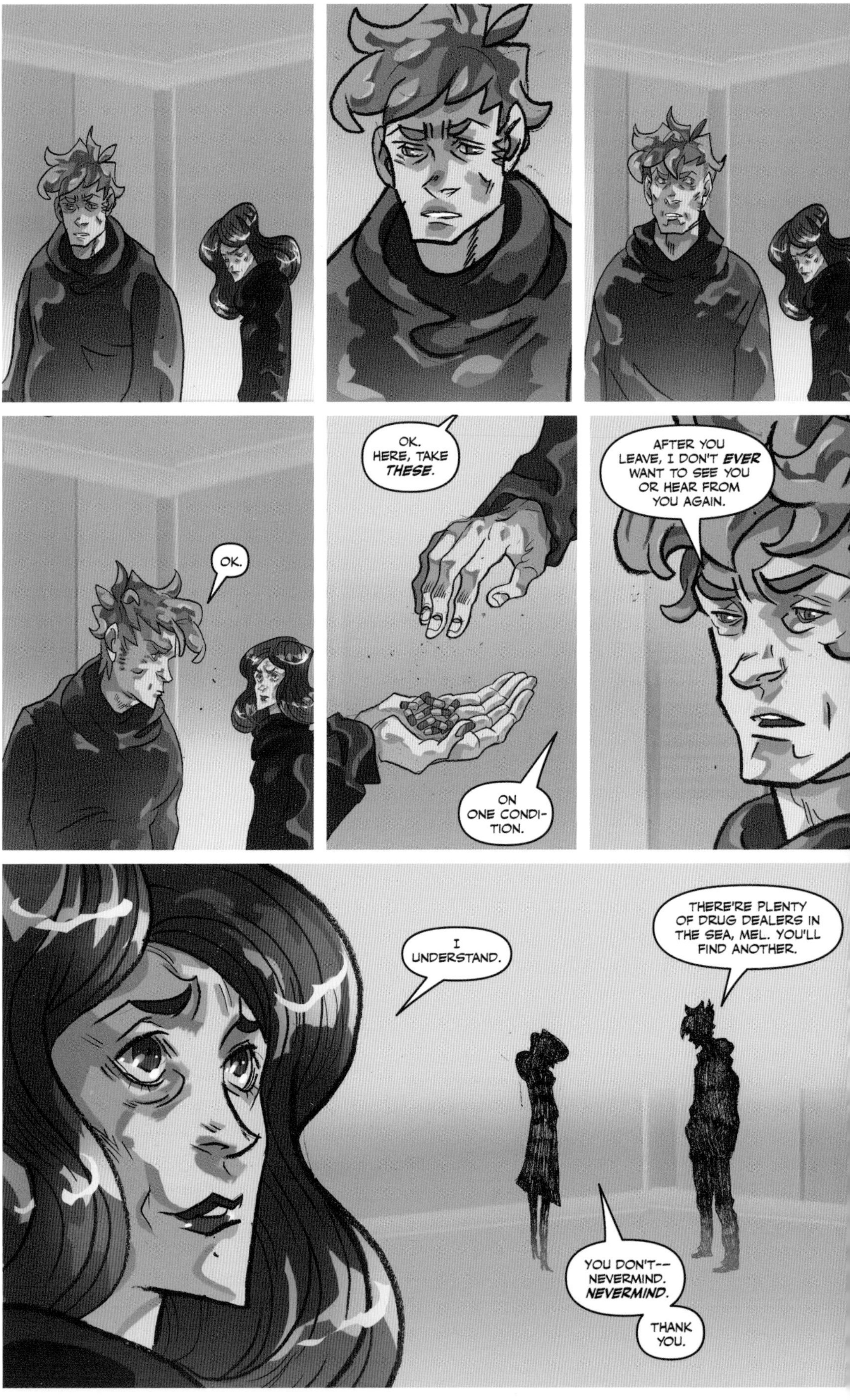
OK.
OK. HERE, TAKE *THESE*.
ON ONE CONDI- TION.
AFTER YOU LEAVE, I DON'T *EVER* WANT TO SEE YOU OR HEAR FROM YOU AGAIN.
I UNDERSTAND.
THERE'RE PLENTY OF DRUG DEALERS IN THE SEA, MEL. YOU'LL FIND ANOTHER.
YOU DON'T-- NEVERMIND. *NEVERMIND*.
THANK YOU.

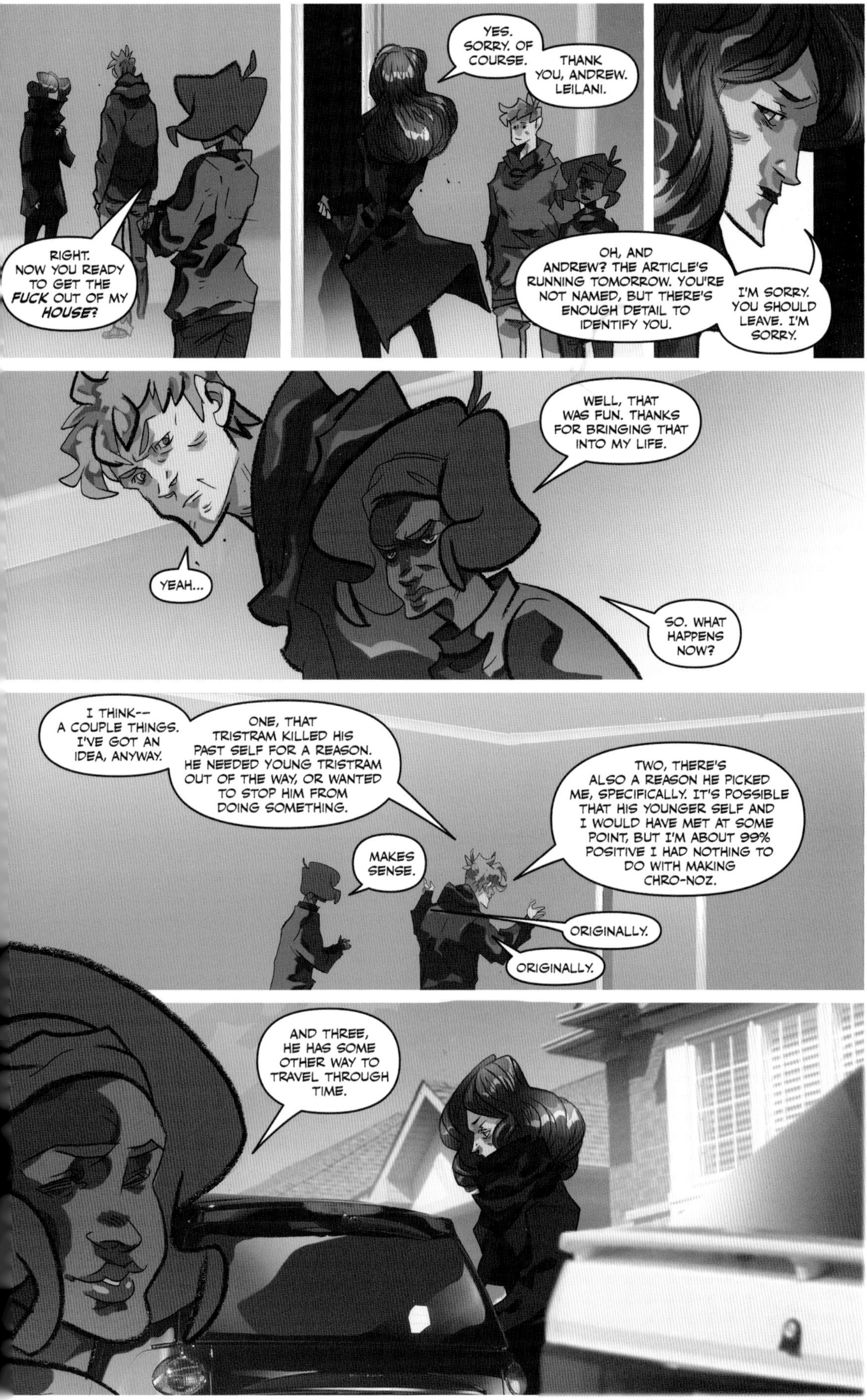
RIGHT. NOW YOU READY TO GET THE *FUCK* OUT OF MY *HOUSE?*
YES. SORRY. OF COURSE.
THANK YOU, ANDREW. LEILANI.
OH, AND ANDREW? THE ARTICLE'S RUNNING TOMORROW. YOU'RE NOT NAMED, BUT THERE'S ENOUGH DETAIL TO IDENTIFY YOU.
I'M SORRY. YOU SHOULD LEAVE. I'M SORRY.
WELL, THAT WAS FUN. THANKS FOR BRINGING THAT INTO MY LIFE.
YEAH...
SO. WHAT HAPPENS NOW?
I THINK-- A COUPLE THINGS. I'VE GOT AN IDEA, ANYWAY.
ONE, THAT TRISTRAM KILLED HIS PAST SELF FOR A REASON. HE NEEDED YOUNG TRISTRAM OUT OF THE WAY, OR WANTED TO STOP HIM FROM DOING SOMETHING.
MAKES SENSE.
TWO, THERE'S ALSO A REASON HE PICKED ME, SPECIFICALLY. IT'S POSSIBLE THAT HIS YOUNGER SELF AND I WOULD HAVE MET AT SOME POINT, BUT I'M ABOUT 99% POSITIVE I HAD NOTHING TO DO WITH MAKING CHRO-NOZ.
ORIGINALLY.
ORIGINALLY.
AND THREE, HE HAS SOME OTHER WAY TO TRAVEL THROUGH TIME.

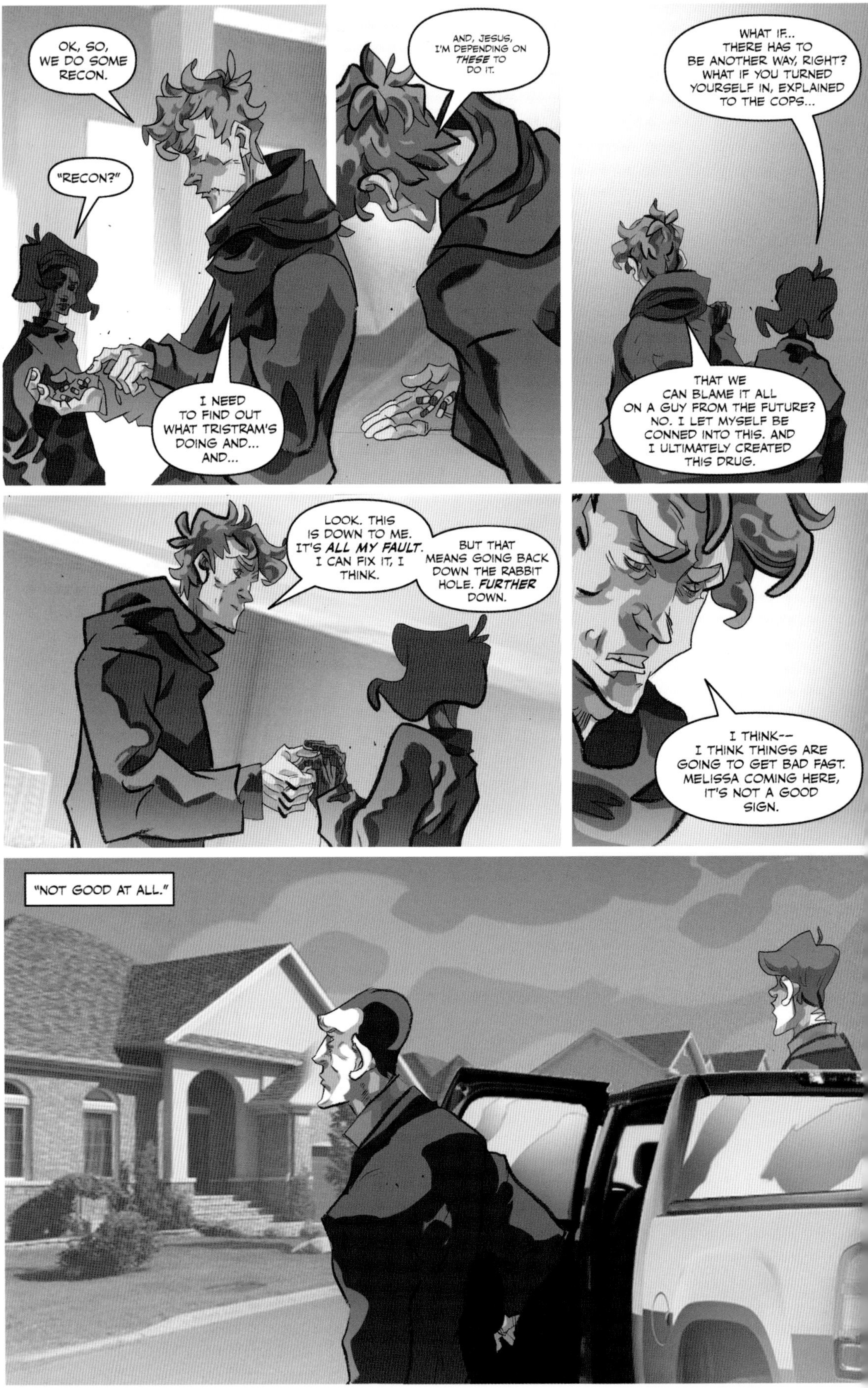
OK, SO, WE DO SOME RECON.
"RECON?"
I NEED TO FIND OUT WHAT TRISTRAM'S DOING AND... AND...
AND, JESUS, I'M DEPENDING ON THESE TO DO IT.
WHAT IF... THERE HAS TO BE ANOTHER WAY, RIGHT? WHAT IF YOU TURNED YOURSELF IN, EXPLAINED TO THE COPS...
THAT WE CAN BLAME IT ALL ON A GUY FROM THE FUTURE? NO. I LET MYSELF BE CONNED INTO THIS. AND I ULTIMATELY CREATED THIS DRUG.
LOOK. THIS IS DOWN TO ME. IT'S ALL MY FAULT. I CAN FIX IT, I THINK.
BUT THAT MEANS GOING BACK DOWN THE RABBIT HOLE. FURTHER DOWN.
I THINK-- I THINK THINGS ARE GOING TO GET BAD FAST. MELISSA COMING HERE, IT'S NOT A GOOD SIGN.
"NOT GOOD AT ALL."

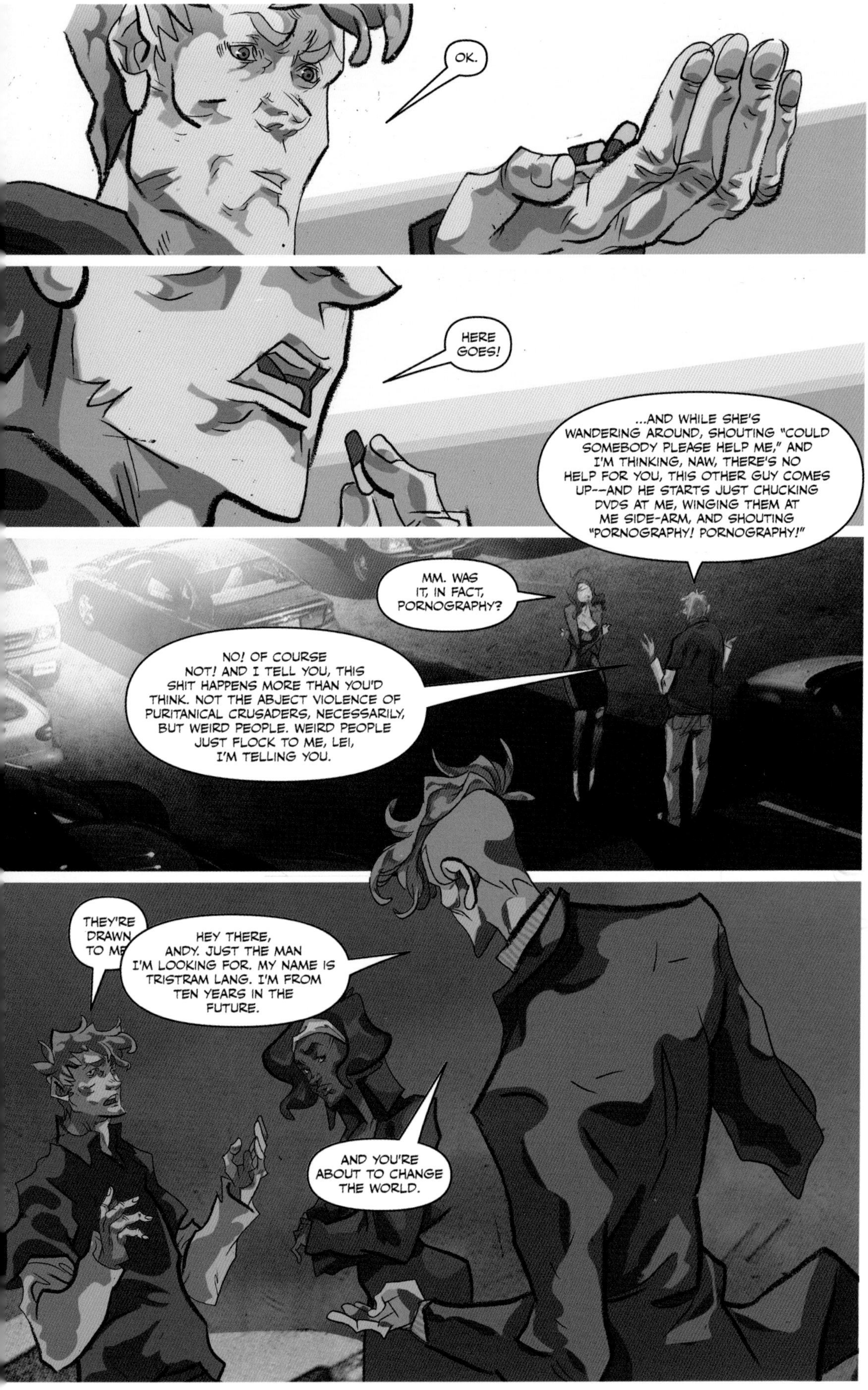
OK.
HERE GOES!
...AND WHILE SHE'S WANDERING AROUND, SHOUTING "COULD SOMEBODY PLEASE HELP ME," AND I'M THINKING, NAW, THERE'S NO HELP FOR YOU, THIS OTHER GUY COMES UP--AND HE STARTS JUST CHUCKING DVDS AT ME, WINGING THEM AT ME SIDE-ARM, AND SHOUTING "PORNOGRAPHY! PORNOGRAPHY!"
MM. WAS IT, IN FACT, PORNOGRAPHY?
NO! OF COURSE NOT! AND I TELL YOU, THIS SHIT HAPPENS MORE THAN YOU'D THINK. NOT THE ABJECT VIOLENCE OF PURITANICAL CRUSADERS, NECESSARILY, BUT WEIRD PEOPLE. WEIRD PEOPLE JUST FLOCK TO ME, LEI, I'M TELLING YOU.
THEY'RE DRAWN TO ME
HEY THERE, ANDY. JUST THE MAN I'M LOOKING FOR. MY NAME IS TRISTRAM LANG. I'M FROM TEN YEARS IN THE FUTURE.
AND YOU'RE ABOUT TO CHANGE THE WORLD.

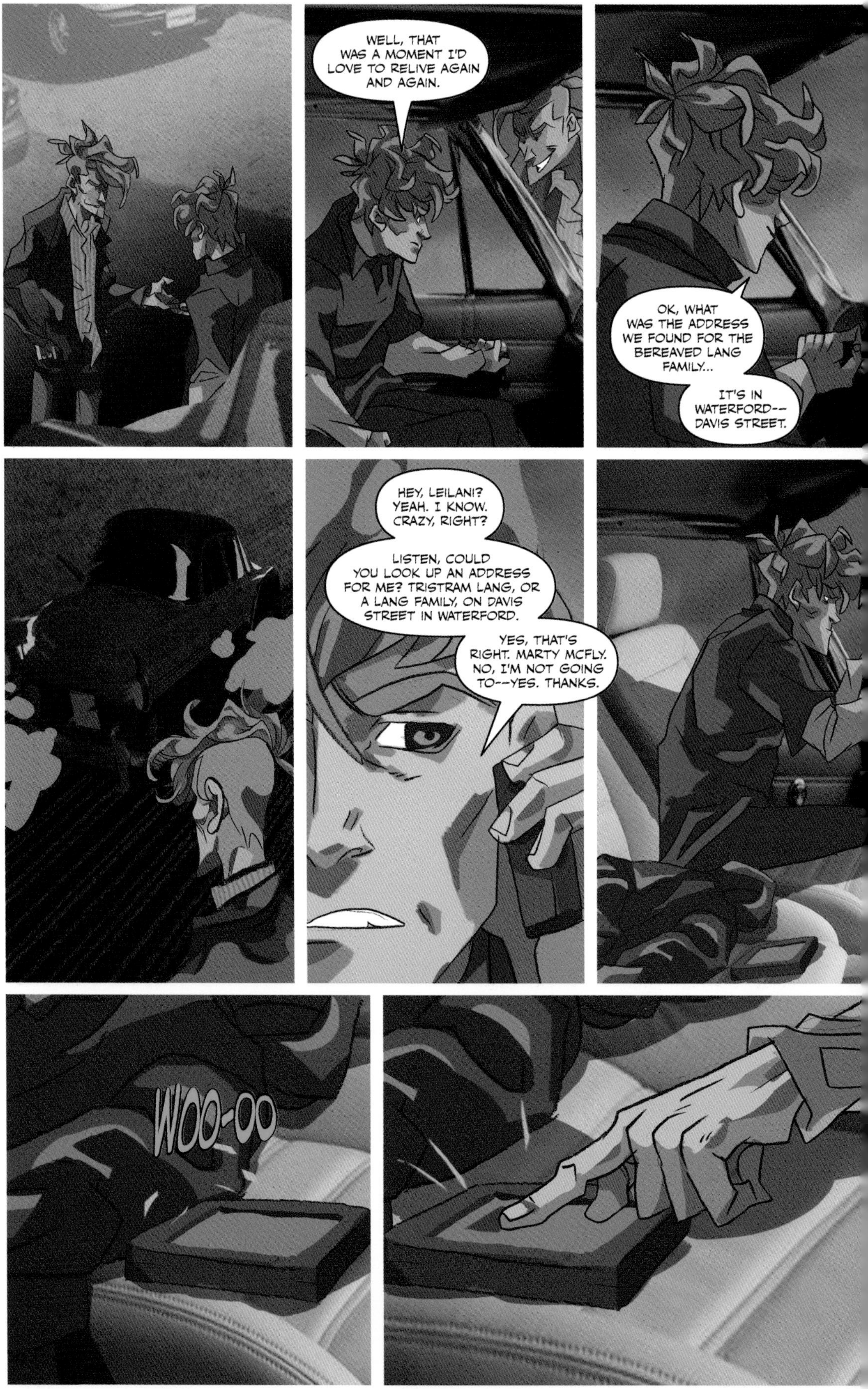
WELL, THAT WAS A MOMENT I'D LOVE TO RELIVE AGAIN AND AGAIN.
OK, WHAT WAS THE ADDRESS WE FOUND FOR THE BEREAVED LANG FAMILY...
IT'S IN WATERFORD-- DAVIS STREET.
HEY, LEILANI? YEAH. I KNOW. CRAZY, RIGHT?
LISTEN, COULD YOU LOOK UP AN ADDRESS FOR ME? TRISTRAM LANG, OR A LANG FAMILY, ON DAVIS STREET IN WATERFORD.
YES, THAT'S RIGHT. MARTY MCFLY. NO, I'M NOT GOING TO--YES. THANKS.
WOO-OO

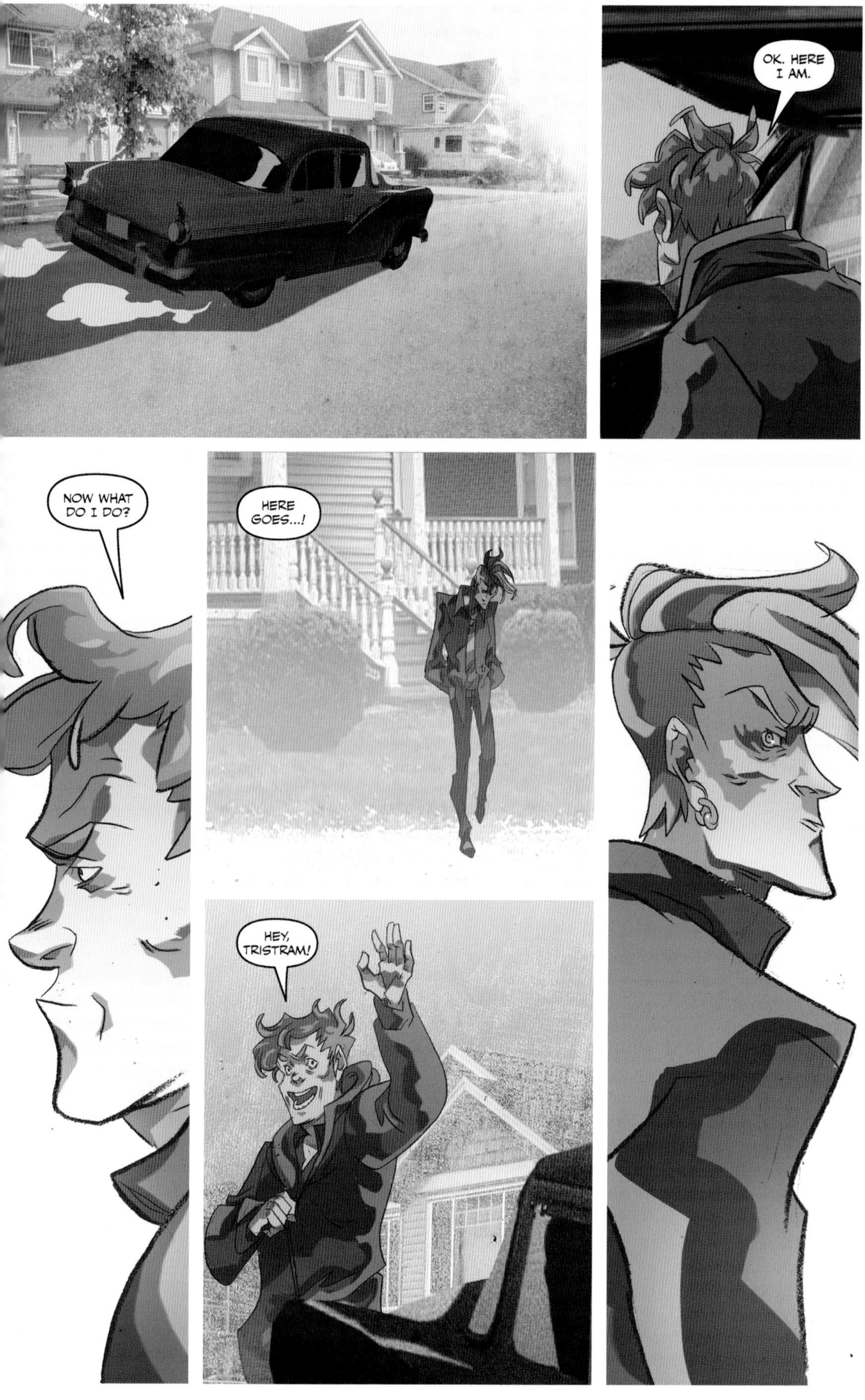
OK. HERE I AM.
NOW WHAT DO I DO?
HERE GOES...!
HEY, TRISTRAM!

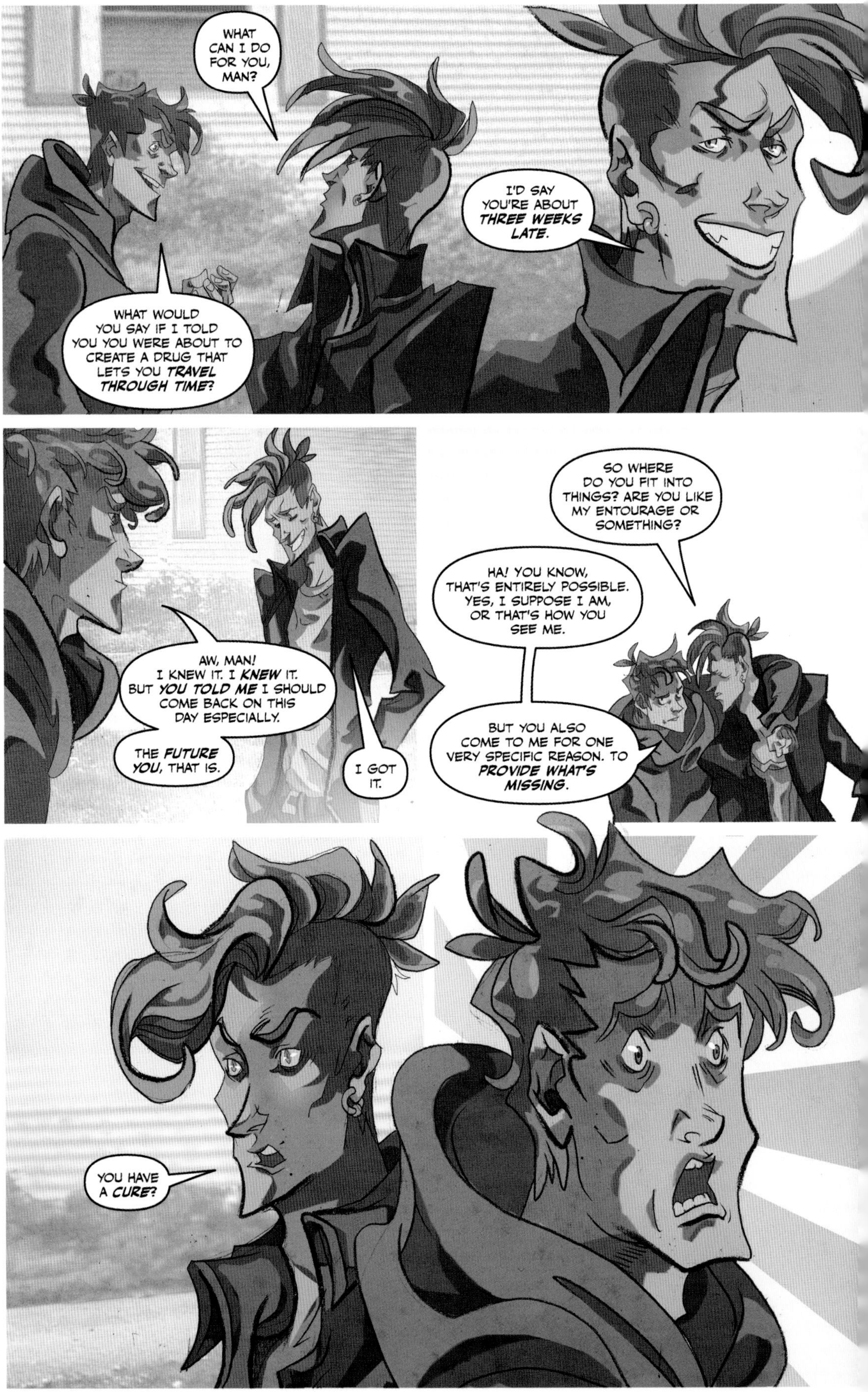

WHAT CAN I DO FOR YOU, MAN?
WHAT WOULD YOU SAY IF I TOLD YOU YOU WERE ABOUT TO CREATE A DRUG THAT LETS YOU TRAVEL THROUGH TIME?
I'D SAY YOU'RE ABOUT THREE WEEKS LATE.
AW, MAN! I KNEW IT. I KNEW IT. BUT YOU TOLD ME I SHOULD COME BACK ON THIS DAY ESPECIALLY.
THE FUTURE YOU, THAT IS.
I GOT IT.
SO WHERE DO YOU FIT INTO THINGS? ARE YOU LIKE MY ENTOURAGE OR SOMETHING?
HA! YOU KNOW, THAT'S ENTIRELY POSSIBLE. YES, I SUPPOSE I AM, OR THAT'S HOW YOU SEE ME.
BUT YOU ALSO COME TO ME FOR ONE VERY SPECIFIC REASON. TO PROVIDE WHAT'S MISSING.
YOU HAVE A CURE?

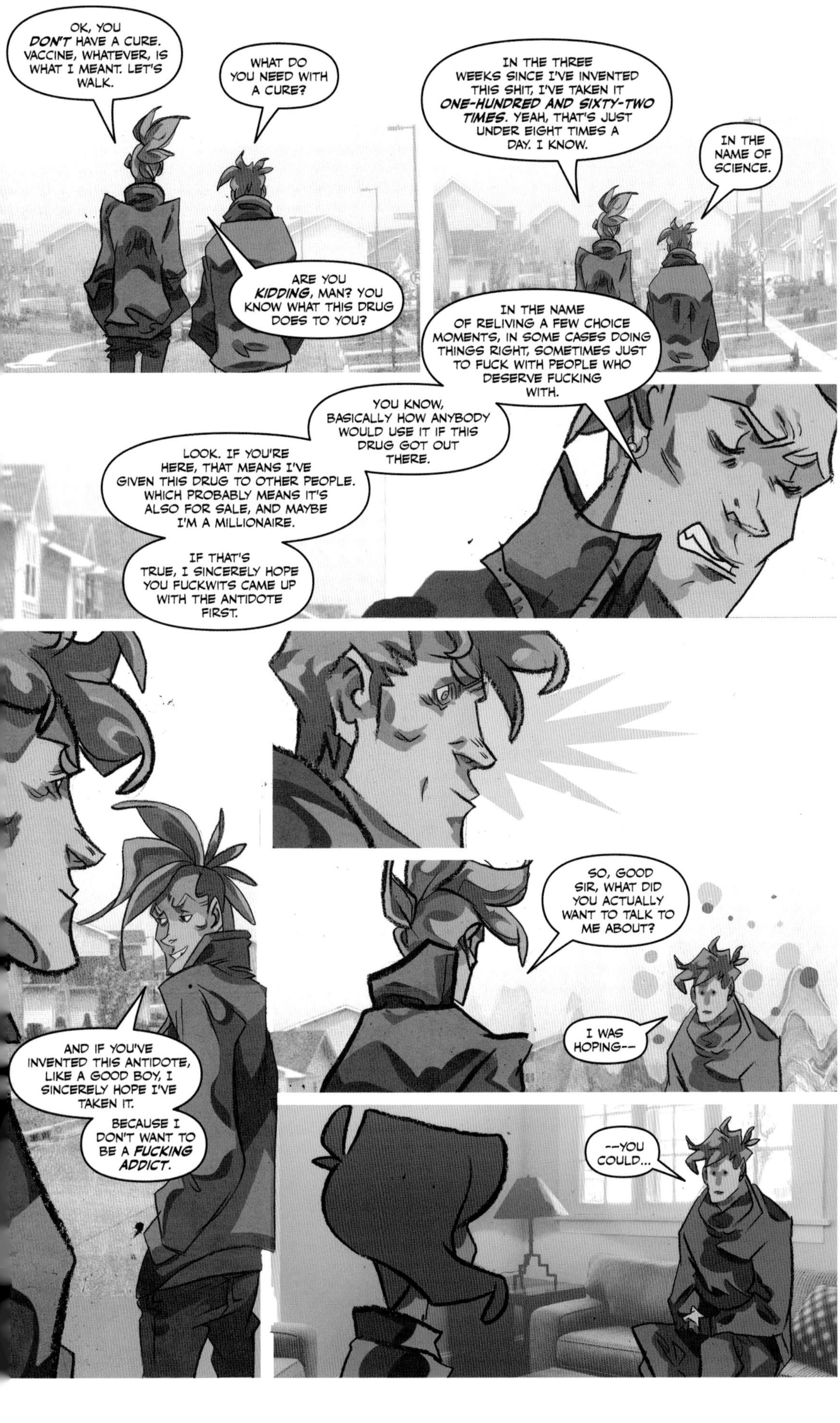
OK, YOU *DON'T* HAVE A CURE. VACCINE, WHATEVER, IS WHAT I MEANT. LET'S WALK.
WHAT DO YOU NEED WITH A CURE?
ARE YOU *KIDDING*, MAN? YOU KNOW WHAT THIS DRUG DOES TO YOU?
IN THE THREE WEEKS SINCE I'VE INVENTED THIS SHIT, I'VE TAKEN IT *ONE-HUNDRED AND SIXTY-TWO TIMES*. YEAH, THAT'S JUST UNDER EIGHT TIMES A DAY. I KNOW.
IN THE NAME OF SCIENCE.
IN THE NAME OF RELIVING A FEW CHOICE MOMENTS, IN SOME CASES DOING THINGS RIGHT, SOMETIMES JUST TO FUCK WITH PEOPLE WHO DESERVE FUCKING WITH.
YOU KNOW, BASICALLY HOW ANYBODY WOULD USE IT IF THIS DRUG GOT OUT THERE.
LOOK. IF YOU'RE HERE, THAT MEANS I'VE GIVEN THIS DRUG TO OTHER PEOPLE. WHICH PROBABLY MEANS IT'S ALSO FOR SALE, AND MAYBE I'M A MILLIONAIRE.
IF THAT'S TRUE, I SINCERELY HOPE YOU FUCKWITS CAME UP WITH THE ANTIDOTE FIRST.
AND IF YOU'VE INVENTED THIS ANTIDOTE, LIKE A GOOD BOY, I SINCERELY HOPE I'VE TAKEN IT.
BECAUSE I DON'T WANT TO BE A *FUCKING ADDICT*.
SO, GOOD SIR, WHAT DID YOU ACTUALLY WANT TO TALK TO ME ABOUT?
I WAS HOPING--
--YOU COULD...

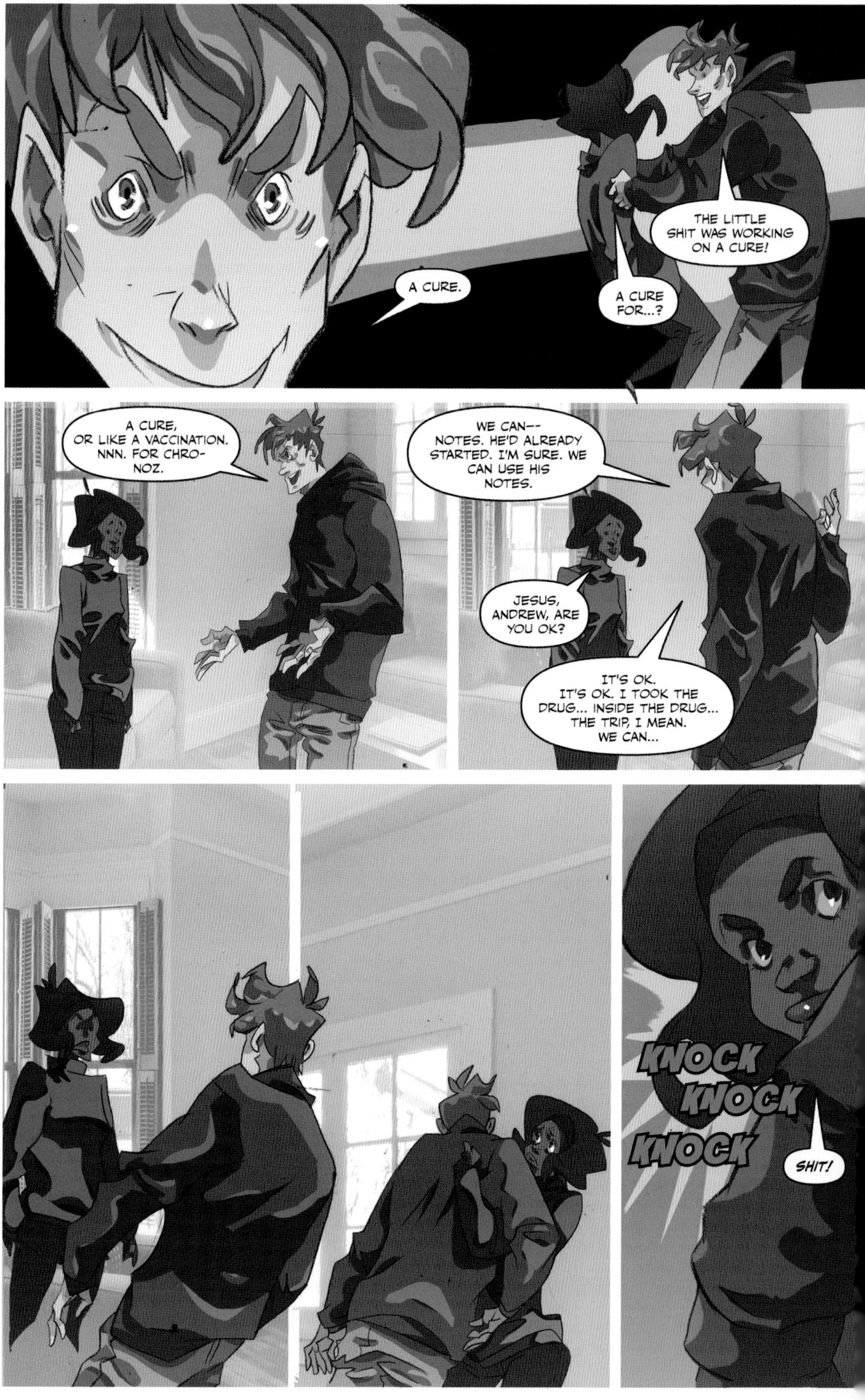
A CURE.
A CURE FOR...?
THE LITTLE SHIT WAS WORKING ON A CURE!
A CURE, OR LIKE A VACCINATION. NNN. FOR CHRO-NOZ.
WE CAN-- NOTES. HE'D ALREADY STARTED. I'M SURE. WE CAN USE HIS NOTES.
JESUS, ANDREW, ARE YOU OK?
IT'S OK. IT'S OK. I TOOK THE DRUG... INSIDE THE DRUG... THE TRIP, I MEAN. WE CAN...
KNOCK
KNOCK
KNOCK
SHIT!

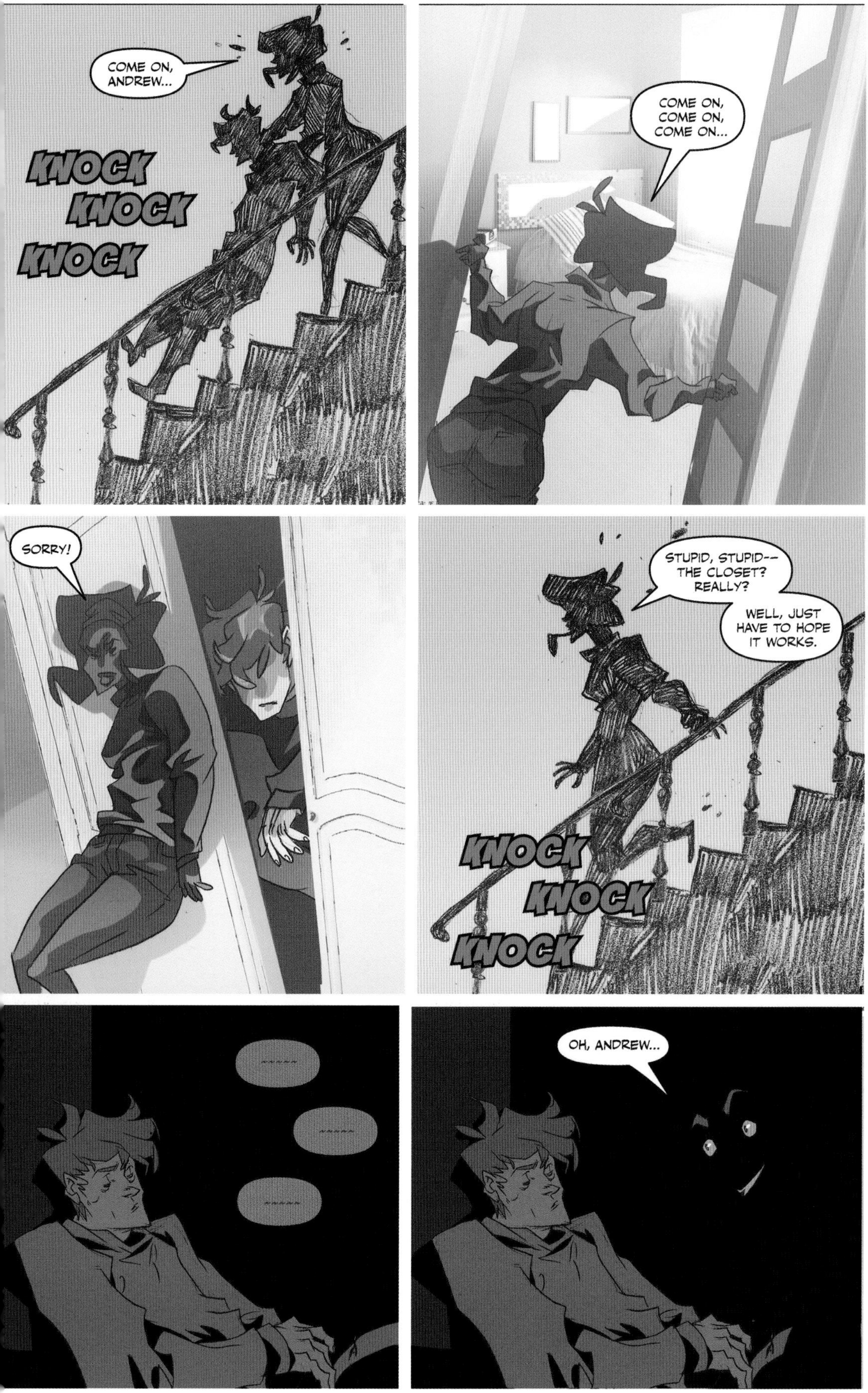
COME ON, ANDREW...
KNOCK
KNOCK
KNOCK
COME ON, COME ON, COME ON...
SORRY!
STUPID, STUPID-- THE CLOSET? REALLY?
WELL, JUST HAVE TO HOPE IT WORKS.
KNOCK
KNOCK
KNOCK
OH, ANDREW...

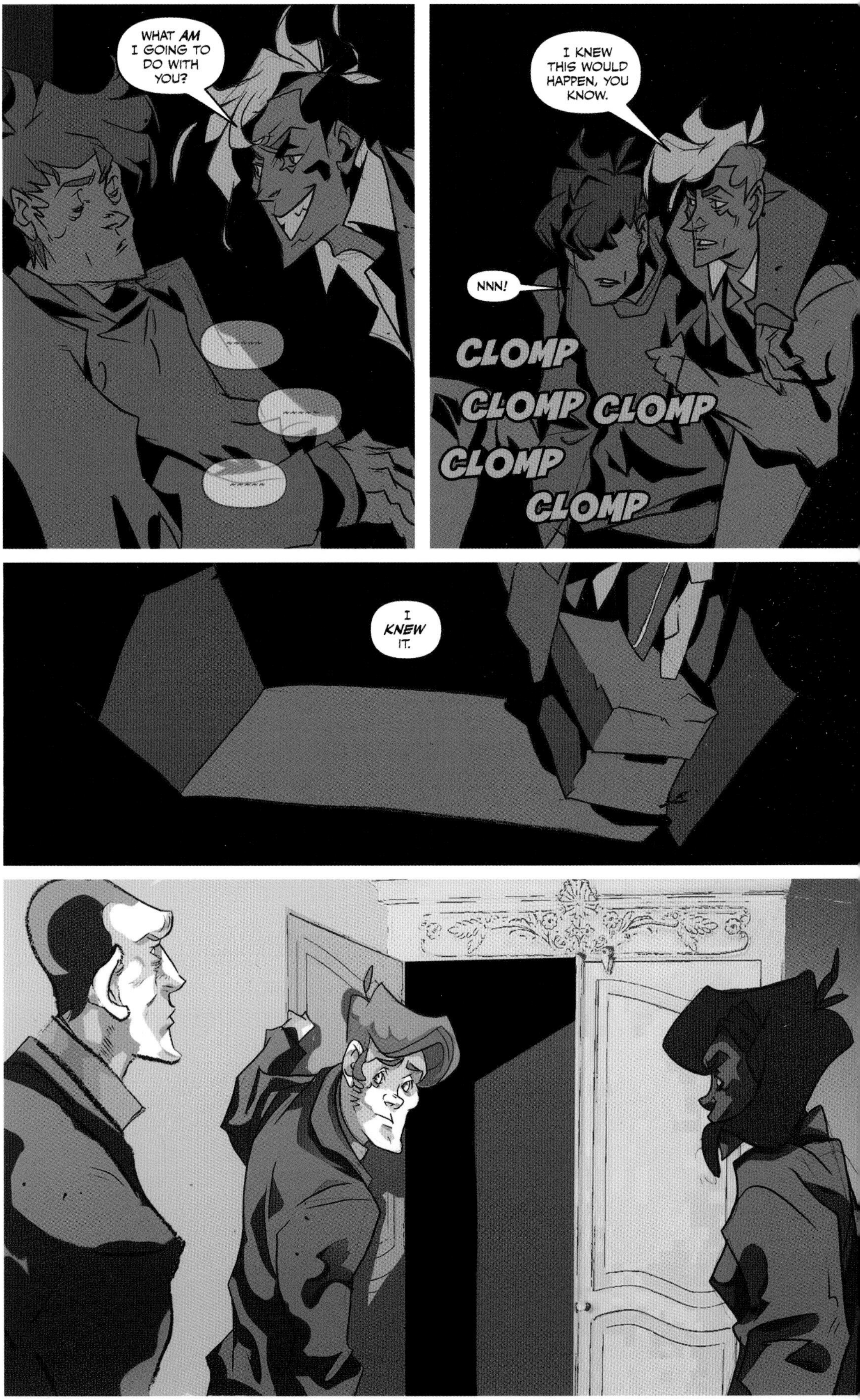
WHAT AM I GOING TO DO WITH YOU?
I KNEW THIS WOULD HAPPEN, YOU KNOW.
NNN!
CLOMP
CLOMP CLOMP
CLOMP
CLOMP
I KNEW IT.

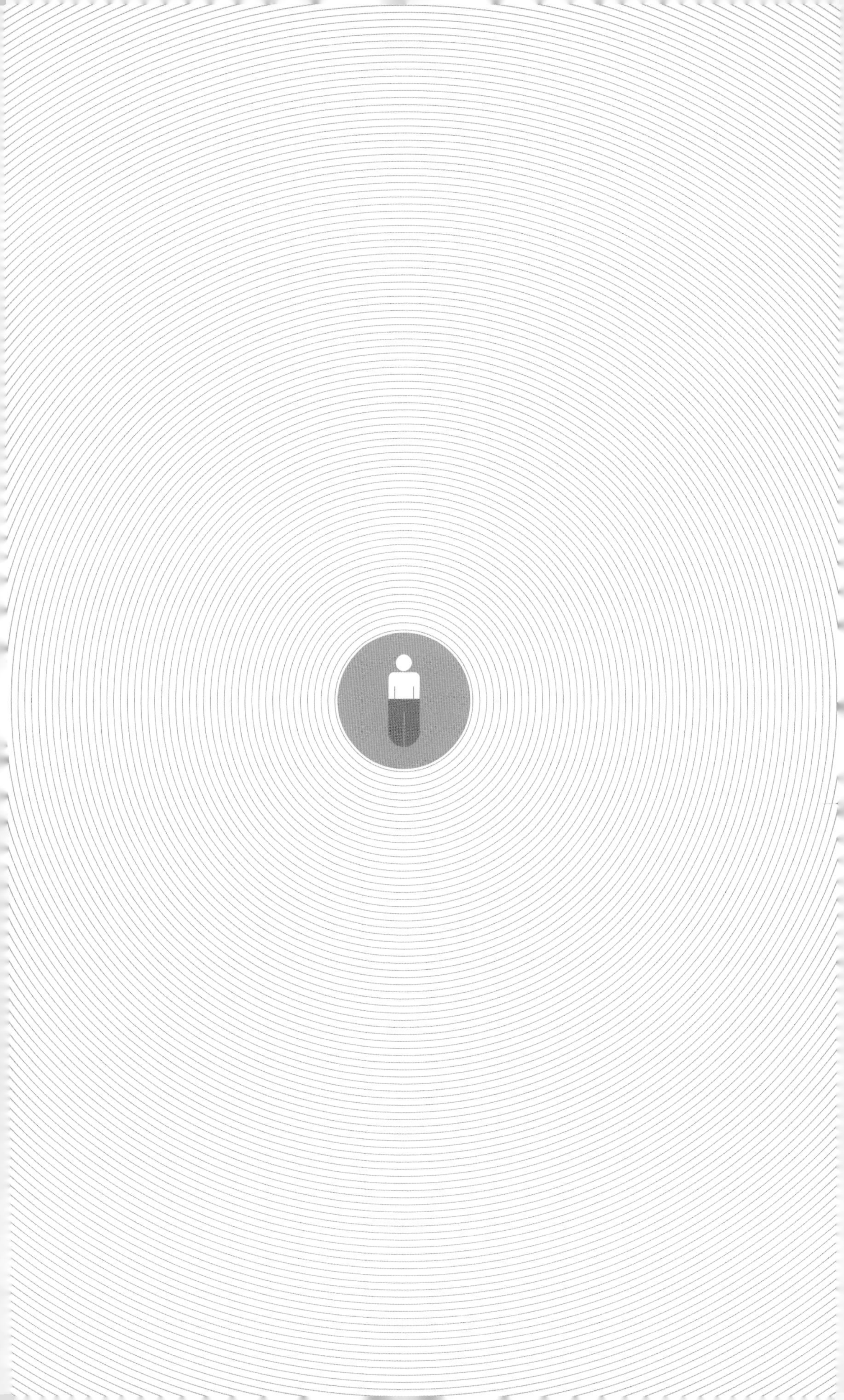

CHAPTER
FOUR

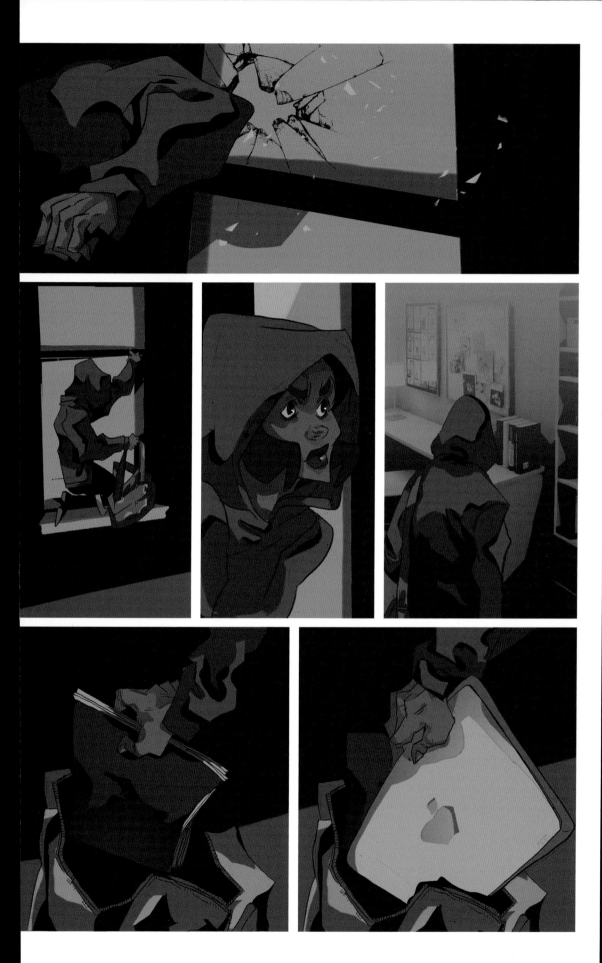

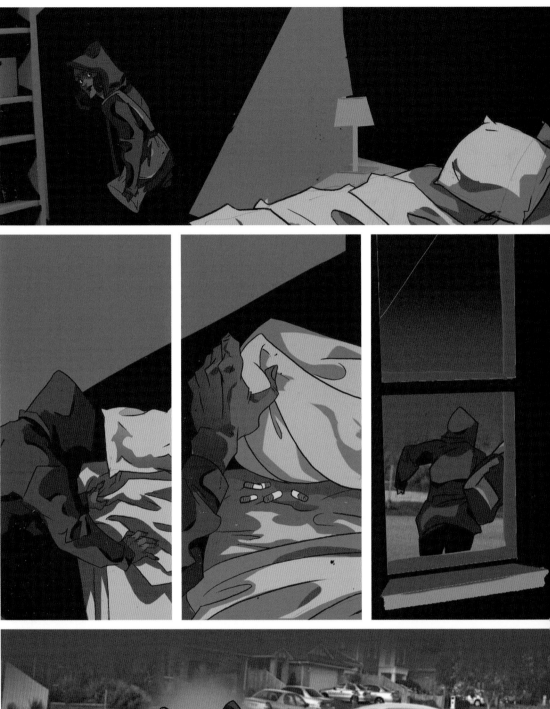

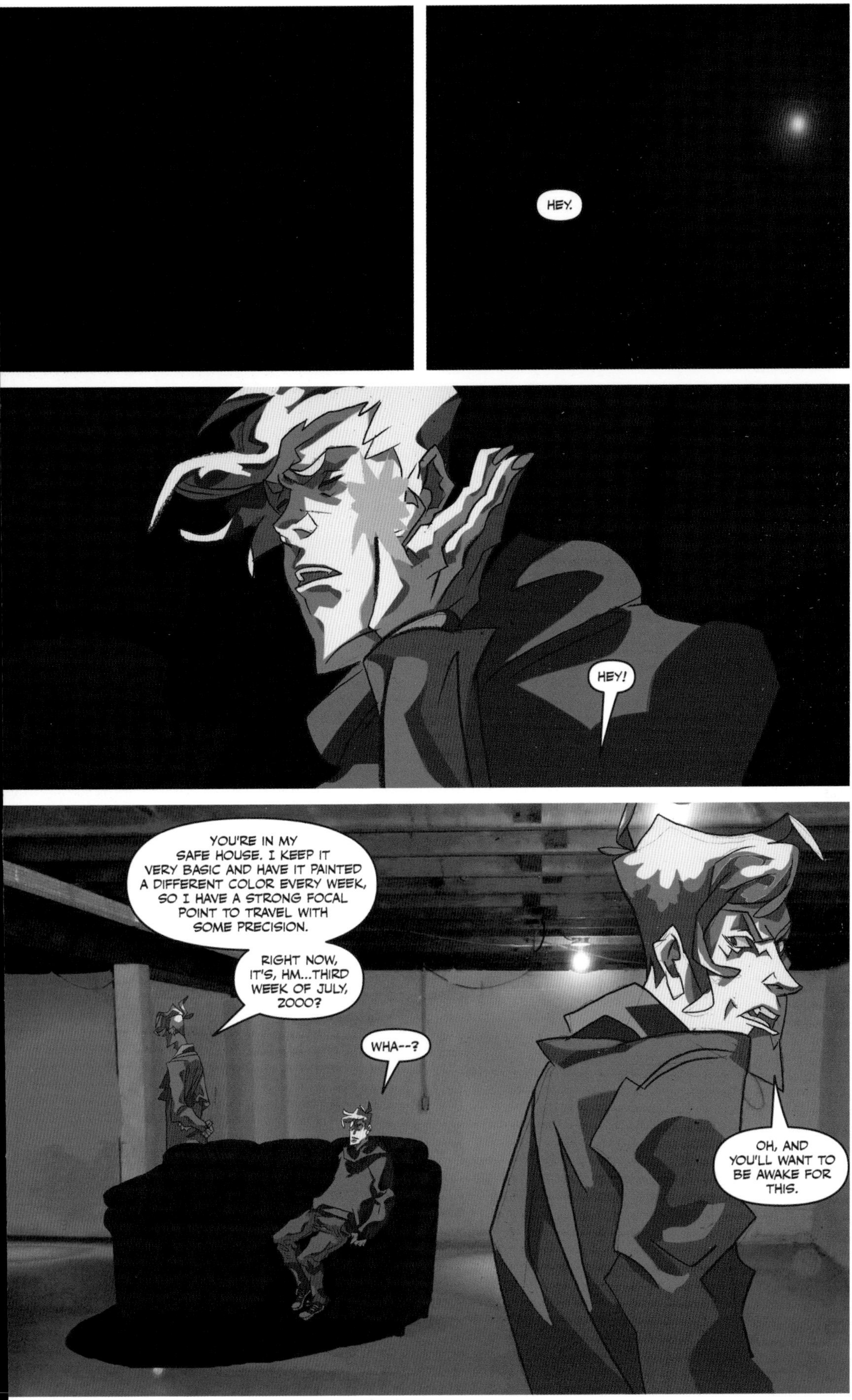
HEY.
HEY!
YOU'RE IN MY SAFE HOUSE. I KEEP IT VERY BASIC AND HAVE IT PAINTED A DIFFERENT COLOR EVERY WEEK, SO I HAVE A STRONG FOCAL POINT TO TRAVEL WITH SOME PRECISION.
RIGHT NOW, IT'S, HM...THIRD WEEK OF JULY, 2000?
WHA--?
OH, AND YOU'LL WANT TO BE AWAKE FOR THIS.

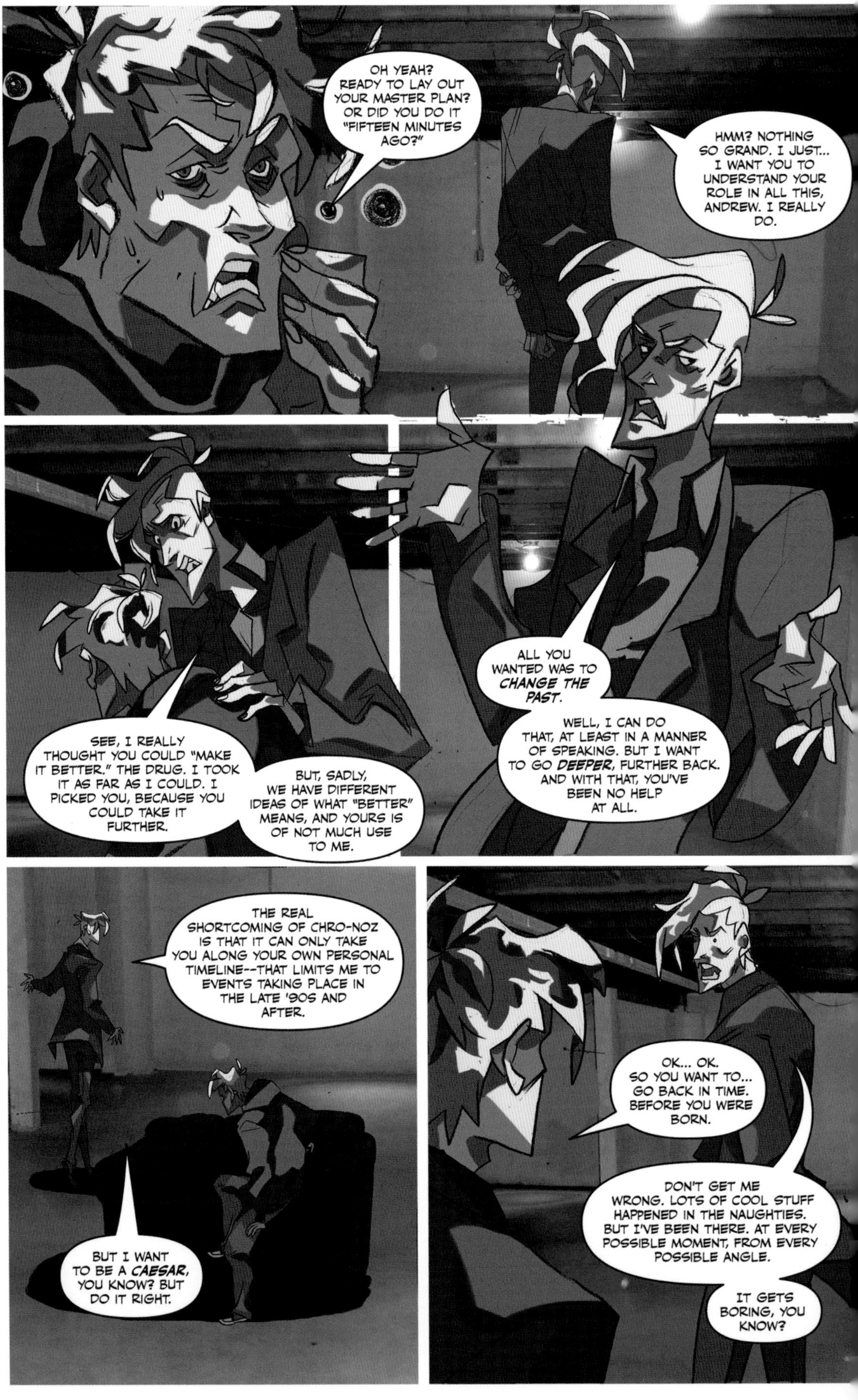
OH YEAH? READY TO LAY OUT YOUR MASTER PLAN? OR DID YOU DO IT "FIFTEEN MINUTES AGO?"
HMM? NOTHING SO GRAND. I JUST... I WANT YOU TO UNDERSTAND YOUR ROLE IN ALL THIS, ANDREW. I REALLY DO.
SEE, I REALLY THOUGHT YOU COULD "MAKE IT BETTER." THE DRUG. I TOOK IT AS FAR AS I COULD. I PICKED YOU, BECAUSE YOU COULD TAKE IT FURTHER.
BUT, SADLY, WE HAVE DIFFERENT IDEAS OF WHAT "BETTER" MEANS, AND YOURS IS OF NOT MUCH USE TO ME.
ALL YOU WANTED WAS TO *CHANGE THE PAST*.
WELL, I CAN DO THAT, AT LEAST IN A MANNER OF SPEAKING. BUT I WANT TO GO *DEEPER*, FURTHER BACK. AND WITH THAT, YOU'VE BEEN NO HELP AT ALL.
THE REAL SHORTCOMING OF CHRO-NOZ IS THAT IT CAN ONLY TAKE YOU ALONG YOUR OWN PERSONAL TIMELINE--THAT LIMITS ME TO EVENTS TAKING PLACE IN THE LATE '90S AND AFTER.
BUT I WANT TO BE A *CAESAR*, YOU KNOW? BUT DO IT RIGHT.
OK... OK. SO YOU WANT TO... GO BACK IN TIME. BEFORE YOU WERE BORN.
DON'T GET ME WRONG. LOTS OF COOL STUFF HAPPENED IN THE NAUGHTIES. BUT I'VE BEEN THERE. AT EVERY POSSIBLE MOMENT, FROM EVERY POSSIBLE ANGLE.
IT GETS BORING, YOU KNOW?

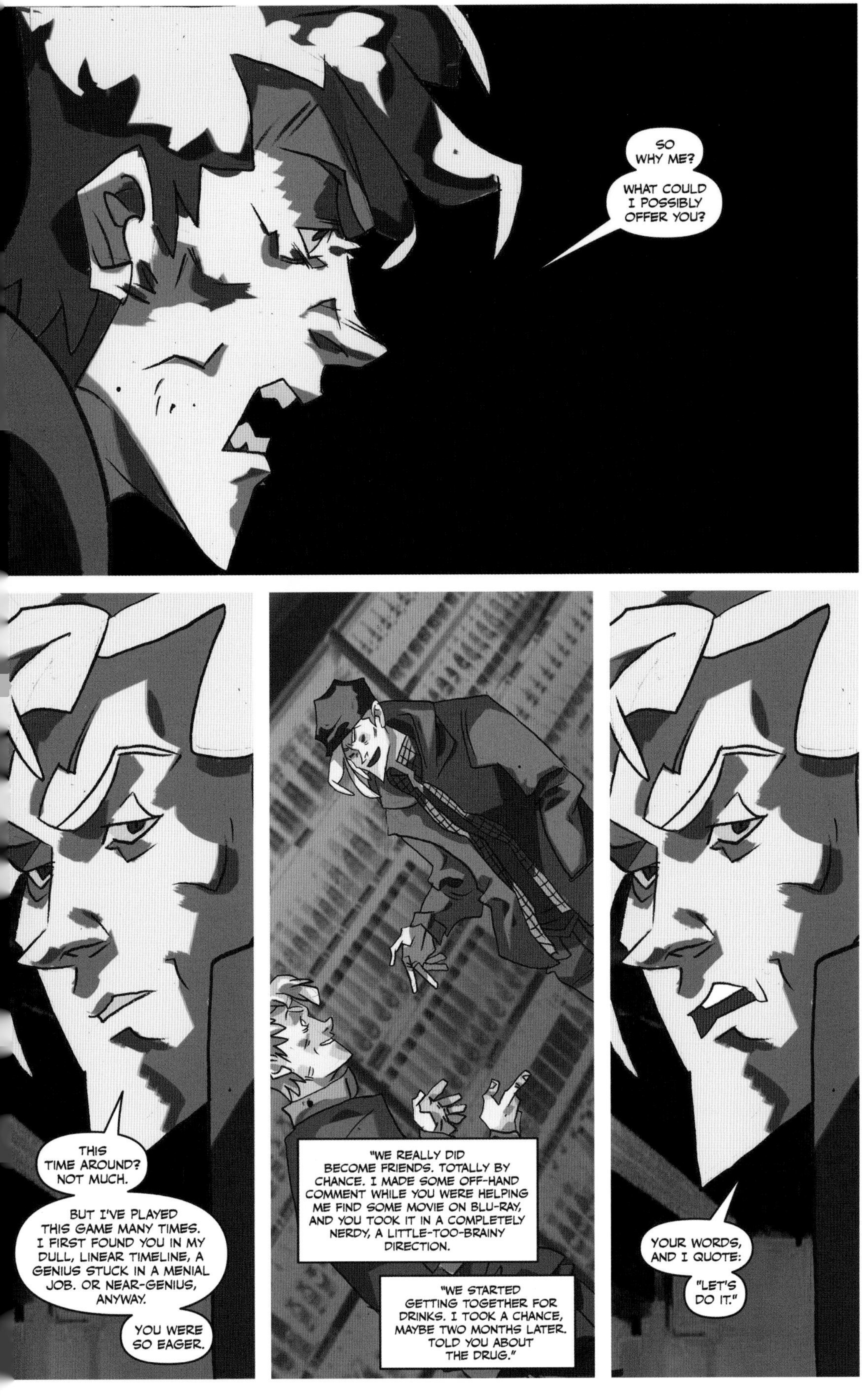
SO WHY ME?
WHAT COULD I POSSIBLY OFFER YOU?
THIS TIME AROUND? NOT MUCH.
BUT I'VE PLAYED THIS GAME MANY TIMES. I FIRST FOUND YOU IN MY DULL, LINEAR TIMELINE, A GENIUS STUCK IN A MENIAL JOB. OR NEAR-GENIUS, ANYWAY.
YOU WERE SO EAGER.
"WE REALLY DID BECOME FRIENDS. TOTALLY BY CHANCE. I MADE SOME OFF-HAND COMMENT WHILE YOU WERE HELPING ME FIND SOME MOVIE ON BLU-RAY, AND YOU TOOK IT IN A COMPLETELY NERDY, A LITTLE-TOO-BRAINY DIRECTION.
"WE STARTED GETTING TOGETHER FOR DRINKS. I TOOK A CHANCE, MAYBE TWO MONTHS LATER. TOLD YOU ABOUT THE DRUG."
YOUR WORDS, AND I QUOTE:
"LET'S DO IT."

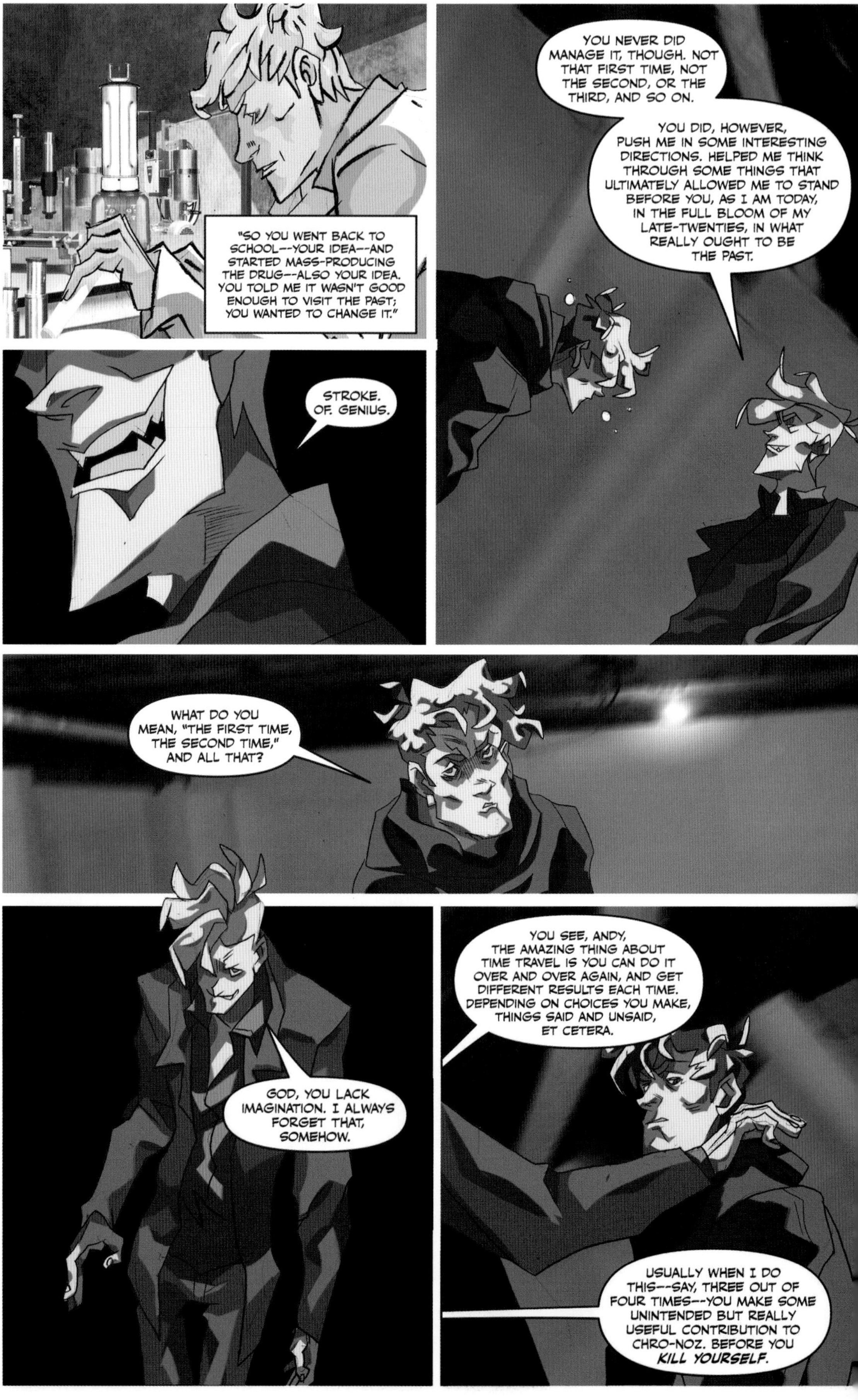
"SO YOU WENT BACK TO SCHOOL--YOUR IDEA--AND STARTED MASS-PRODUCING THE DRUG--ALSO YOUR IDEA. YOU TOLD ME IT WASN'T GOOD ENOUGH TO VISIT THE PAST; YOU WANTED TO CHANGE IT."
STROKE. OF. GENIUS.
YOU NEVER DID MANAGE IT, THOUGH. NOT THAT FIRST TIME, NOT THE SECOND, OR THE THIRD, AND SO ON.
YOU DID, HOWEVER, PUSH ME IN SOME INTERESTING DIRECTIONS. HELPED ME THINK THROUGH SOME THINGS THAT ULTIMATELY ALLOWED ME TO STAND BEFORE YOU, AS I AM TODAY, IN THE FULL BLOOM OF MY LATE-TWENTIES, IN WHAT REALLY OUGHT TO BE THE PAST.
WHAT DO YOU MEAN, "THE FIRST TIME, THE SECOND TIME," AND ALL THAT?
GOD, YOU LACK IMAGINATION. I ALWAYS FORGET THAT, SOMEHOW.
YOU SEE, ANDY, THE AMAZING THING ABOUT TIME TRAVEL IS YOU CAN DO IT OVER AND OVER AGAIN, AND GET DIFFERENT RESULTS EACH TIME. DEPENDING ON CHOICES YOU MAKE, THINGS SAID AND UNSAID, ET CETERA.
USUALLY WHEN I DO THIS--SAY, THREE OUT OF FOUR TIMES--YOU MAKE SOME UNINTENDED BUT REALLY USEFUL CONTRIBUTION TO CHRO-NOZ. BEFORE YOU ***KILL YOURSELF***.

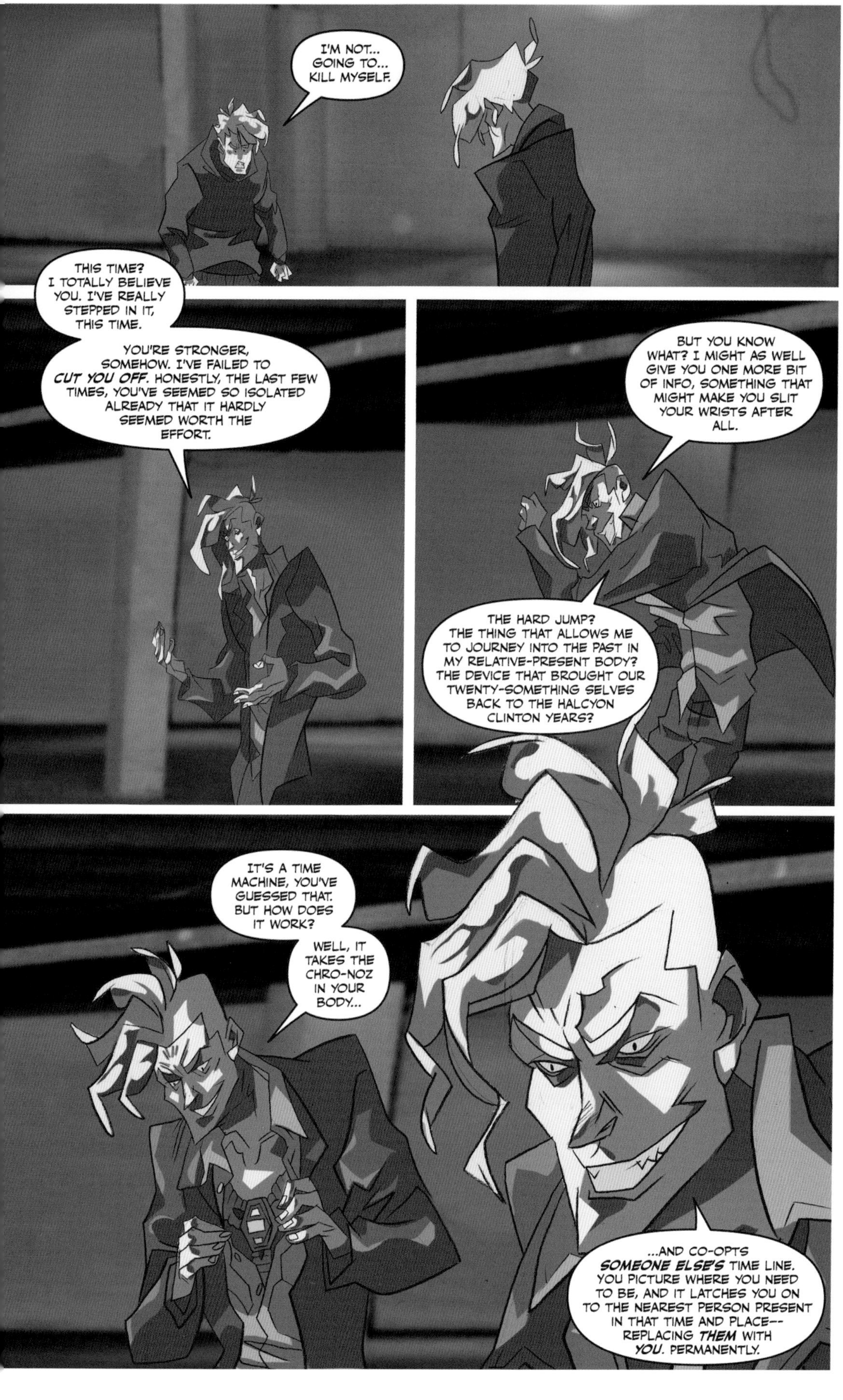
I'M NOT... GOING TO... KILL MYSELF.
THIS TIME? I TOTALLY BELIEVE YOU. I'VE REALLY STEPPED IN IT, THIS TIME.
YOU'RE STRONGER, SOMEHOW. I'VE FAILED TO *CUT YOU OFF*. HONESTLY, THE LAST FEW TIMES, YOU'VE SEEMED SO ISOLATED ALREADY THAT IT HARDLY SEEMED WORTH THE EFFORT.
BUT YOU KNOW WHAT? I MIGHT AS WELL GIVE YOU ONE MORE BIT OF INFO, SOMETHING THAT MIGHT MAKE YOU SLIT YOUR WRISTS AFTER ALL.
THE HARD JUMP? THE THING THAT ALLOWS ME TO JOURNEY INTO THE PAST IN MY RELATIVE-PRESENT BODY? THE DEVICE THAT BROUGHT OUR TWENTY-SOMETHING SELVES BACK TO THE HALCYON CLINTON YEARS?
IT'S A TIME MACHINE, YOU'VE GUESSED THAT. BUT HOW DOES IT WORK?
WELL, IT TAKES THE CHRO-NOZ IN YOUR BODY...
...AND CO-OPTS ***SOMEONE ELSE'S*** TIME LINE. YOU PICTURE WHERE YOU NEED TO BE, AND IT LATCHES YOU ON TO THE NEAREST PERSON PRESENT IN THAT TIME AND PLACE-- REPLACING ***THEM*** WITH ***YOU***. PERMANENTLY.

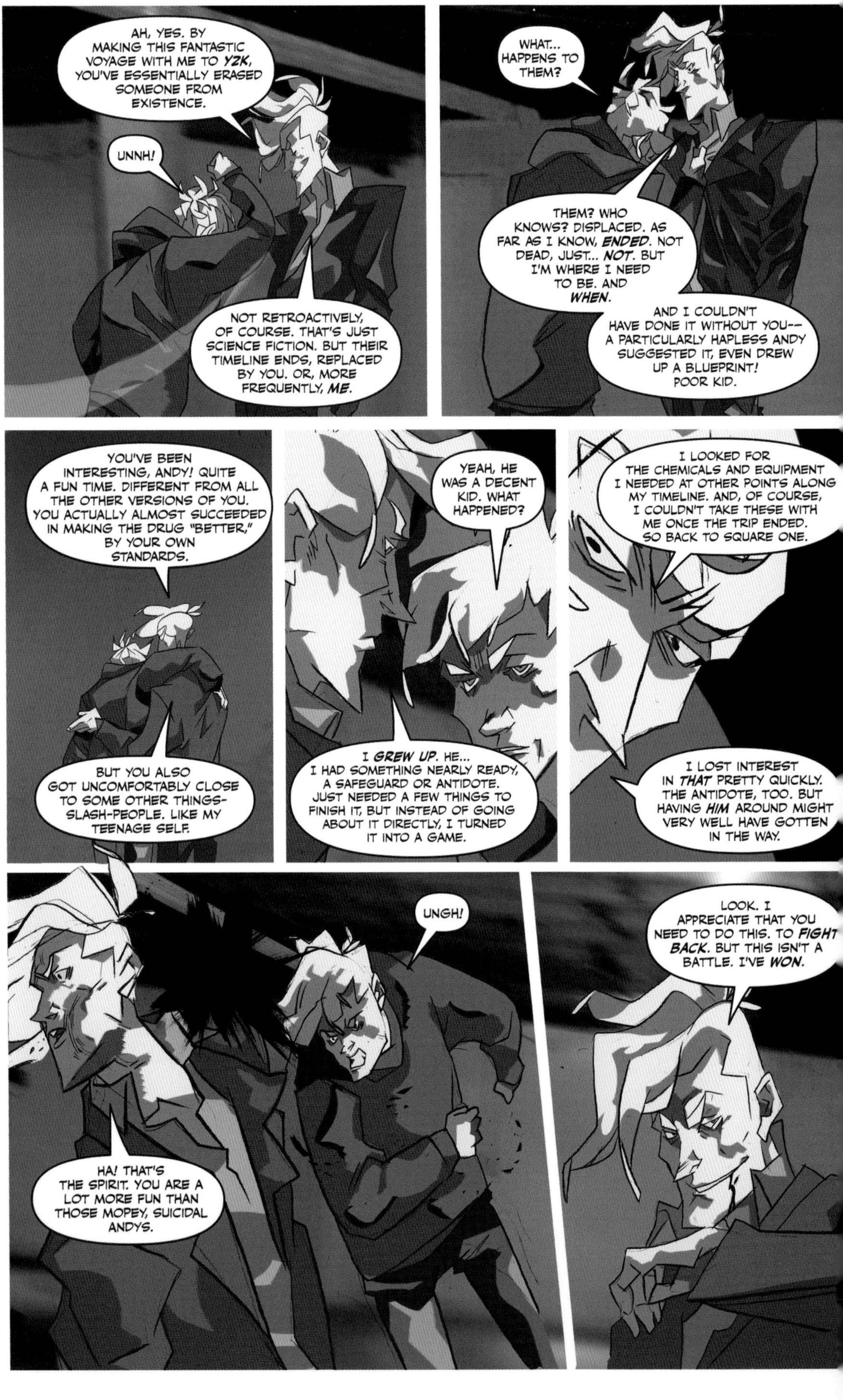
AH, YES. BY MAKING THIS FANTASTIC VOYAGE WITH ME TO YZK, YOU'VE ESSENTIALLY ERASED SOMEONE FROM EXISTENCE.
UNNH!
NOT RETROACTIVELY, OF COURSE. THAT'S JUST SCIENCE FICTION. BUT THEIR TIMELINE ENDS, REPLACED BY YOU. OR, MORE FREQUENTLY, ME.
WHAT... HAPPENS TO THEM?
THEM? WHO KNOWS? DISPLACED. AS FAR AS I KNOW, ENDED. NOT DEAD, JUST... NOT. BUT I'M WHERE I NEED TO BE. AND WHEN.
AND I COULDN'T HAVE DONE IT WITHOUT YOU-- A PARTICULARLY HAPLESS ANDY SUGGESTED IT, EVEN DREW UP A BLUEPRINT! POOR KID.
YOU'VE BEEN INTERESTING, ANDY! QUITE A FUN TIME. DIFFERENT FROM ALL THE OTHER VERSIONS OF YOU. YOU ACTUALLY ALMOST SUCCEEDED IN MAKING THE DRUG "BETTER," BY YOUR OWN STANDARDS.
BUT YOU ALSO GOT UNCOMFORTABLY CLOSE TO SOME OTHER THINGS-SLASH-PEOPLE. LIKE MY TEENAGE SELF.
YEAH, HE WAS A DECENT KID. WHAT HAPPENED?
I GREW UP. HE... I HAD SOMETHING NEARLY READY, A SAFEGUARD OR ANTIDOTE. JUST NEEDED A FEW THINGS TO FINISH IT, BUT INSTEAD OF GOING ABOUT IT DIRECTLY, I TURNED IT INTO A GAME.
I LOOKED FOR THE CHEMICALS AND EQUIPMENT I NEEDED AT OTHER POINTS ALONG MY TIMELINE. AND, OF COURSE, I COULDN'T TAKE THESE WITH ME ONCE THE TRIP ENDED. SO BACK TO SQUARE ONE.
I LOST INTEREST IN THAT PRETTY QUICKLY. THE ANTIDOTE, TOO. BUT HAVING HIM AROUND MIGHT VERY WELL HAVE GOTTEN IN THE WAY.
UNGH!
HA! THAT'S THE SPIRIT. YOU ARE A LOT MORE FUN THAN THOSE MOPEY, SUICIDAL ANDYS.
LOOK. I APPRECIATE THAT YOU NEED TO DO THIS. TO FIGHT BACK. BUT THIS ISN'T A BATTLE. I'VE WON.

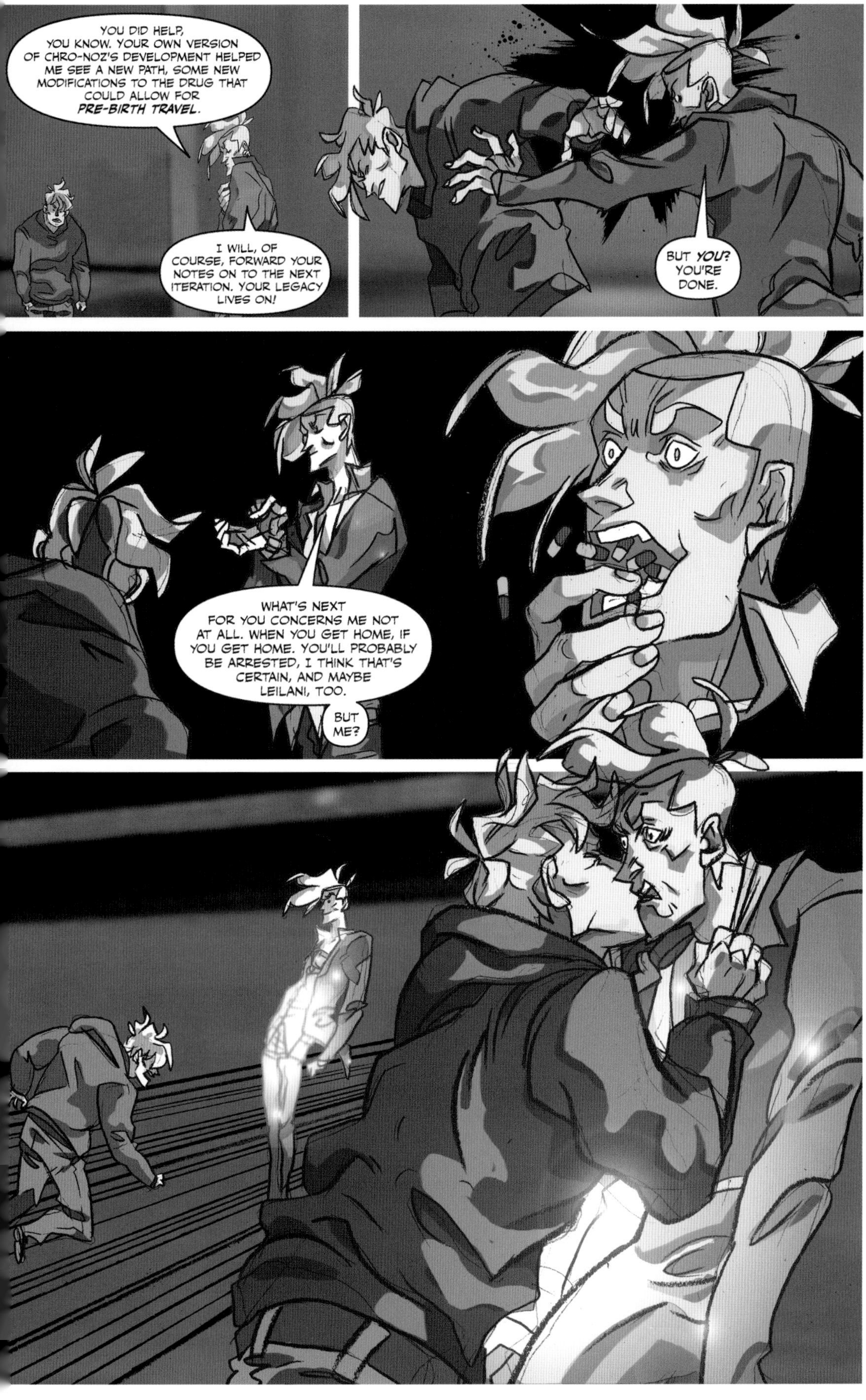
YOU DID HELP, YOU KNOW. YOUR OWN VERSION OF CHRO-NOZ'S DEVELOPMENT HELPED ME SEE A NEW PATH, SOME NEW MODIFICATIONS TO THE DRUG THAT COULD ALLOW FOR *PRE-BIRTH TRAVEL*.
I WILL, OF COURSE, FORWARD YOUR NOTES ON TO THE NEXT ITERATION. YOUR LEGACY LIVES ON!
BUT *YOU*? YOU'RE DONE.
WHAT'S NEXT FOR YOU CONCERNS ME NOT AT ALL. WHEN YOU GET HOME, IF YOU GET HOME. YOU'LL PROBABLY BE ARRESTED, I THINK THAT'S CERTAIN, AND MAYBE LEILANI, TOO.
BUT ME?

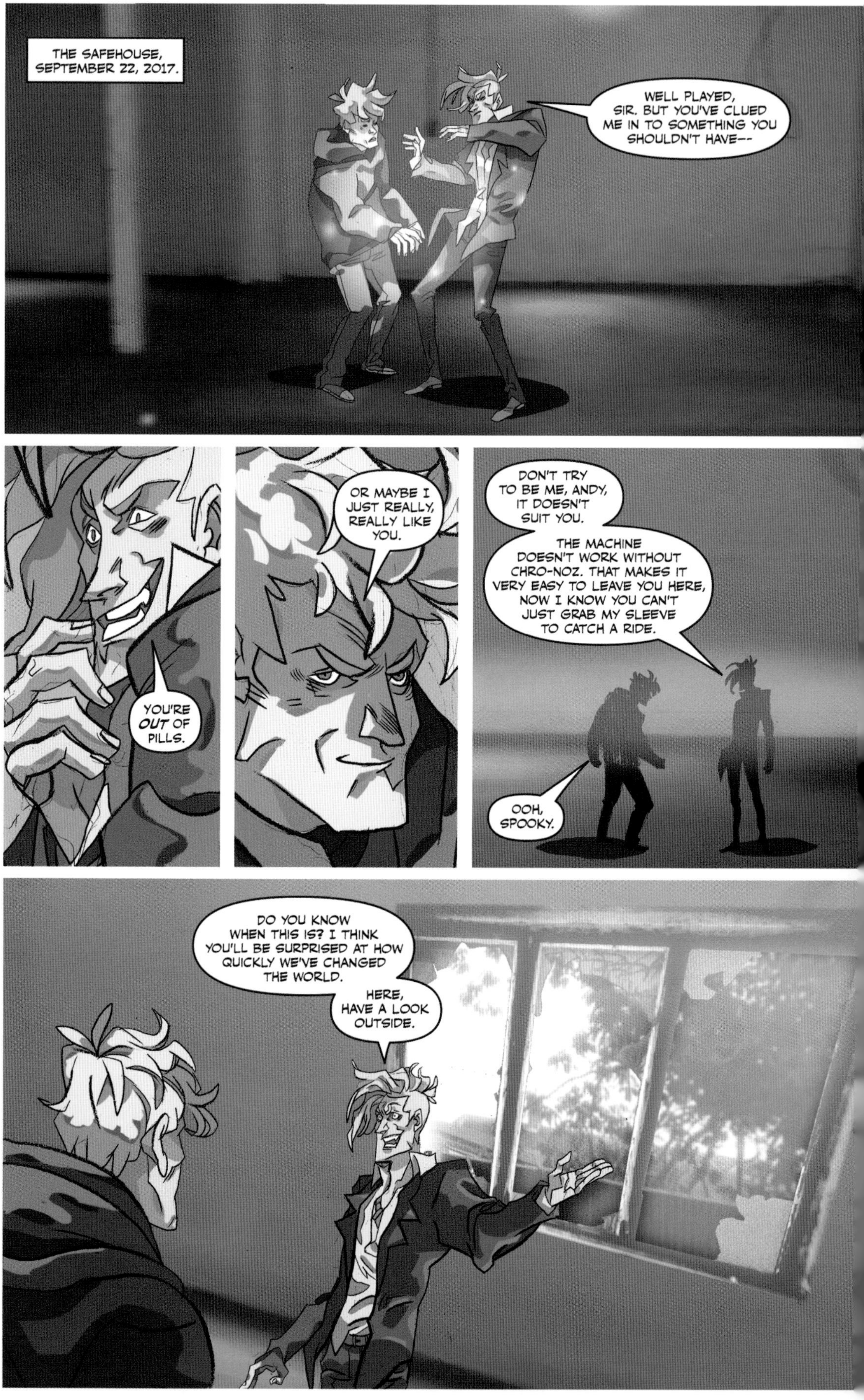
THE SAFEHOUSE, SEPTEMBER 22, 2017.
WELL PLAYED, SIR. BUT YOU'VE CLUED ME IN TO SOMETHING YOU SHOULDN'T HAVE--
YOU'RE *OUT* OF PILLS.
OR MAYBE I JUST REALLY, REALLY LIKE YOU.
DON'T TRY TO BE ME, ANDY, IT DOESN'T SUIT YOU.
THE MACHINE DOESN'T WORK WITHOUT CHRO-NOZ. THAT MAKES IT VERY EASY TO LEAVE YOU HERE, NOW I KNOW YOU CAN'T JUST GRAB MY SLEEVE TO CATCH A RIDE.
OOH, SPOOKY.
DO YOU KNOW WHEN THIS IS? I THINK YOU'LL BE SURPRISED AT HOW QUICKLY WE'VE CHANGED THE WORLD.
HERE, HAVE A LOOK OUTSIDE.

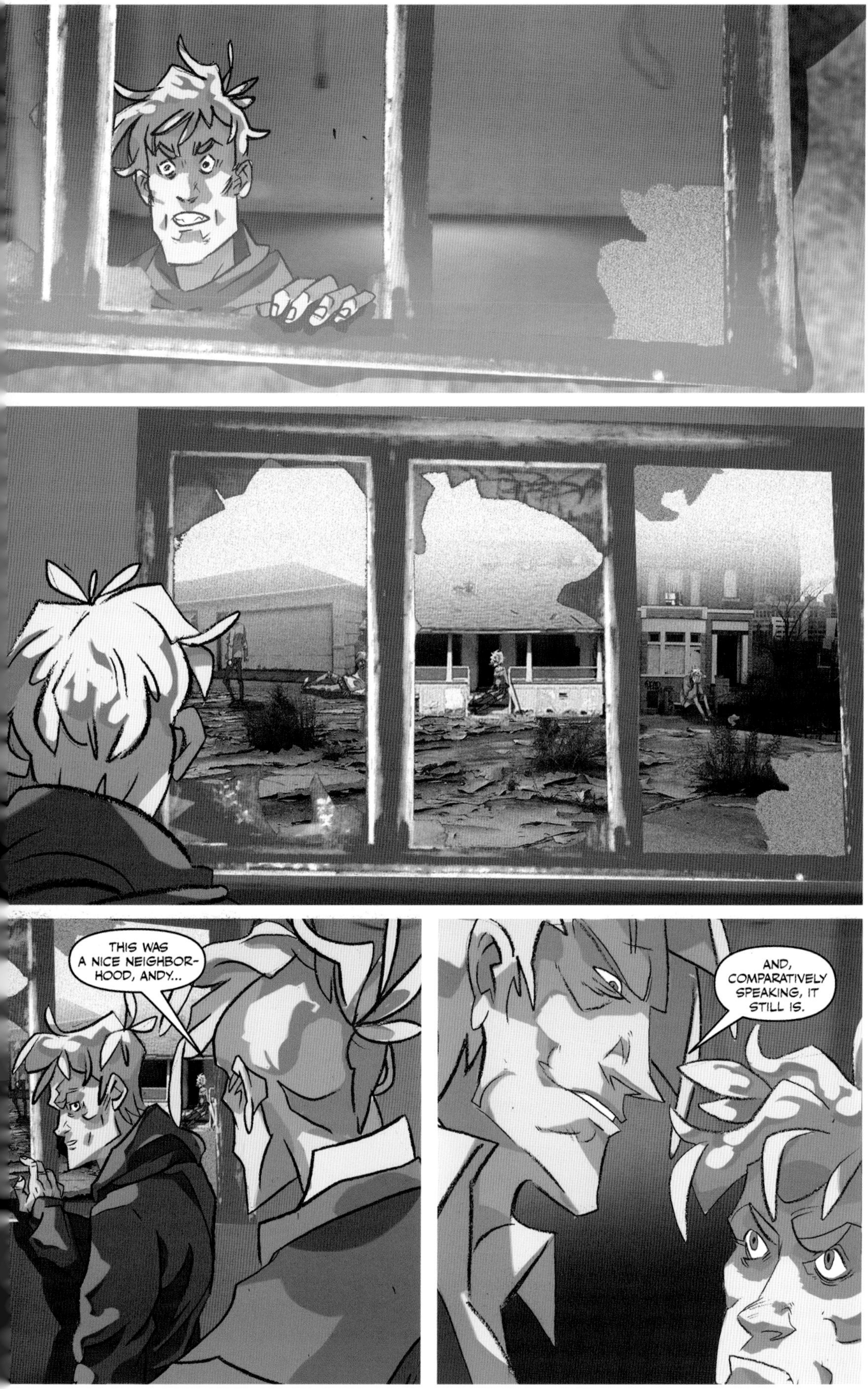
THIS WAS A NICE NEIGHBOR-HOOD, ANDY...
AND, COMPARATIVELY SPEAKING, IT STILL IS.

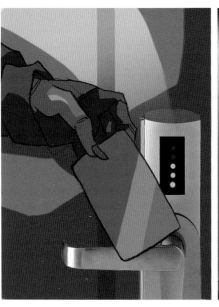

SCIENCE!

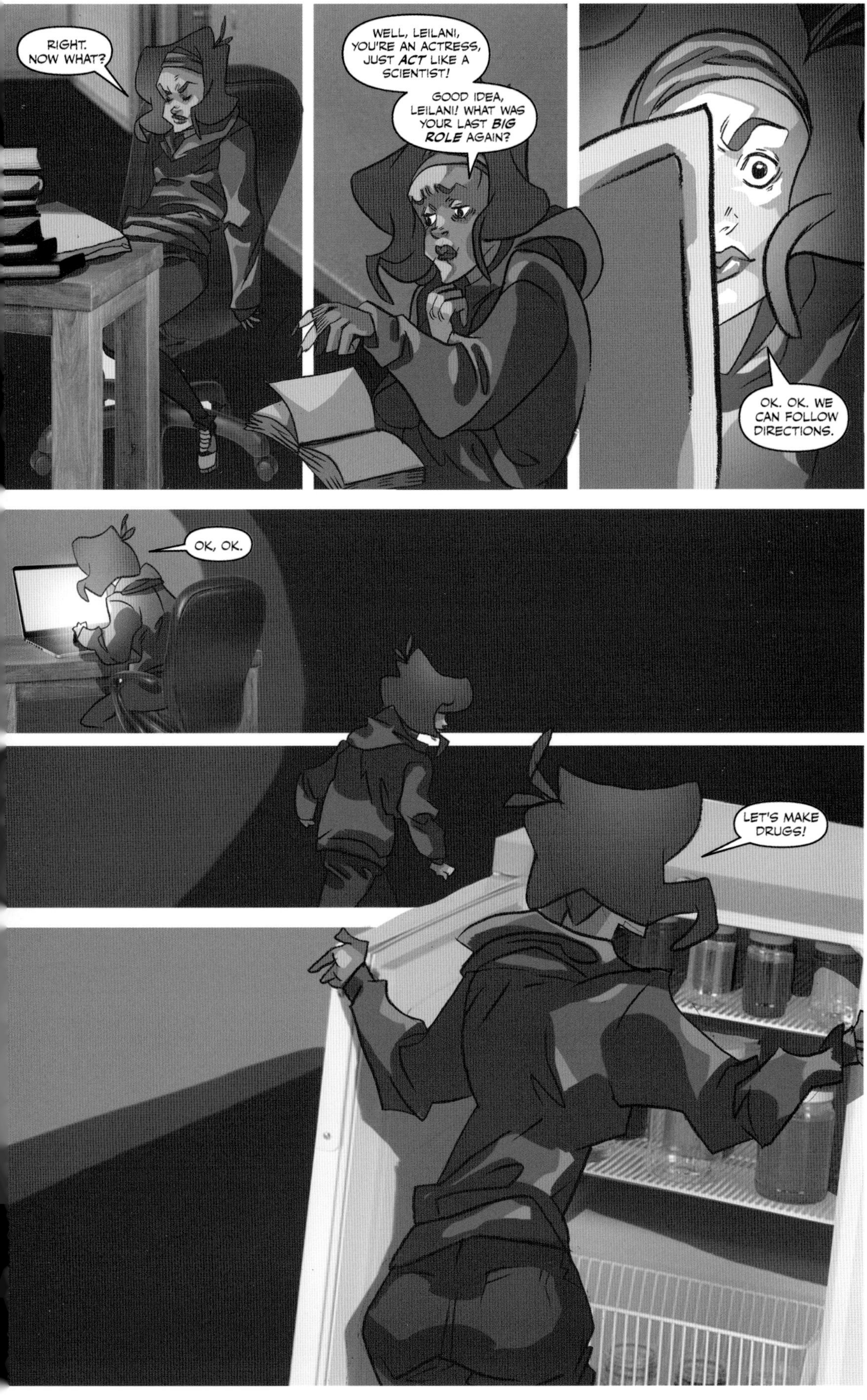
RIGHT. NOW WHAT?
WELL, LEILANI, YOU'RE AN ACTRESS, JUST ACT LIKE A SCIENTIST!
GOOD IDEA, LEILANI! WHAT WAS YOUR LAST BIG ROLE AGAIN?
OK. OK. WE CAN FOLLOW DIRECTIONS.
OK, OK.
LET'S MAKE DRUGS!

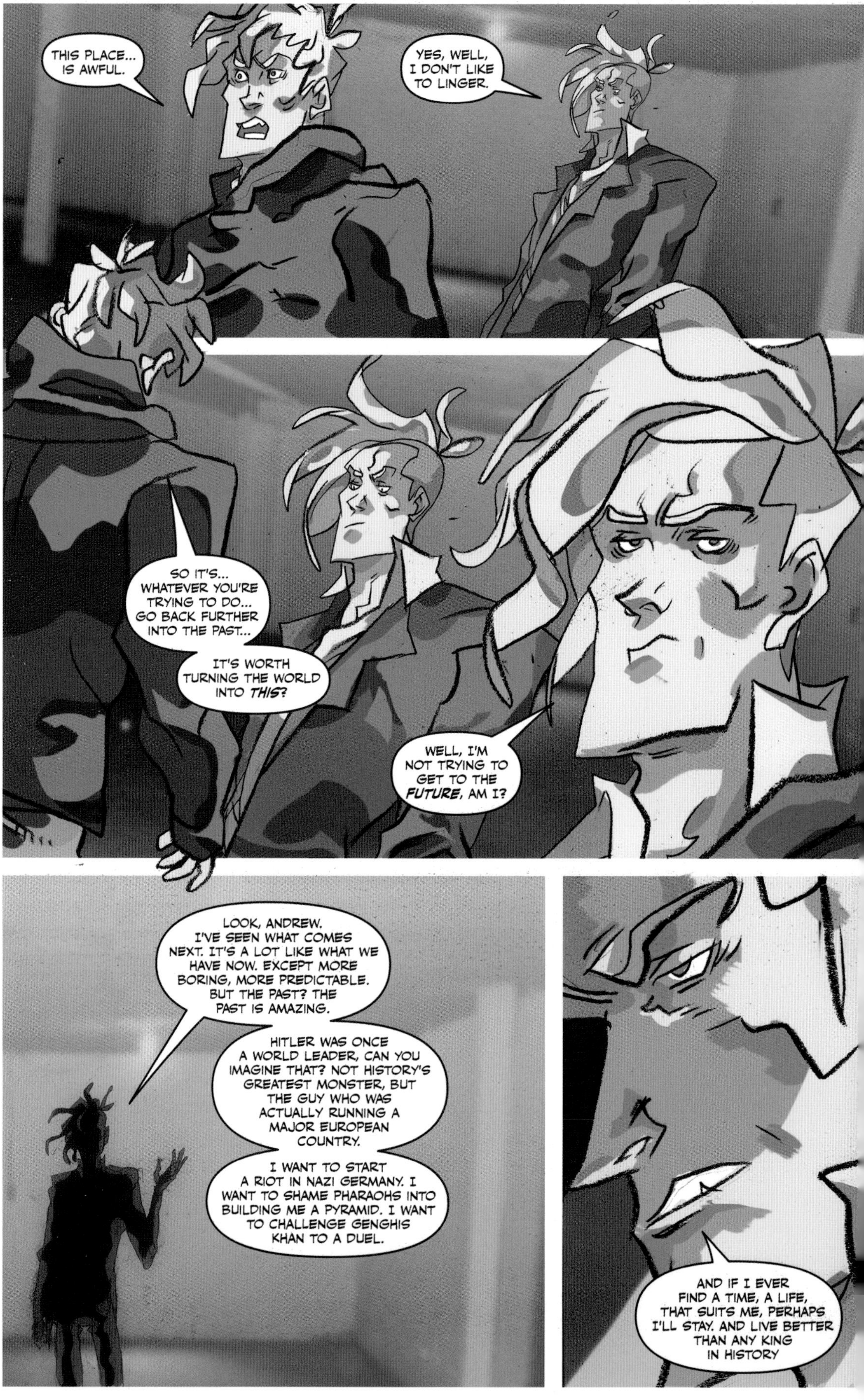
THIS PLACE... IS AWFUL.
YES, WELL, I DON'T LIKE TO LINGER.
SO IT'S... WHATEVER YOU'RE TRYING TO DO... GO BACK FURTHER INTO THE PAST...
IT'S WORTH TURNING THE WORLD INTO *THIS*?
WELL, I'M NOT TRYING TO GET TO THE *FUTURE*, AM I?
LOOK, ANDREW. I'VE SEEN WHAT COMES NEXT. IT'S A LOT LIKE WHAT WE HAVE NOW. EXCEPT MORE BORING, MORE PREDICTABLE. BUT THE PAST? THE PAST IS AMAZING.
HITLER WAS ONCE A WORLD LEADER, CAN YOU IMAGINE THAT? NOT HISTORY'S GREATEST MONSTER, BUT THE GUY WHO WAS ACTUALLY RUNNING A MAJOR EUROPEAN COUNTRY.
I WANT TO START A RIOT IN NAZI GERMANY. I WANT TO SHAME PHARAOHS INTO BUILDING ME A PYRAMID. I WANT TO CHALLENGE GENGHIS KHAN TO A DUEL.
AND IF I EVER FIND A TIME, A LIFE, THAT SUITS ME, PERHAPS I'LL STAY. AND LIVE BETTER THAN ANY KING IN HISTORY

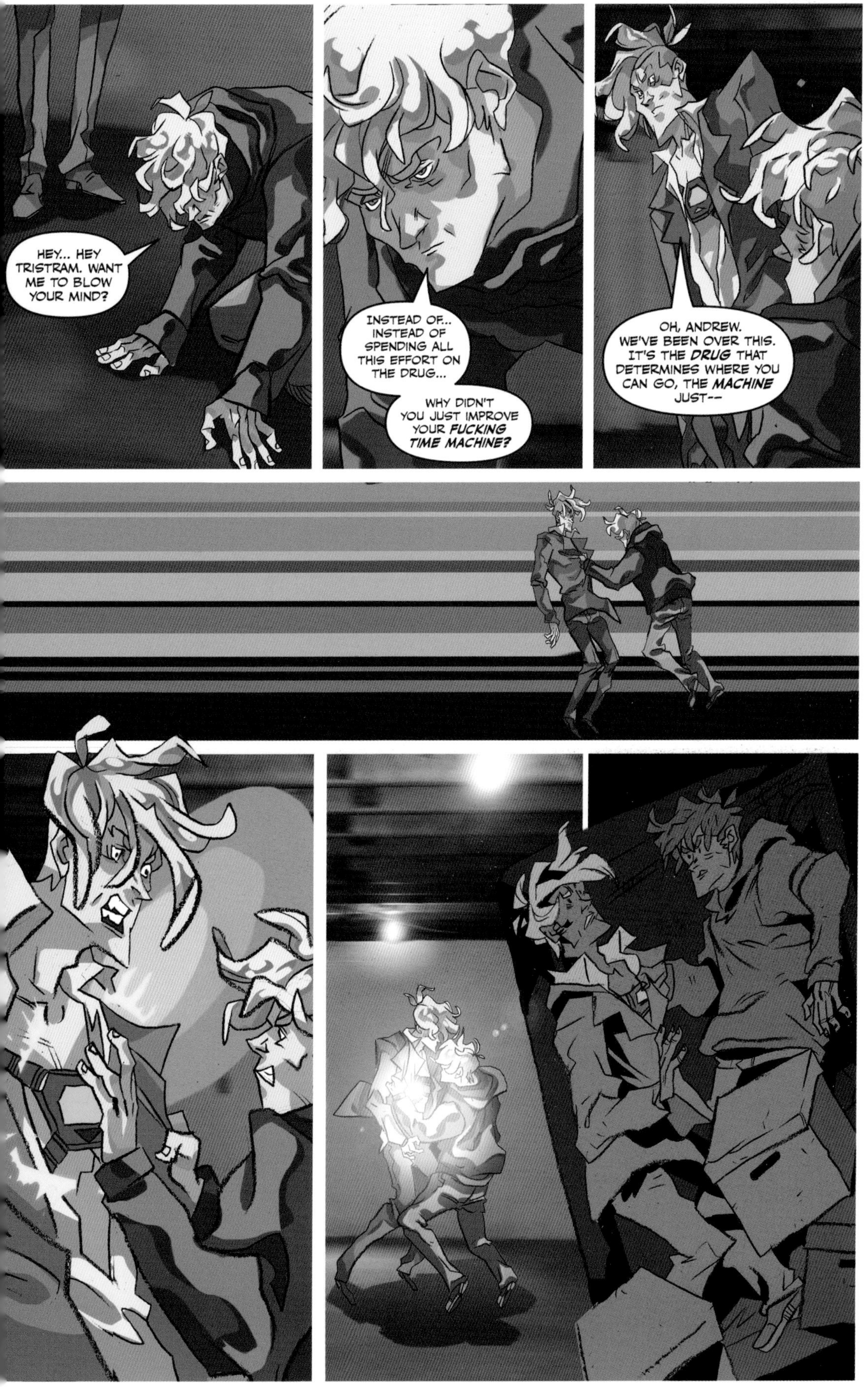
HEY... HEY TRISTRAM. WANT ME TO BLOW YOUR MIND?
INSTEAD OF... INSTEAD OF SPENDING ALL THIS EFFORT ON THE DRUG...
WHY DIDN'T YOU JUST IMPROVE YOUR ***FUCKING TIME MACHINE?***
OH, ANDREW. WE'VE BEEN OVER THIS. IT'S THE ***DRUG*** THAT DETERMINES WHERE YOU CAN GO, THE ***MACHINE*** JUST--

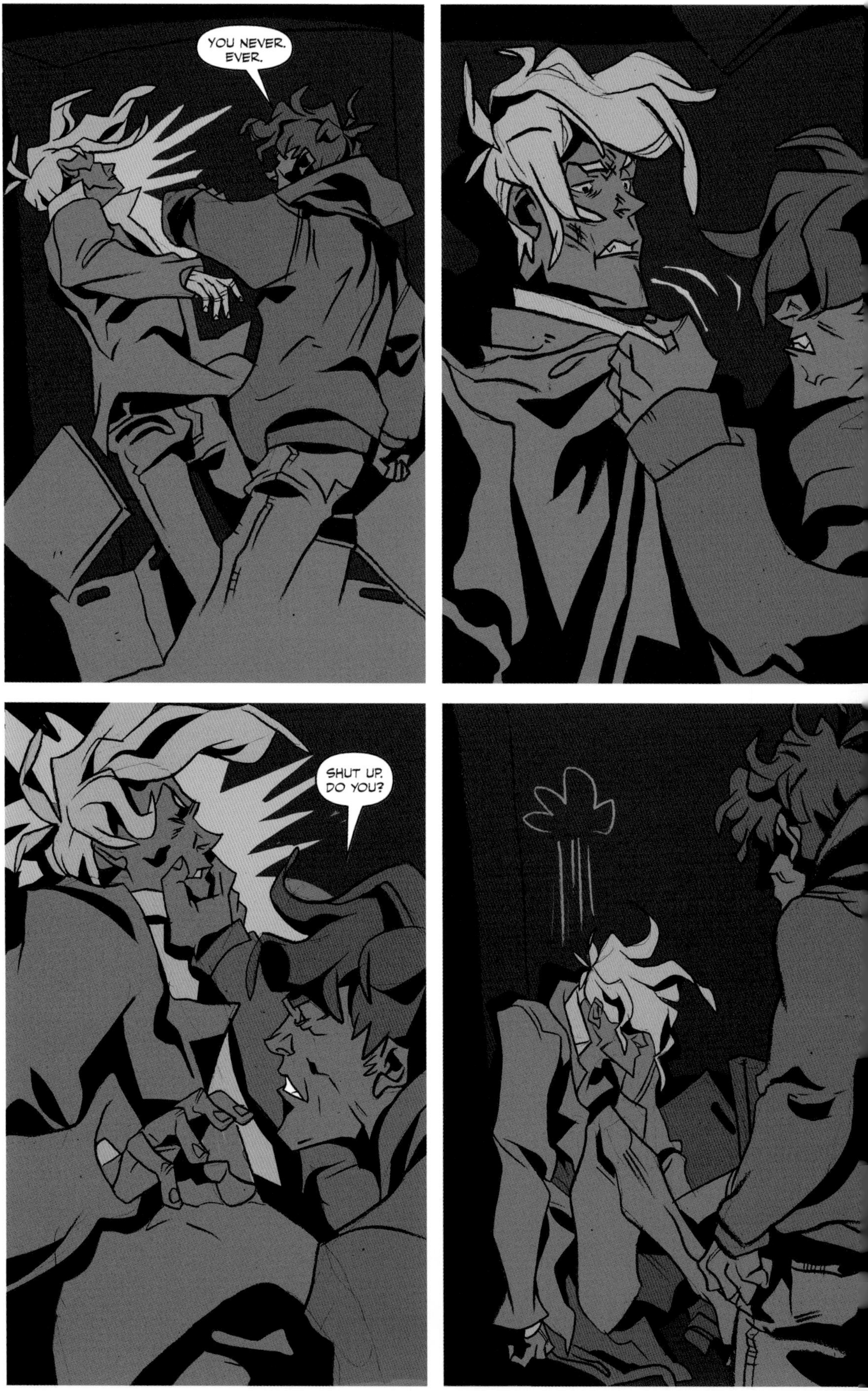
YOU NEVER. EVER.
SHUT UP. DO YOU?

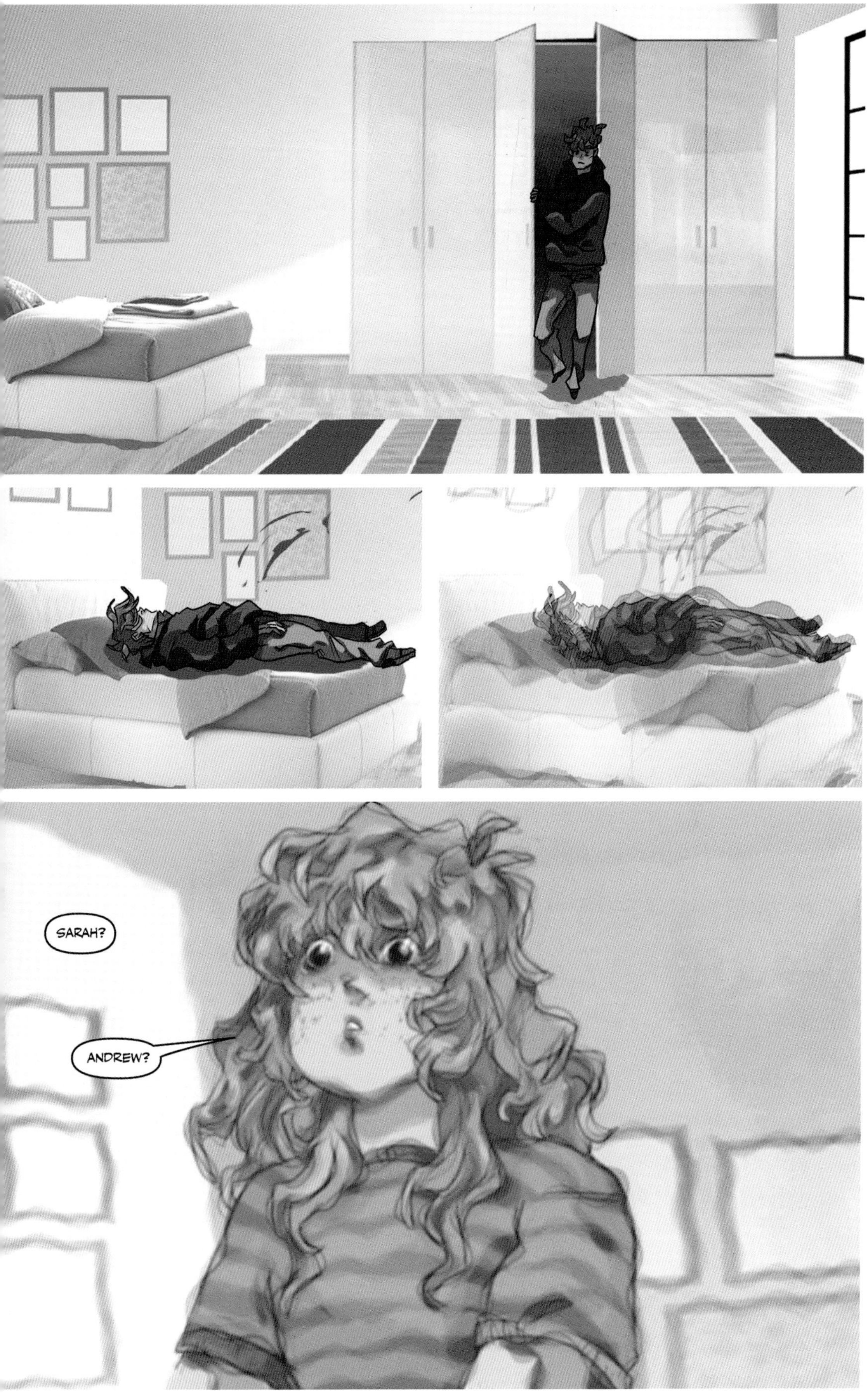
SARAH?
ANDREW?

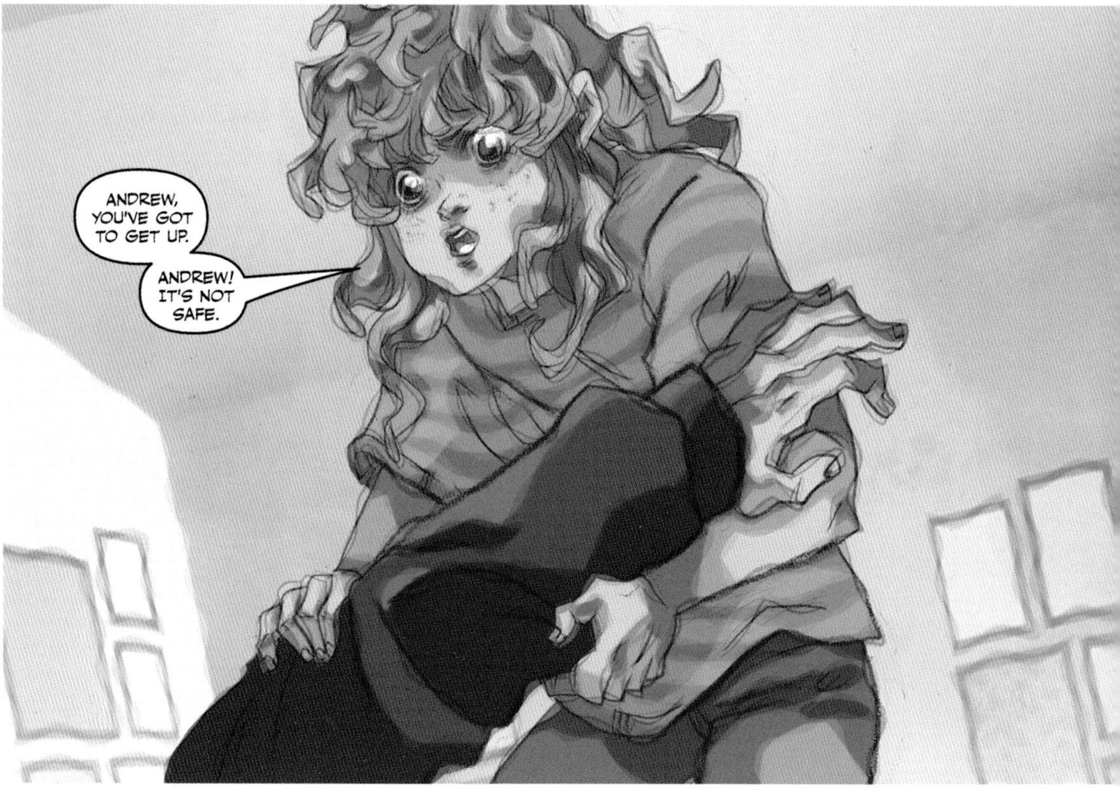
ANDREW, YOU'VE GOT TO GET UP.
ANDREW! IT'S NOT SAFE.

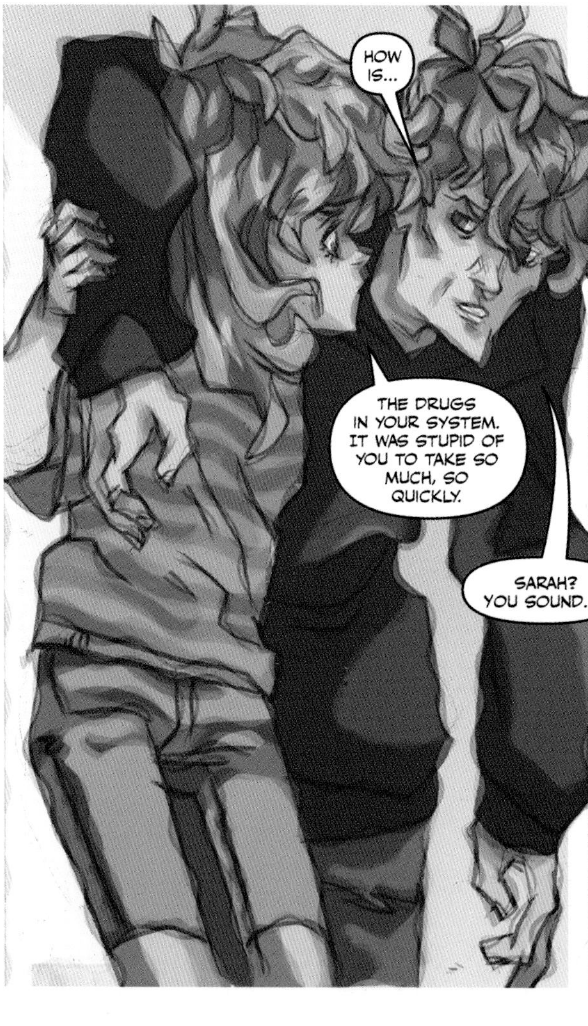
HOW IS...
THE DRUGS IN YOUR SYSTEM. IT WAS STUPID OF YOU TO TAKE SO MUCH, SO QUICKLY.
SARAH? YOU SOUND...?

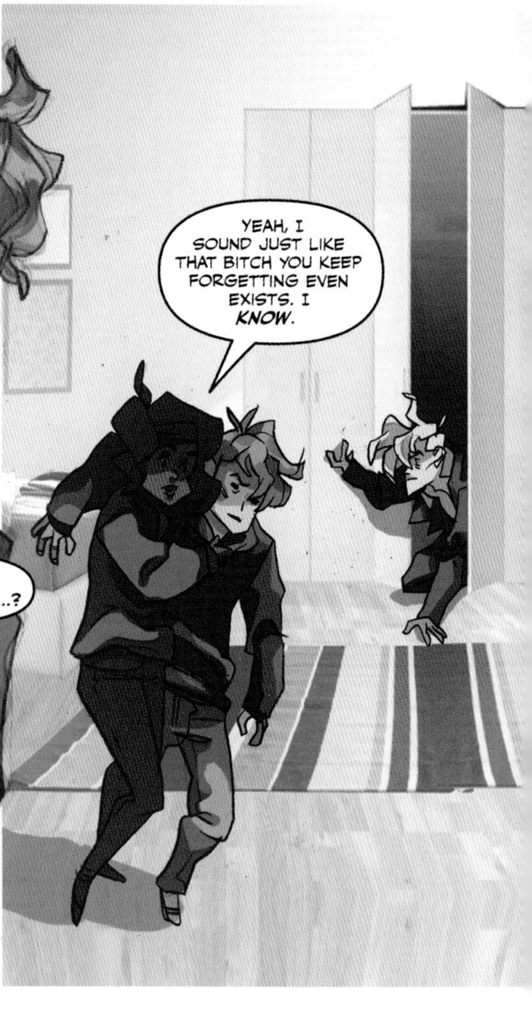
YEAH, I SOUND JUST LIKE THAT BITCH YOU KEEP FORGETTING EVEN EXISTS. I *KNOW*.

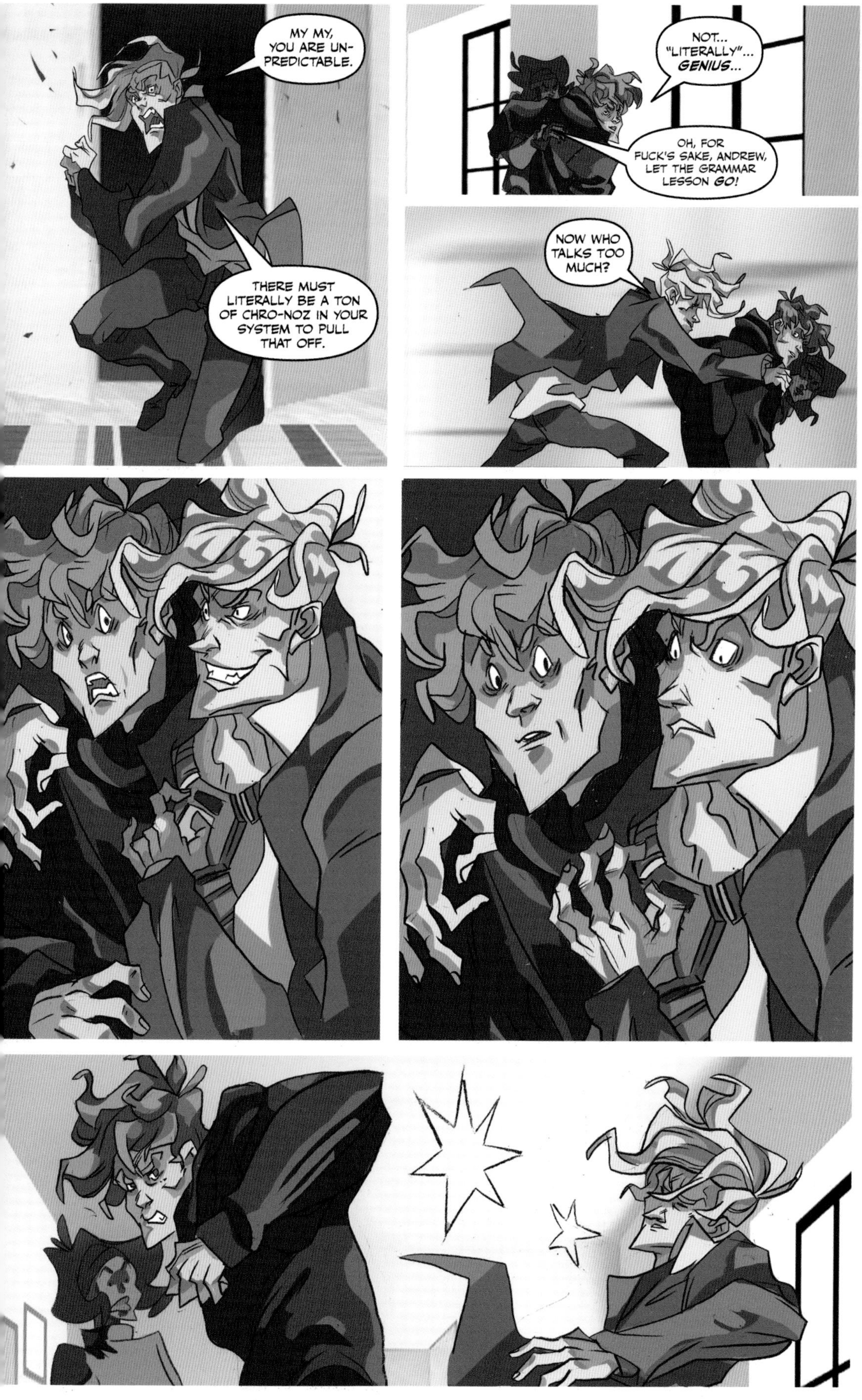
MY MY, YOU ARE UN-PREDICTABLE.
THERE MUST LITERALLY BE A TON OF CHRO-NOZ IN YOUR SYSTEM TO PULL THAT OFF.
NOT... "LITERALLY"... GENIUS...
OH, FOR FUCK'S SAKE, ANDREW, LET THE GRAMMAR LESSON GO!
NOW WHO TALKS TOO MUCH?

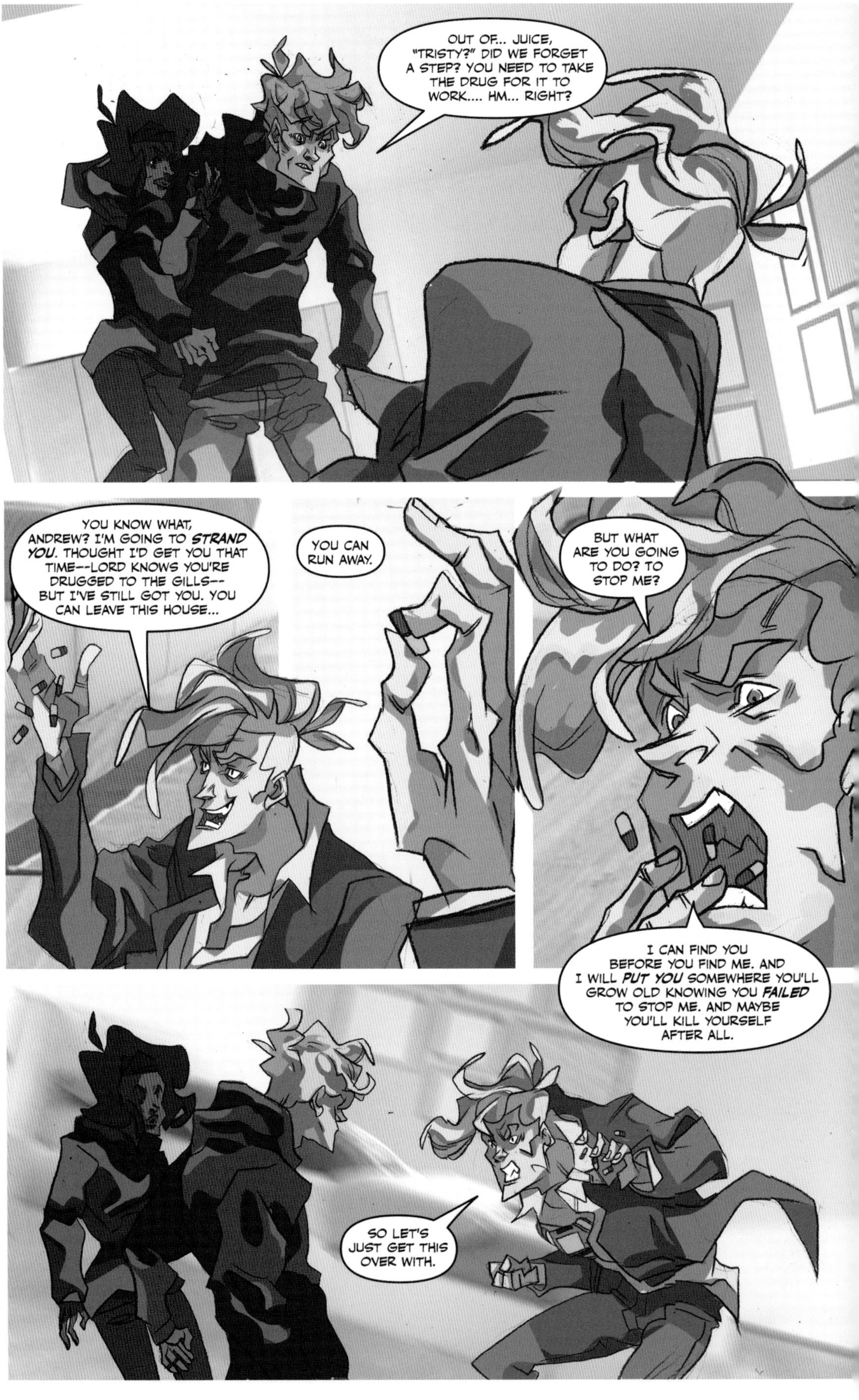
OUT OF... JUICE, "TRISTY?" DID WE FORGET A STEP? YOU NEED TO TAKE THE DRUG FOR IT TO WORK.... HM... RIGHT?
YOU KNOW WHAT, ANDREW? I'M GOING TO STRAND YOU. THOUGHT I'D GET YOU THAT TIME--LORD KNOWS YOU'RE DRUGGED TO THE GILLS-- BUT I'VE STILL GOT YOU. YOU CAN LEAVE THIS HOUSE...
YOU CAN RUN AWAY.
BUT WHAT ARE YOU GOING TO DO? TO STOP ME?
I CAN FIND YOU BEFORE YOU FIND ME. AND I WILL PUT YOU SOMEWHERE YOU'LL GROW OLD KNOWING YOU FAILED TO STOP ME. AND MAYBE YOU'LL KILL YOURSELF AFTER ALL.
SO LET'S JUST GET THIS OVER WITH.

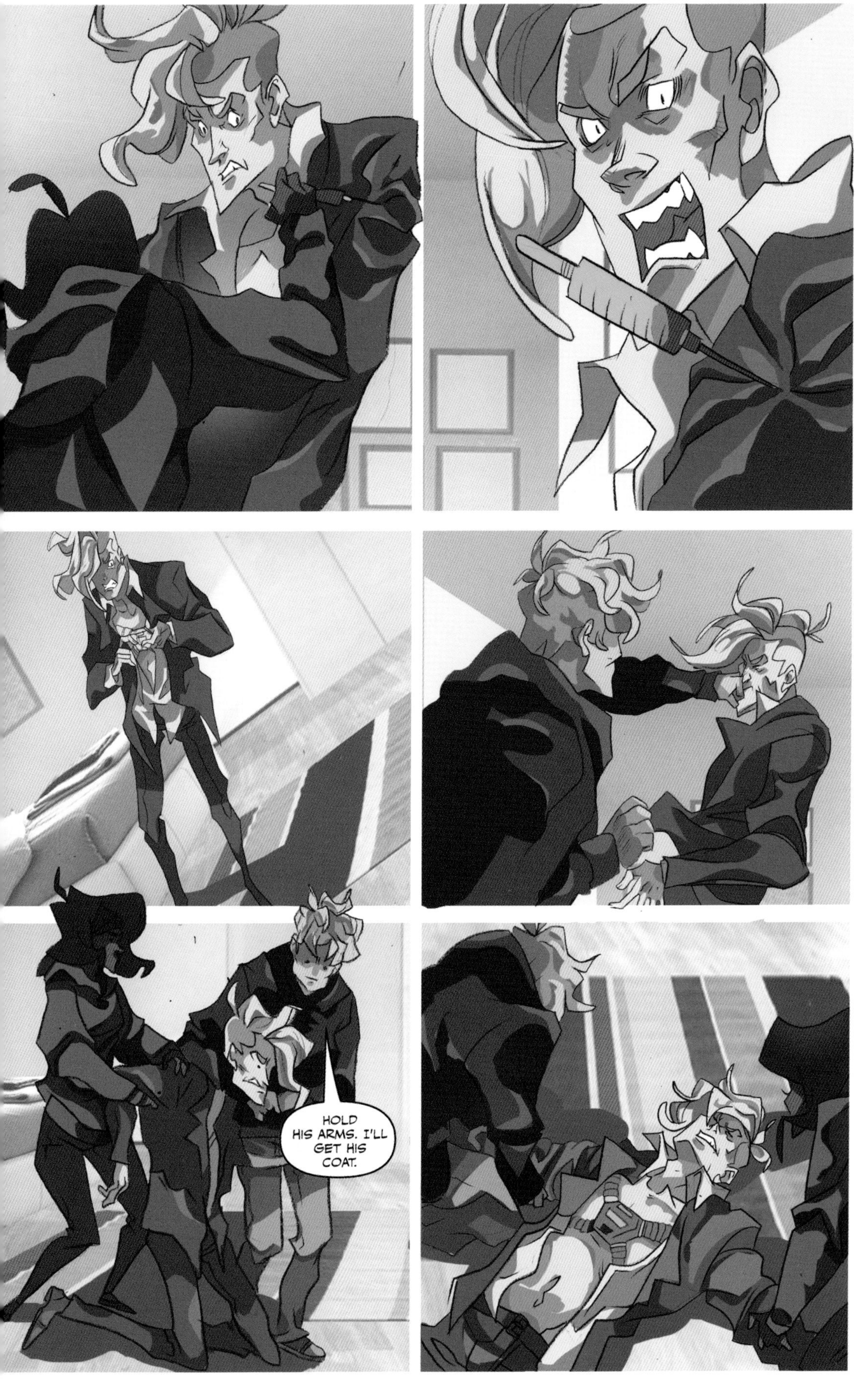
HOLD HIS ARMS. I'LL GET HIS COAT.

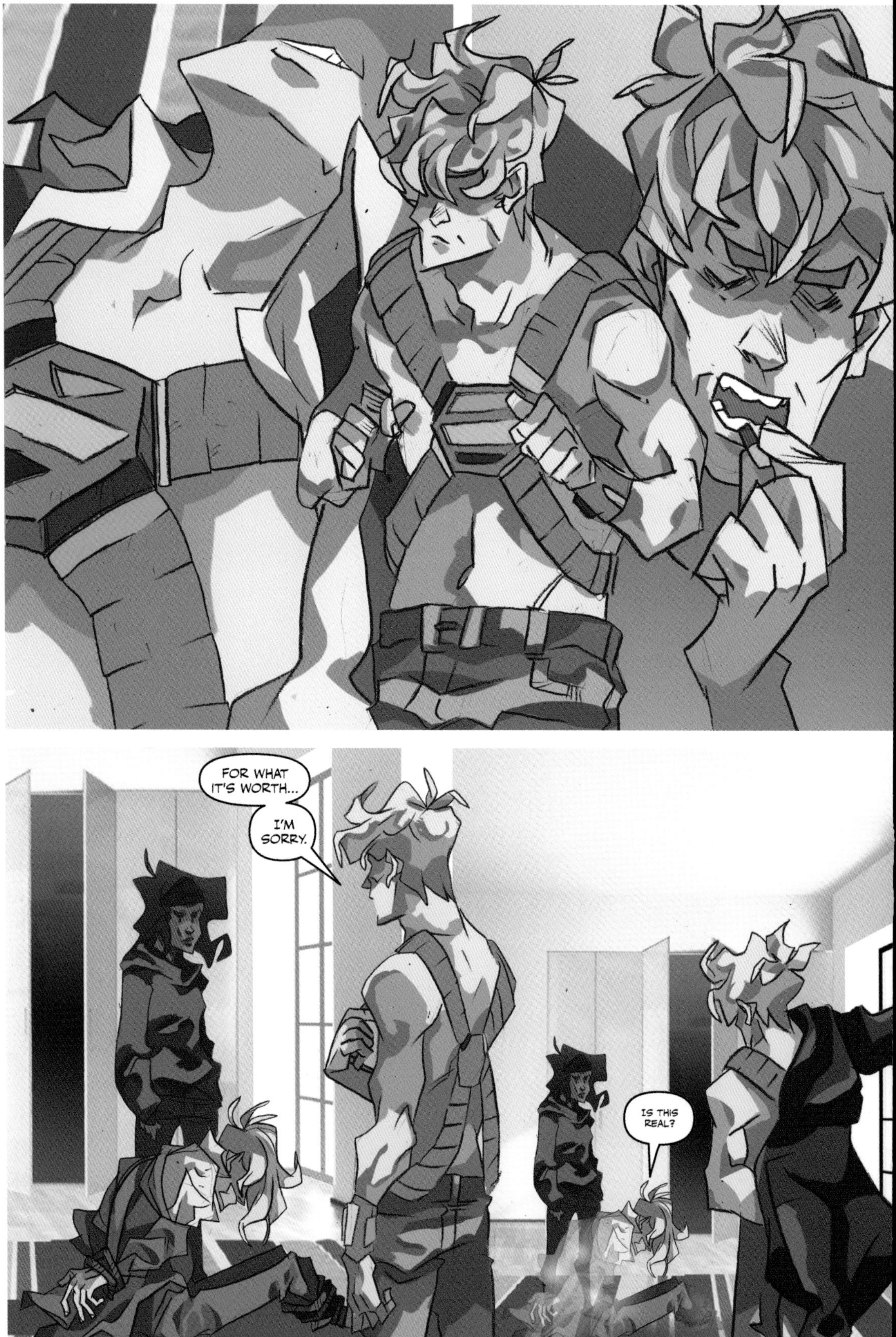
FOR WHAT IT'S WORTH...
I'M SORRY.
IS THIS REAL?

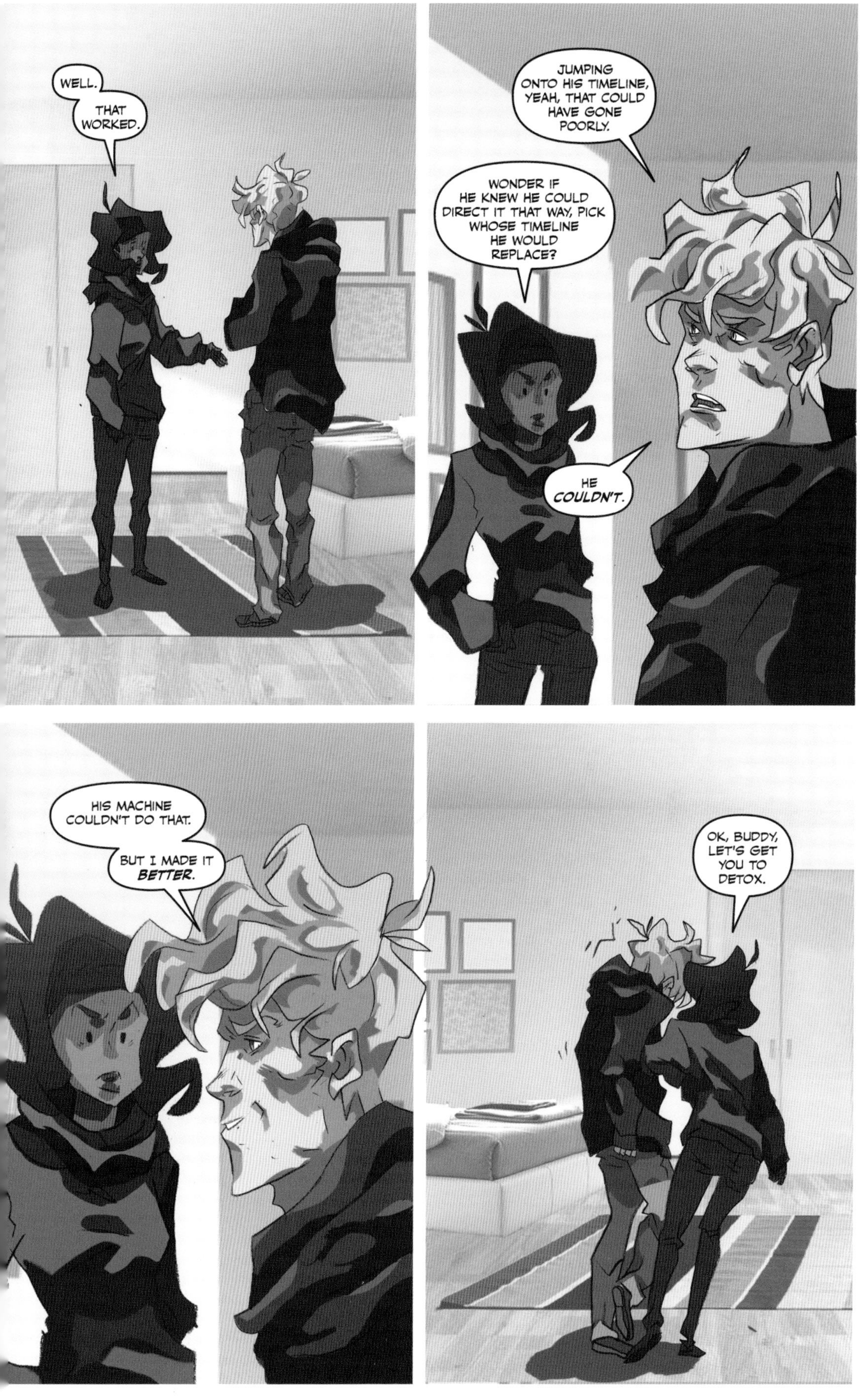
WELL.
THAT WORKED.
JUMPING ONTO HIS TIMELINE, YEAH, THAT COULD HAVE GONE POORLY.
WONDER IF HE KNEW HE COULD DIRECT IT THAT WAY, PICK WHOSE TIMELINE HE WOULD REPLACE?
HE COULDN'T.
HIS MACHINE COULDN'T DO THAT.
BUT I MADE IT BETTER.
OK, BUDDY, LET'S GET YOU TO DETOX.

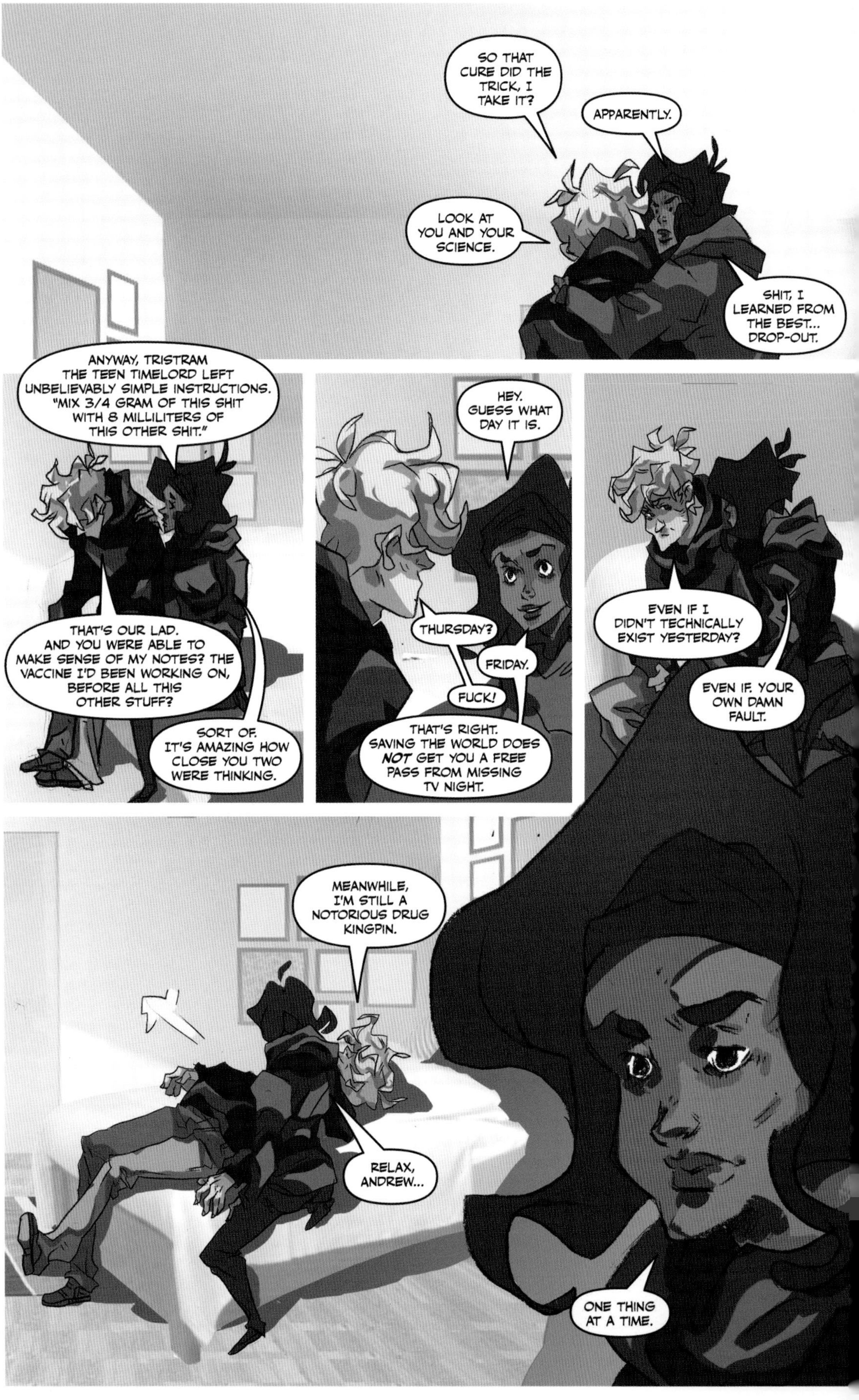
SO THAT CURE DID THE TRICK, I TAKE IT?
APPARENTLY.
LOOK AT YOU AND YOUR SCIENCE.
SHIT, I LEARNED FROM THE BEST... DROP-OUT.
ANYWAY, TRISTRAM THE TEEN TIMELORD LEFT UNBELIEVABLY SIMPLE INSTRUCTIONS. "MIX 3/4 GRAM OF THIS SHIT WITH 8 MILLILITERS OF THIS OTHER SHIT."
THAT'S OUR LAD. AND YOU WERE ABLE TO MAKE SENSE OF MY NOTES? THE VACCINE I'D BEEN WORKING ON, BEFORE ALL THIS OTHER STUFF?
SORT OF. IT'S AMAZING HOW CLOSE YOU TWO WERE THINKING.
HEY. GUESS WHAT DAY IT IS.
THURSDAY?
FRIDAY.
FUCK!
THAT'S RIGHT. SAVING THE WORLD DOES *NOT* GET YOU A FREE PASS FROM MISSING TV NIGHT.
EVEN IF I DIDN'T TECHNICALLY EXIST YESTERDAY?
EVEN IF. YOUR OWN DAMN FAULT.
MEANWHILE, I'M STILL A NOTORIOUS DRUG KINGPIN.
RELAX, ANDREW...
ONE THING AT A TIME.

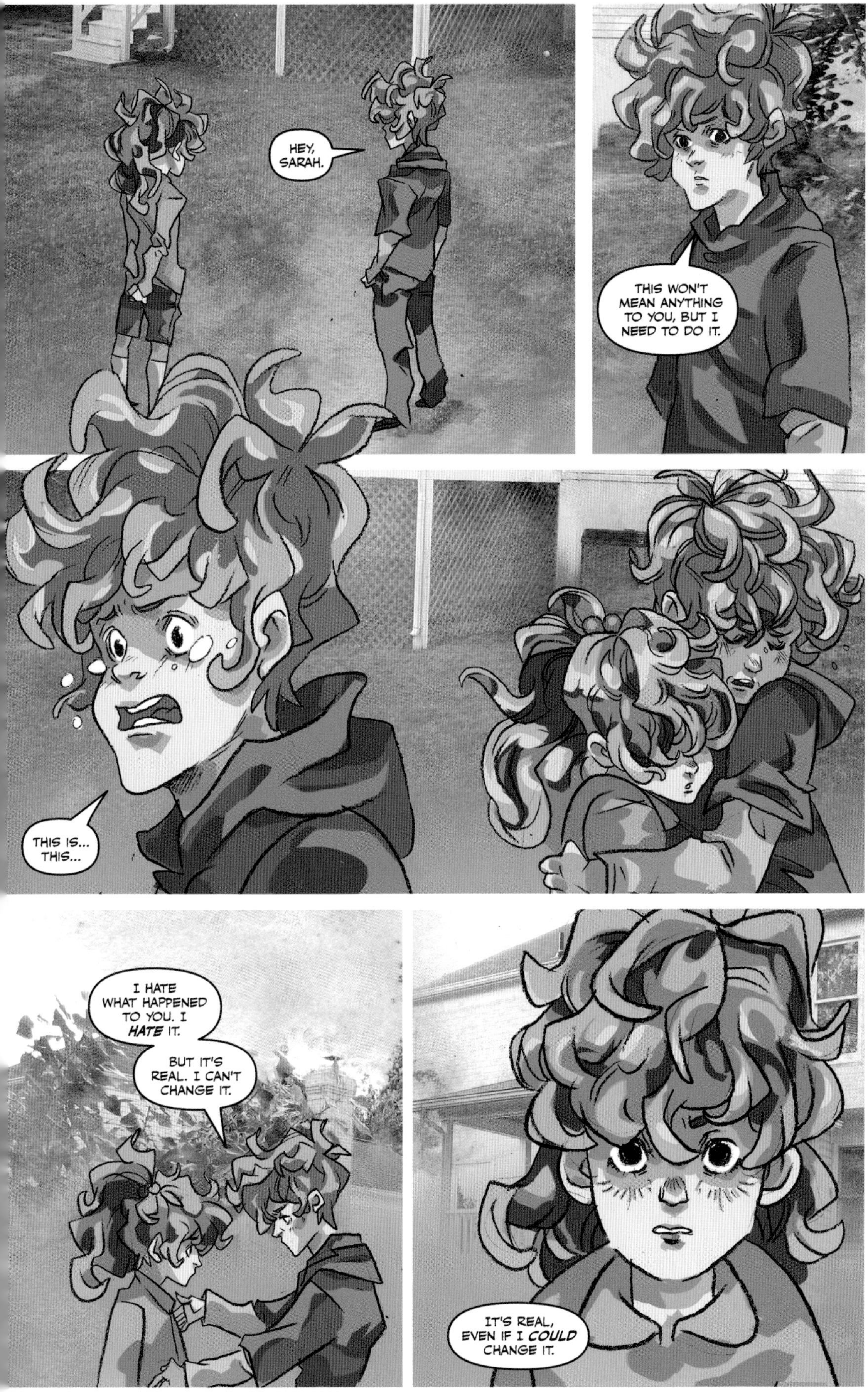
HEY, SARAH.
THIS WON'T MEAN ANYTHING TO YOU, BUT I NEED TO DO IT.
THIS IS... THIS...
I HATE WHAT HAPPENED TO YOU. I *HATE* IT.
BUT IT'S REAL. I CAN'T CHANGE IT.
IT'S REAL, EVEN IF I *COULD* CHANGE IT.

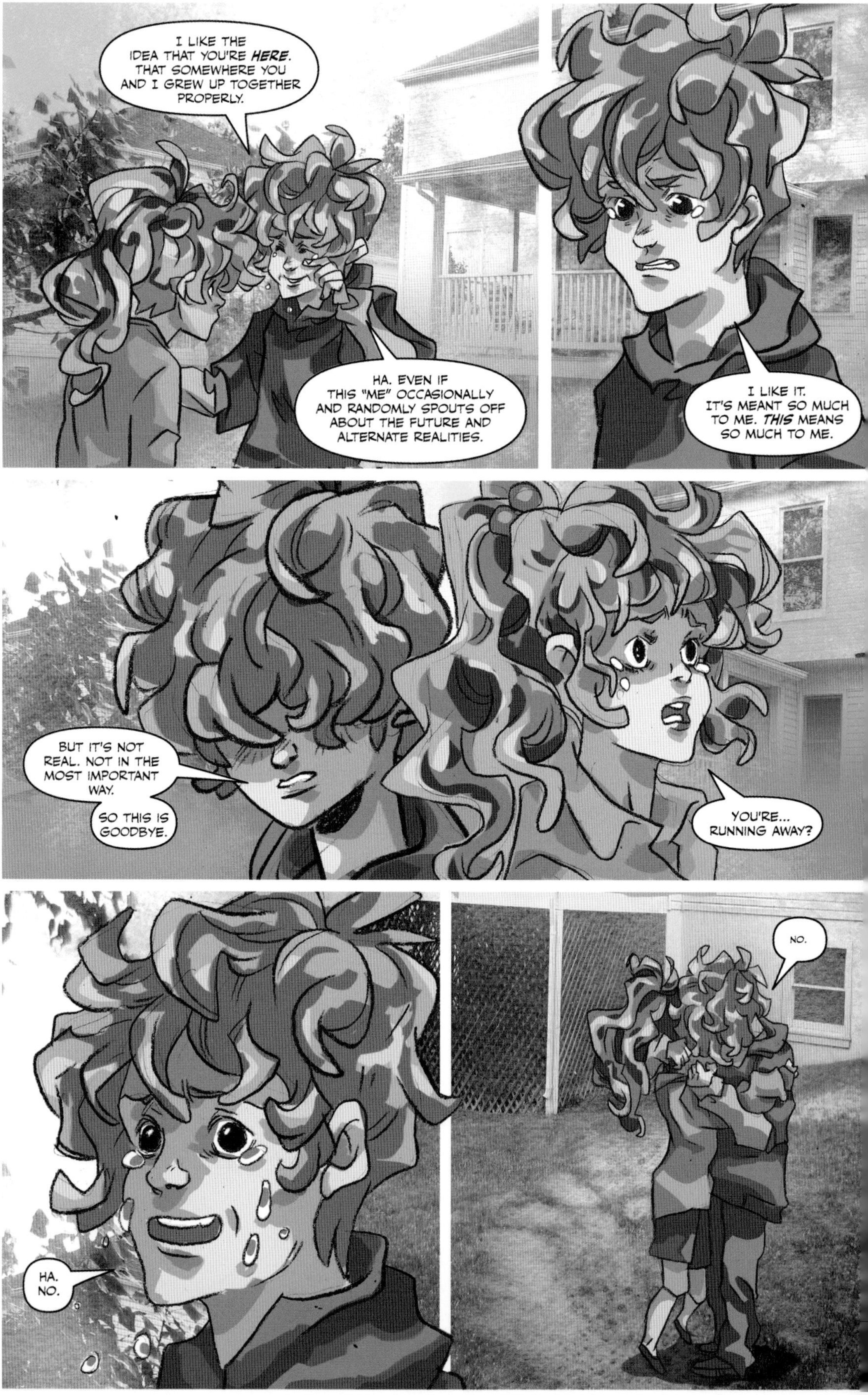
I LIKE THE IDEA THAT YOU'RE *HERE*. THAT SOMEWHERE YOU AND I GREW UP TOGETHER PROPERLY.
HA. EVEN IF THIS "ME" OCCASIONALLY AND RANDOMLY SPOUTS OFF ABOUT THE FUTURE AND ALTERNATE REALITIES.
I LIKE IT. IT'S MEANT SO MUCH TO ME. *THIS* MEANS SO MUCH TO ME.
BUT IT'S NOT REAL. NOT IN THE MOST IMPORTANT WAY.
SO THIS IS GOODBYE.
YOU'RE... RUNNING AWAY?
HA. NO.
NO.

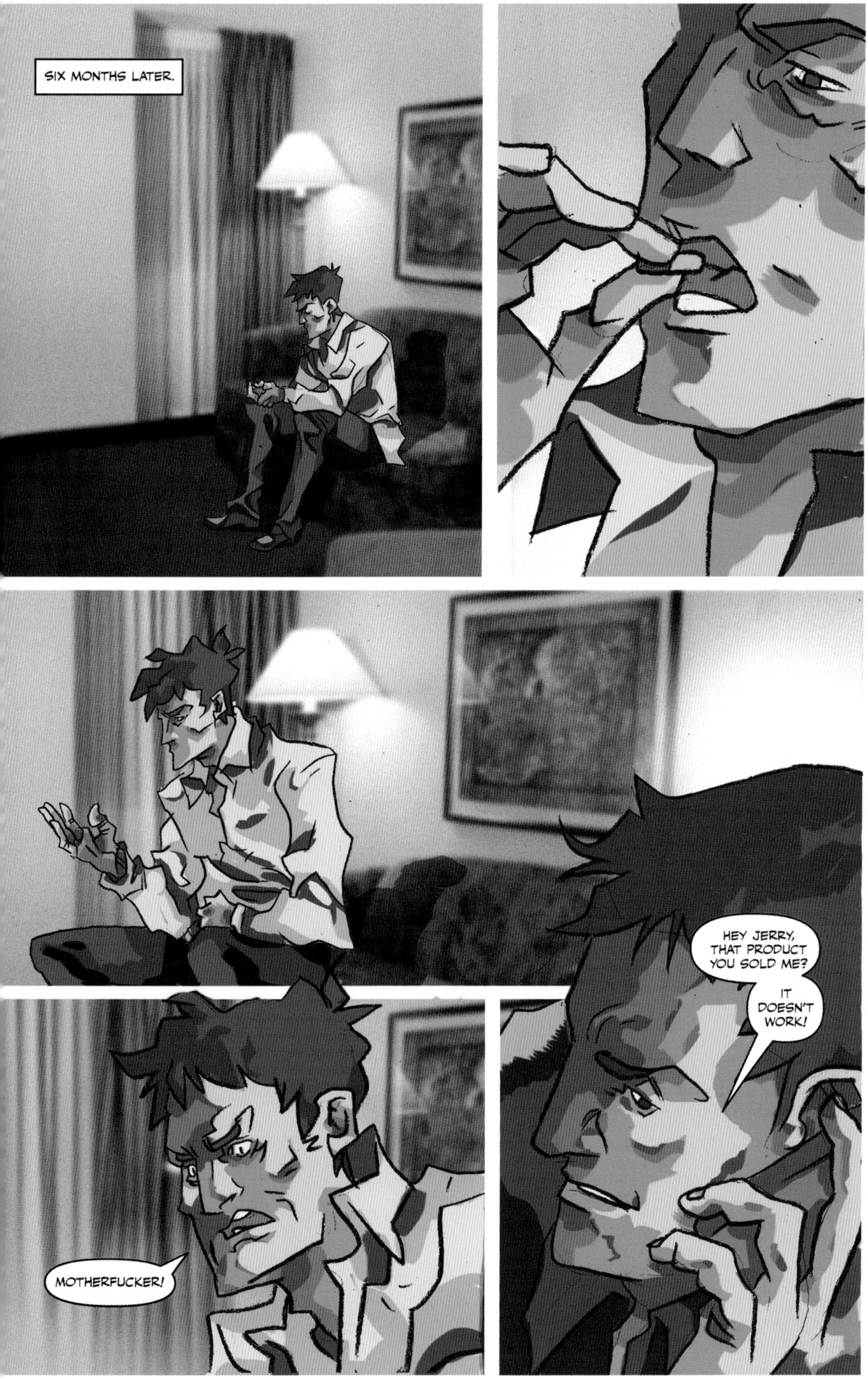
SIX MONTHS LATER.
HEY JERRY, THAT PRODUCT YOU SOLD ME?
IT DOESN'T WORK!
MOTHERFUCKER!

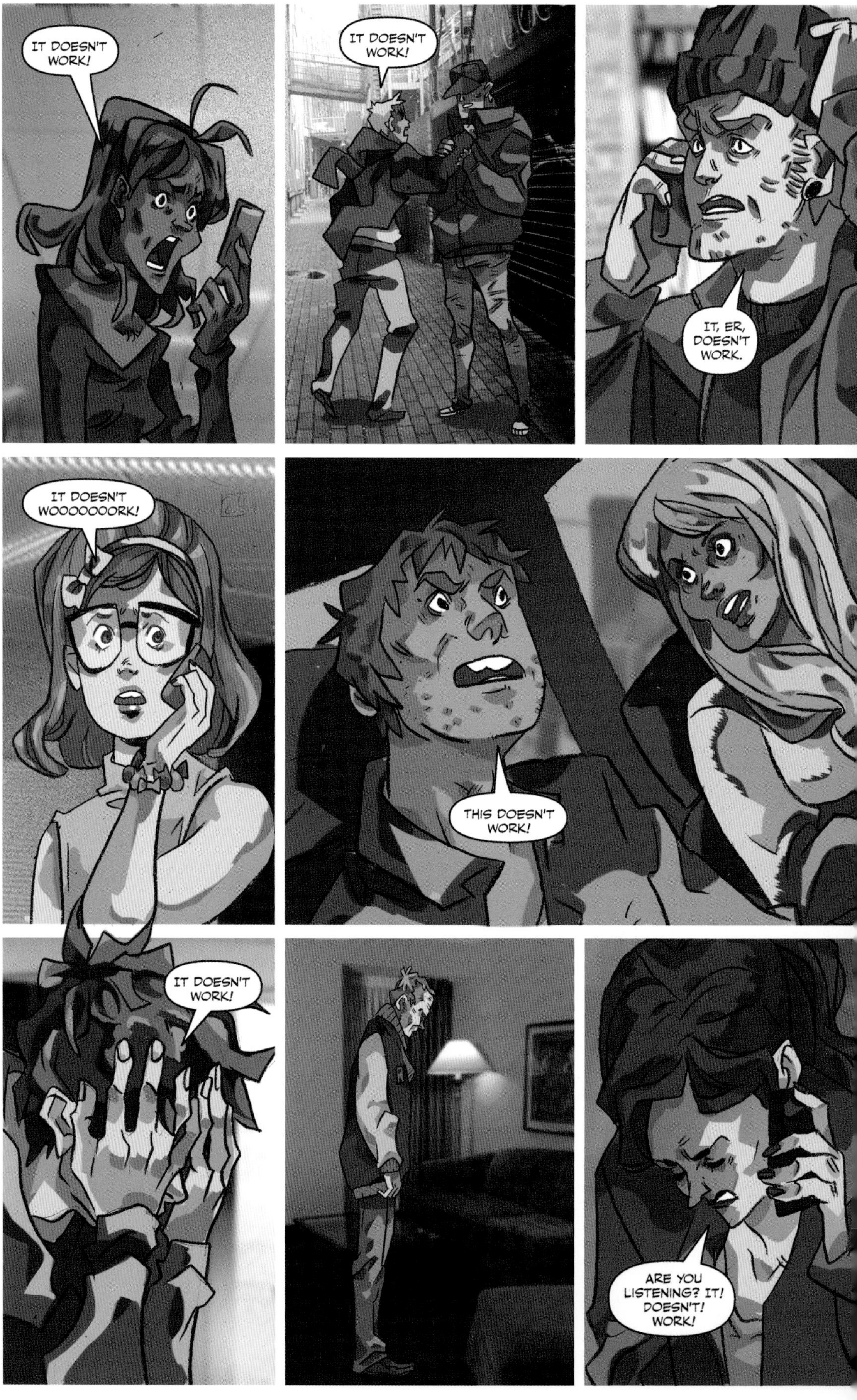
IT DOESN'T WORK!
IT DOESN'T WORK!
IT, ER, DOESN'T WORK.
IT DOESN'T WOOOOOOORK!
THIS DOESN'T WORK!
IT DOESN'T WORK!
ARE YOU LISTENING? IT! DOESN'T! WORK!

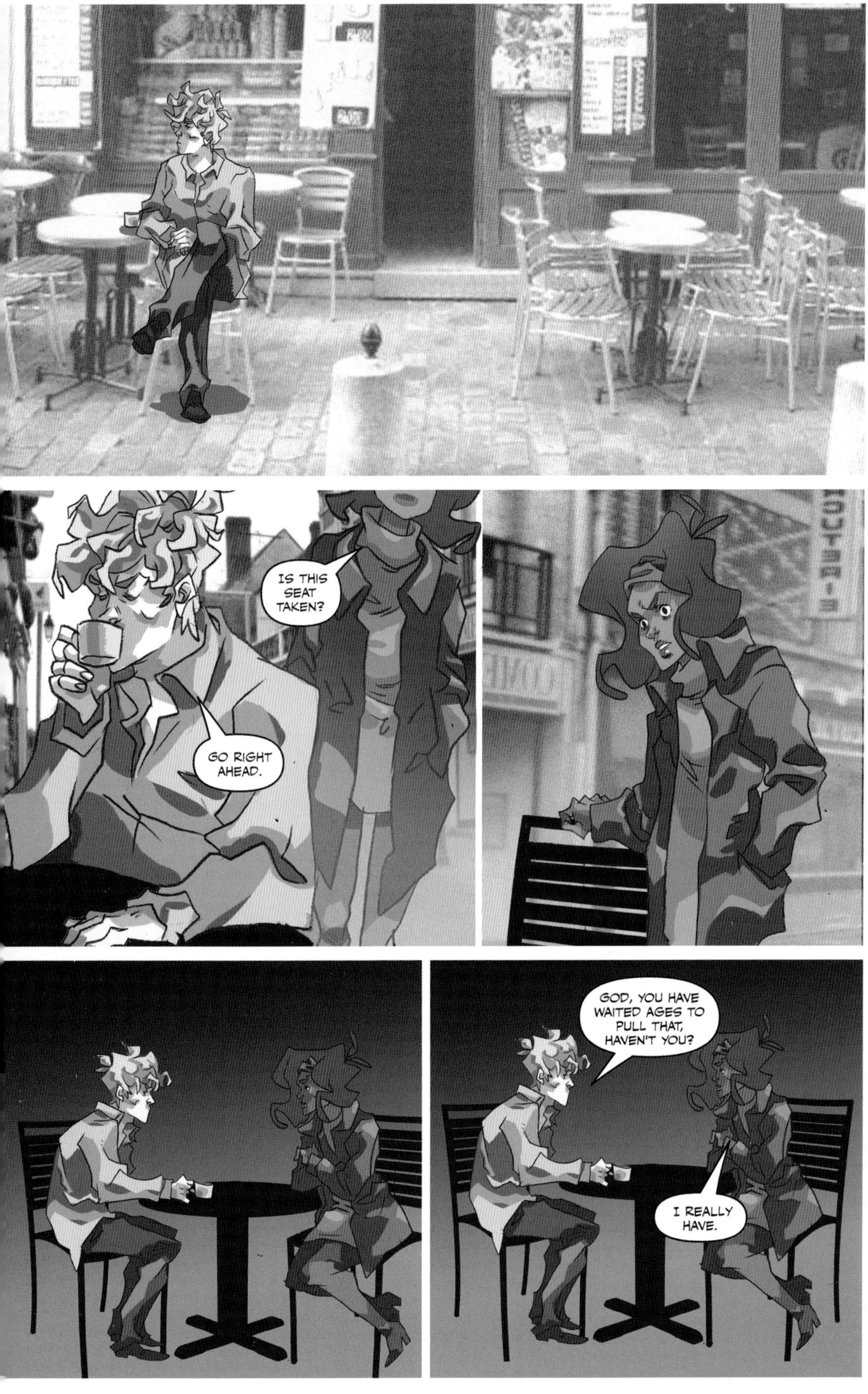
IS THIS SEAT TAKEN?
GO RIGHT AHEAD.
GOD, YOU HAVE WAITED AGES TO PULL THAT, HAVEN'T YOU?
I REALLY HAVE.

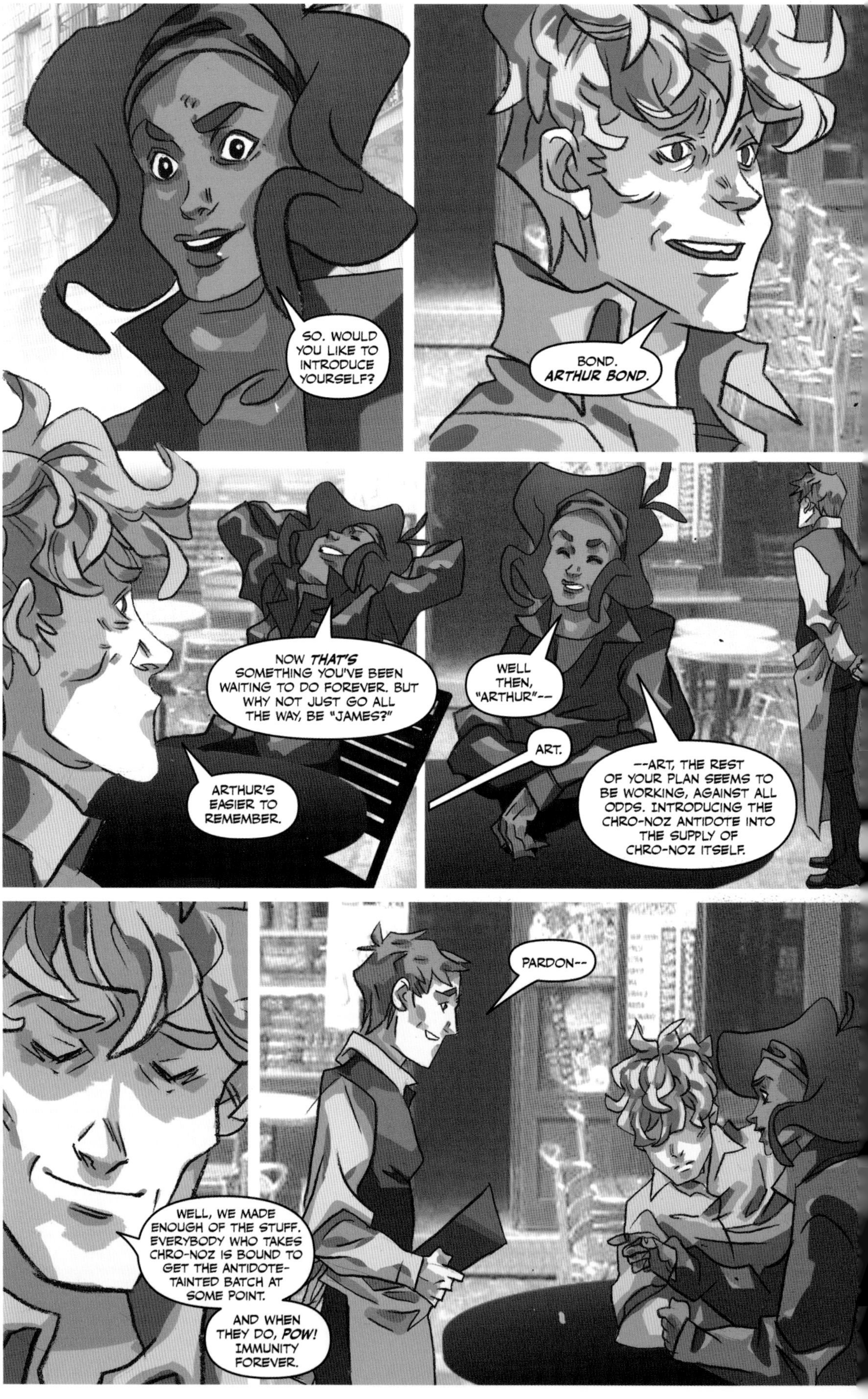
SO. WOULD YOU LIKE TO INTRODUCE YOURSELF?
BOND. *ARTHUR BOND.*
NOW *THAT'S* SOMETHING YOU'VE BEEN WAITING TO DO FOREVER. BUT WHY NOT JUST GO ALL THE WAY, BE "JAMES?"
ARTHUR'S EASIER TO REMEMBER.
WELL THEN, "ARTHUR"--
ART.
--ART, THE REST OF YOUR PLAN SEEMS TO BE WORKING, AGAINST ALL ODDS. INTRODUCING THE CHRO-NOZ ANTIDOTE INTO THE SUPPLY OF CHRO-NOZ ITSELF.
WELL, WE MADE ENOUGH OF THE STUFF. EVERYBODY WHO TAKES CHRO-NOZ IS BOUND TO GET THE ANTIDOTE-TAINTED BATCH AT SOME POINT.
AND WHEN THEY DO, *POW!* IMMUNITY FOREVER.
PARDON--

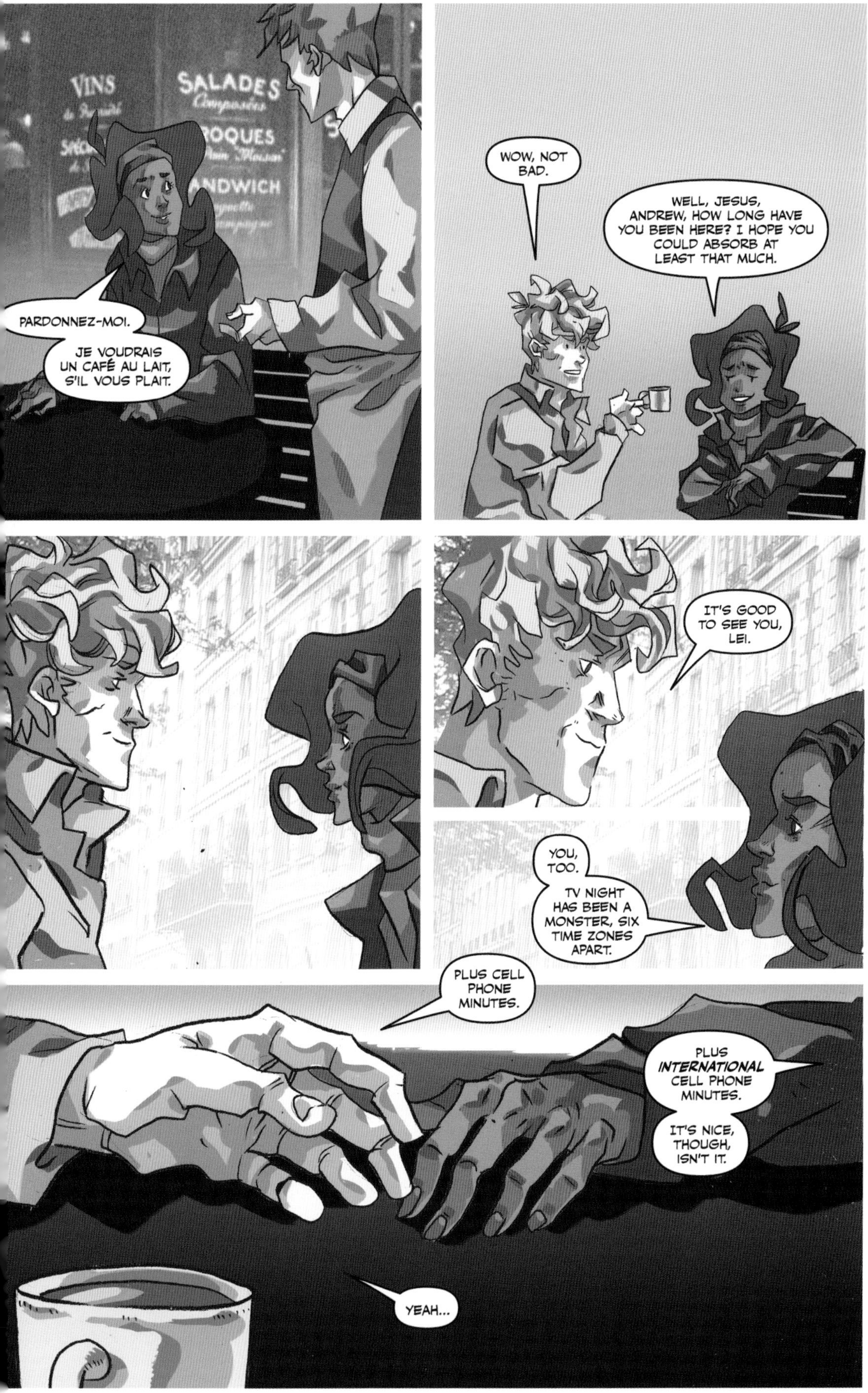
VINS
SALADES
PARDONNEZ-MOI.
JE VOUDRAIS UN CAFÉ AU LAIT, S'IL VOUS PLAIT.
WOW, NOT BAD.
WELL, JESUS, ANDREW, HOW LONG HAVE YOU BEEN HERE? I HOPE YOU COULD ABSORB AT LEAST THAT MUCH.
IT'S GOOD TO SEE YOU, LEI.
YOU, TOO.
TV NIGHT HAS BEEN A MONSTER, SIX TIME ZONES APART.
PLUS CELL PHONE MINUTES.
PLUS *INTERNATIONAL* CELL PHONE MINUTES.
IT'S NICE, THOUGH, ISN'T IT.
YEAH...

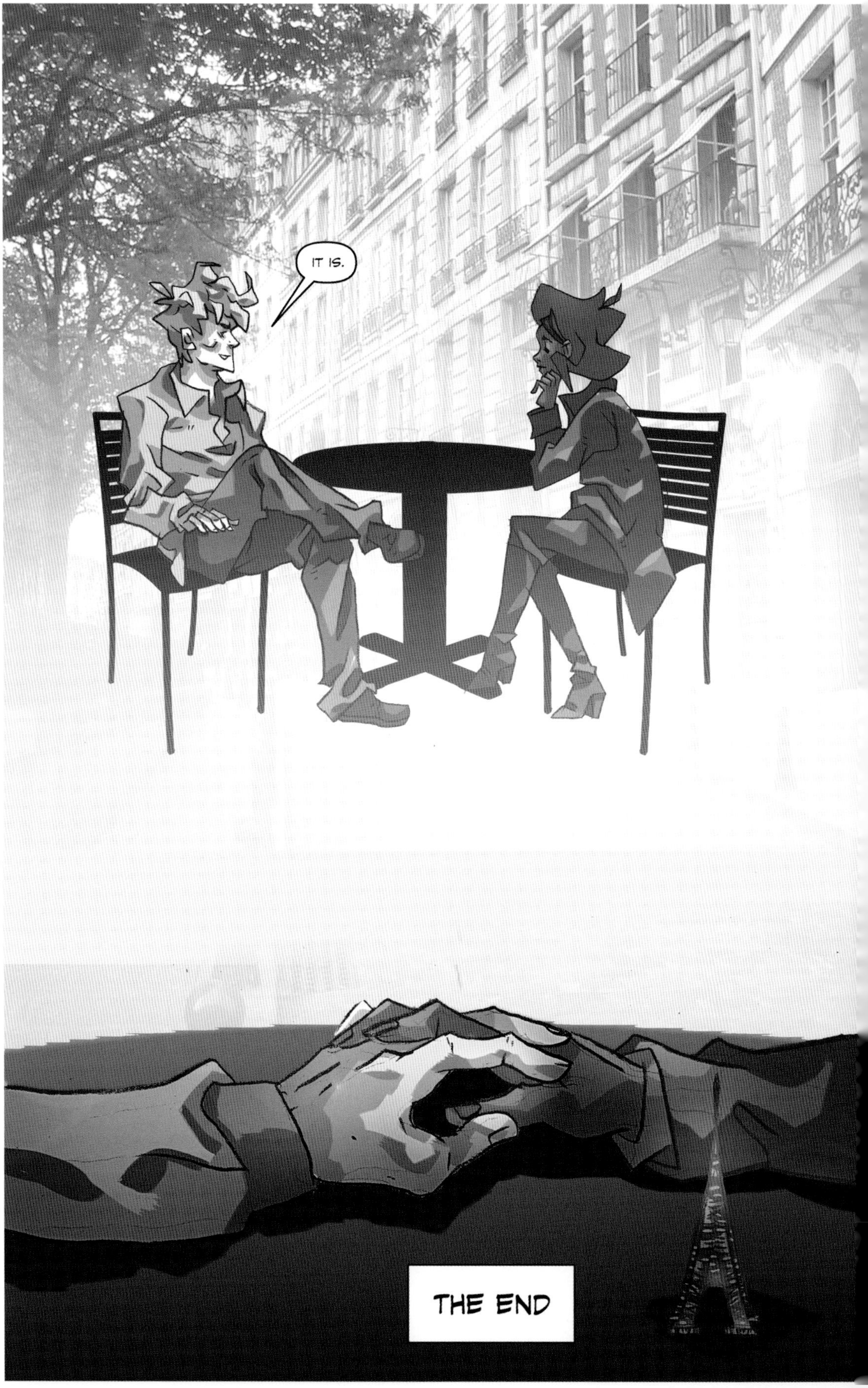
IT IS.
THE END

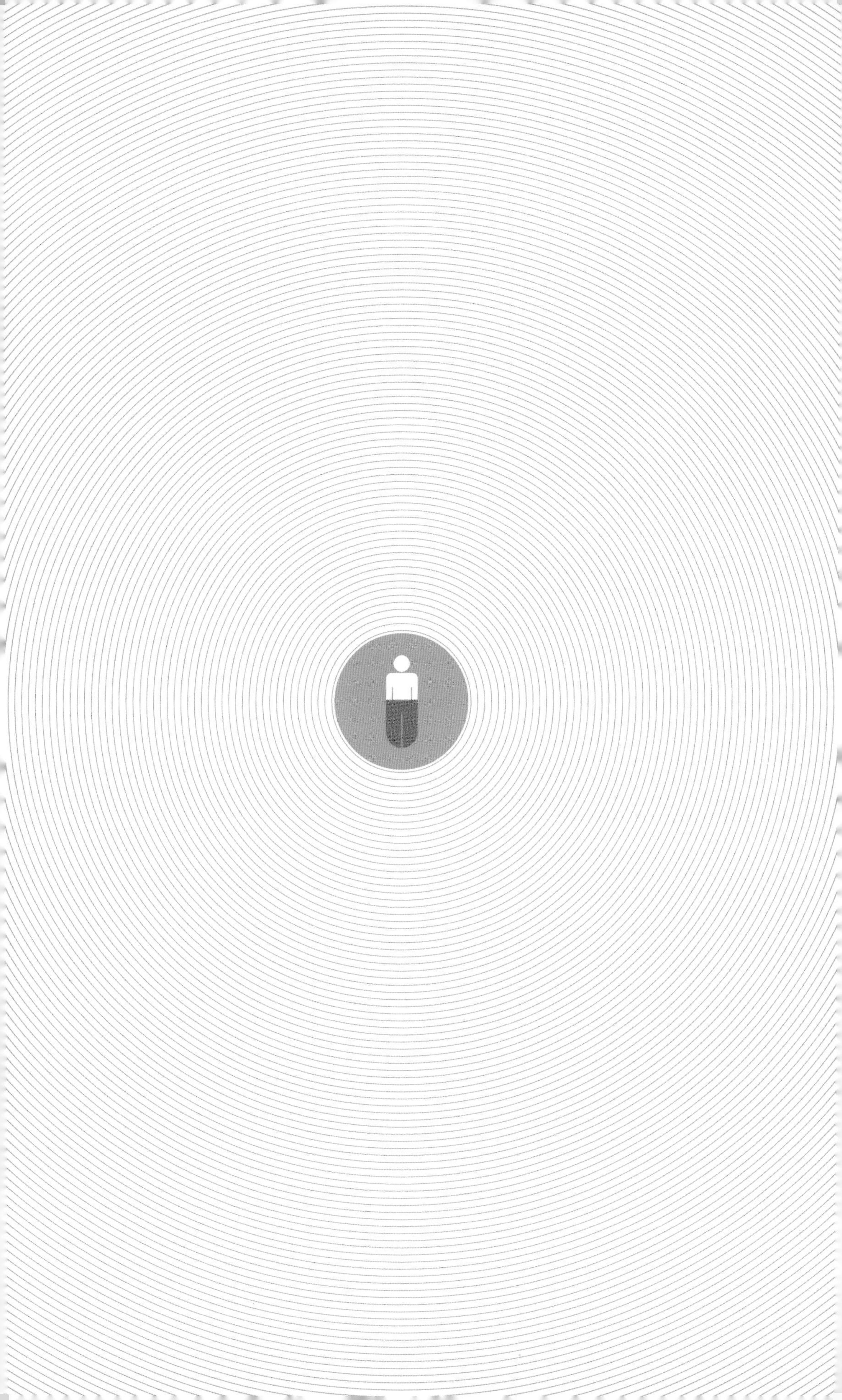

**SHAUN MANNING** is the creator and writer of *Interesting Drug* for Archaia and *Hell, Nebraska* on Comixology. His work has appeared in *Dark Horse Presents*, Top Shelf 2.0, *Hope: New Orleans*, and *The Looking Glass Wars: Hatter M*, as well as in several literary magazines, on stage, and on BBC Radio 4. Shaun took home first prize for a reading from his comedy novella *Pizza Good Times in Edinburgh, Scotland*; the trophy was a bottle of whiskey. He currently lives in Ann Arbor with his wife Truly, daughter Lila, and the family hamster.

**ANNA WIESZCZYK** is a comic book artist currently residing in Kraków, Poland. She has drawn for as far back as she can remember. She studied graphic design for five years, but since her major interest was always comics, she decided to follow her interests instead of enslaving herself to an advertising agency. Her works have been published in the United States and Poland. Anna's favorite hobby is reading hermetic tarot. Her personal works are inspired mostly by thoughts of Carl Jung and Maria Louiza von Franz. She believes that the most important thing in life is a strong sense of understanding oneself.

**S.M.**
Special thanks to Rebecca
Taylor and the Archaia crew for
making this the best book it could be; to
Andy Schmidt and Comics Experience for
productive workshopping at the earliest stages;
to Jonah Weiland for bringing me on to an amazing
team in the heart of the medium I love; and most
of all to Truly and Lila, my wife and daughter, whose
boundless support and encouragement made the
whole endeavor possible.

**A.W.**
I'd like to thank the people who support me:
my sister, Olga, and my parents. And also
a huge thanks to all our readers!

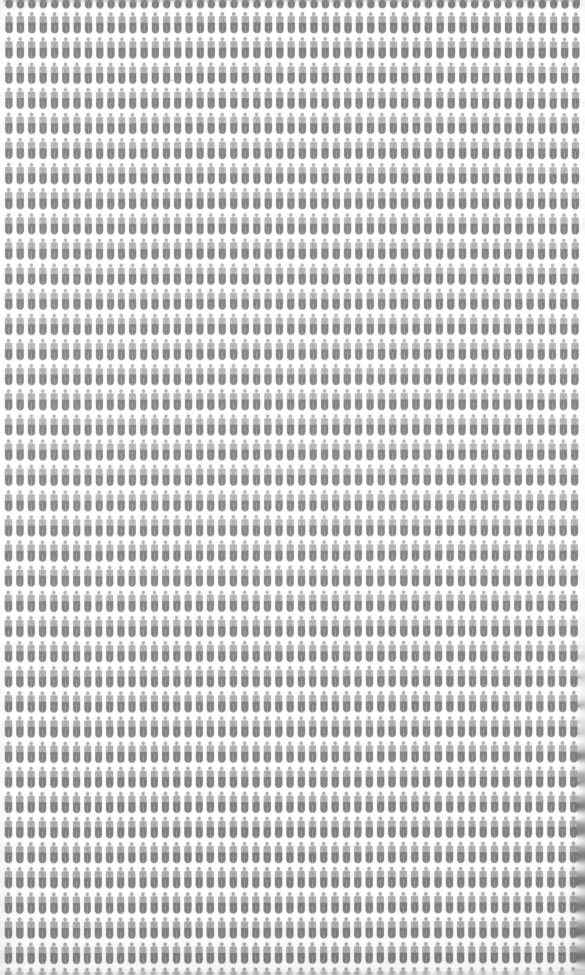